Baku
to
Baker Street

Baku
to
Baker Street

The Memoirs of Flora Solomon

by Herself and Barnet Litvinoff

COLLINS
8 Grafton Street, London W1
1984

William Collins Sons and Co. Ltd
London * Glasgow * Sydney * Auckland
Toronto * Johannesburg

British Library Cataloguing in Publication Data

Solomon, Flora
Baku to Baker Street
1. Solomon, Flora   2. England–Biography
I. Title   II. Litvinoff, Barnet
942.082'092'4   CT788.S/

ISBN 0-00-217094-9

First published 1984
© Flora Solomon and Barnet Litvinoff 1984

Photoset in Palatino by
Rowland Phototypesetting Ltd
Bury St Edmunds, Suffolk
and printed in Great Britain by
William Collins Sons and Co. Ltd, Glasgow

*Dedicated with love and pride
to my son Peter Benenson,
founder of Amnesty International*

"Where there is no vision, the people perish"

Proverbs, Ch. 29, v.18.

Contents

Illustrations

Foreword

I do not believe for a moment that the world has been waiting with bated breath for this account of my life, though I have been pressed by my family and many friends, including those in the publishing world, to open my heart and tell, as they say, all. Or nearly all. The dentist grinding away at my teeth, the bank manager pensively surveying my affairs, and the cleaning lady who comes to operate my Hoover, have all informed me that they would be the first to rush out for a copy of my book. Well, flattery will get you everywhere, so here is the result. It has been a voyage of discovery, for we are all strangers to ourselves. And living one's life twice, first by experiencing it and again by recording it, is not for the coward soul.

Don't look here for a description of how I composed great music, or discovered a cure for the common cold, or brought emancipation to womankind. I didn't. During one period of my life I inhabited a society accomplished in the art of frittering wealth away, but who cares? I can think of better ways of wasting money now that I have to keep a close watch over my weekly budget. A French politician, asked what he did in his country's revolution, replied: 'I survived.' That's me too, though I don't go back so far, merely to a couple of Russian revolutions.

To a certain degree mine is a woman's story. It tells how women could do little while the world travelled the road to catastrophe in masculine blinkers and plagued by masculine vanities. Life was pampering me, a severe handicap if you are in search of a purpose.

When fortune brought me to earth through a back-door of Marks and Spencer I began to realize how the mass of women lived and laboured. Previously, what I required in a High Street store was purchased for me by a lady's maid. Now I became a servant of sorts myself, to grant me an education unavailable at any university.

Paradoxically, this is where my account ceases to be a

13

woman's story. Call it welfare work (a deadening description) if you like, or the class struggle, or even a tale of escape. For me it was an adventure. I was a butterfly in the First World War, a lady with a soup ladle and a burning anger picking her way through ruined cities in the Second, eventually finding myself engrossed in the problems of human relations in industry. What were my qualifications? Struggle as I might, I can find only three: A Russian soul, a Jewish heart and a British passport.

I have spoken frankly, of many people beside myself. At my age the one indulgence remaining is honesty. To friends and others omitted from this story, I offer my regrets. To those included, my gratitude.

14

1 The Benensons

We are almost an extinct species, those of us who consult our memories rather than the history books to recall Imperial Russia when she claimed Tolstoy as her living conscience. And when the Tsar was for worshipping, not the firing-squad.

This is not because of our venerable years; nowadays to overleap the biblical span of three score and ten by decades is a commonplace. Our rarity comes from the waning of that Russian atmospheric which nurtured a particular breed, neither townsmen nor frontiersmen, in whom the sublime mingled with the barbarous. My younger days were situated in an intersection between feudalism and modernity. Men galloped across the steppes in a kind of trembling courage so that they might write a poem or impale a child. Women inhabited a secret domain of deceit and desire, some within the orbit of the boudoir, some enslaved by unrelenting toil in their hovels of mud, some to despatch a messenger a thousand miles to arrange a tryst or secure an inheritance.

Russia was untamed and beautiful, disciplined yet ungovernable. If her music revealed a spiritless sentimentality it had qualities that were universally admired, and this helped to satisfy my country's yearning for acceptance as a civilized nation. But at every turn Russia was reminded of the misery, poverty and cruelty which was her heritage, and which she feared would be her legacy. Change came slowly, innovation was unwelcome, so the Russia I was born into also lay blanketed in tedium.

My personality was determined by three cities, and I have always thought of them as a troika speeding driverless across time. I was the passenger being carried she knew not where. They were Minsk, home of my father and his father's father; Baku, city of oil, earthquakes and tribal warfare; and St Petersburg, the northern capital, which introduced me to the torments of wakening womanhood.

I was however born in a fourth city, Pinsk. It was 1895, the same year of birth as the ill-fated Princess Olga, first child of the Empress Alexandra, whom I therefore adopted mentally as my foster-twin. Pinsk was my mother's town before she was taken away to serve my father as his wife. She had returned to produce her child among her own. From the beginning I banished Pinsk from my perceptions, lest it dare claim any association with me. I had concluded that my mother, Sophie Goldberg, was what she was because of Pinsk, while my father, Grigori Benenson, seemed the human representation of Minsk.

Pinsk was a crabbed, wretched little town with pretensions but no character. Or so I decided. Minsk was a large, important metropolis – had to be, because father was tall and powerful, known throughout Russia as a go-getter. Pinsk was an extended village overpopulated by clerics and struggling for an identity when I emerged there, while Minsk, two hundred miles away, already boasted great industries, theatres, and social revolutionaries. Being further from Warsaw and closer to Moscow, Minsk sat squarely in Russia proper and it was rumoured that some Jews there actually consumed food on *Yom Kippur*.

Thus, in my childish estimate, was my mother's relationship to her husband. It was in the nature of things that she should exist only to cosset and support him, and I naturally wondered whether this was the role of all women towards all men. For Pinsk appeared to be grateful to be associated with Minsk, recognizing that it must be less decisive, of smaller girth, somewhat wary of the dawning twentieth century, more pious, and demonstrably inferior in every way. All this was idiotic of course, but I dredge it from my ancient prejudices to establish that with the passage of time I was not going to hold mother with real regard, while father would do no wrong.

In truth, Pinsk and Minsk had a great deal in common in those days – much more than divided them. Catherine the Great, who was a German princess, did not realize when she plundered the territory of Poland in the hope of making Russia a European rather than an Oriental empire, that she could not have the land without the people. And along with the people went millions of that most unwelcome tribe, my tribe, the Jews.

To any visitor from Mars or even St Petersburg at the turn of the century, Pinsk and Minsk would both appear, in the main, Jewish towns. They fell within a great stretch of territory known for administrative purposes as the Pale of Settlement, and which many Jews considered their prison-cage. From the Baltic to the Black Sea we were regulated, with only rare exceptions, to live there, work there, die there. Imperial edict allowed a Jew to reside with his family outside the Pale of Settlement if he qualified through a learned profession to perform services deemed of value to the state, or if he was a merchant belonging to one of the influential guilds, or if he had undergone the maximum period of military service. Some students had the right too, and a few artisans.

Such was the law. But Russian laws were made for bending, and in practice Jews with drive and ambition or restlessness and cunning swarmed across all the provinces of the vast empire. Religious piety kept many within the Pale, as did poverty, physical inertia, ignorance, and the shackles of worldly possessions. Older generations, like old lags anywhere, were happiest in their prison-cage. Then there was the herd instinct; it held millions to Pinsk, Minsk, and a hundred other ghettoes.

The way Jews mostly got out of the Pale of Settlement was by emigration. From the early 1880s they packed up in their thousands and left the country, to seek their fortunes and a breath of fresh air in Western Europe or America. I have a host of cousins, first, second and third, in the United States, whom I have never met.

There was another avenue of escape. Russian anti-Semitism was without racial basis, and Jews had freedom of residence anywhere if they elected for baptism. Forget that you were born a Hebrew, Russia said, go to church, and you are one of us. Quite a number took this course, with a sort of placid resignation. They had not been very good Jews, and they did not make very good Christians.

Gazing balefully upon the overflowing ghettoes was a man who in my childhood enjoyed the title of Chief Procurator of the Holy Synod. This was Constantin Pobedonostev, mentor to Tsar Nicholas, and the Jews feared him as a latter-day Torquemada. His proposal to solve Russia's Jewish problem became famous: a third should emigrate, a third should embrace Christianity, and a third should die of starvation. Well, there was plenty of starvation: Jews subsisted as wandering pedlars, or by cobbling their neighbours' boots, or on charity. Conversion crumbled our nation within a nation at the edges, and at times the emigration swelled to a great flood, with endless lines of wretches, clutching their bedding and their prayer books, shuffling their way to

17

the frontiers. Still, millions of Jews obstinately, exasperatingly, remained.

A pogrom here and there, periodic expulsion from country areas, shipment of the young (and the more stupid!) to distant parts as soldiers of the Tsar to garrison his far-flung provinces, they multiplied nevertheless, as in the Egypt of the Pharaohs, occupying whole districts between Riga and Odessa. Jews packed the market-place with their pathetic merchandise, traded in livestock, arranged their marriages, conspired for revolution, and waited for the Messiah.

Fatalism formed part of the Russian yoke. Yet the empire was a measureless expanse and the aristocracy proof that here was wealth to be had beyond exhaustion. Jews too could make money, change it, conceal it, lend it and bribe their way to more. A few became millionaires. Thousands more threw material possessions and religion alike in the teeth of their elders. They vowed to change the system, if not by politics then by the bomb, mostly to be pounced upon by the secret police and pay for their dream of turning the country into a better place with exile to Siberia. The Empress Catherine had fed into the stomach of Mother Russia a lump of indigestible humanity. At the time of my birth in 1895 we were five million Jews, and every one a source of irritation and resentment.

My father's family, far from being confined by the Jewish condition to a pale-faced existence bound by ritual and docility, lived in close proximity to the soil. Minsk stood in uncontained marshland, wild with fruit bushes and thickly spread with pine, fir and oak. Grigori Benenson grew up in the open. A keen fisherman, he was, like his father the bearded Ossip, tall and robust. Shortly after his sister Leah married Sophie Goldberg's brother, he took Sophie for his bride. I doubt whether he thought long before making up his mind. I never saw him perplexed by dilemma, in decisions great and small. The Talmud teaches that there are two sides to every question, but my father had never studied the sacred text. Caution was the least quality that could be attributed to him.

The Benensons traced their story back to a succession of rabbis, or rather wonder-rabbis – mystics with direct access to God, similar to the Russian holy men who wandered the villages distributing amulets against the evil eye. But father emphasized that my grandfather had put all this obscurantism behind him. He spoke and wrote Russian as well as Yiddish, and despite the

18

disadvantage of being a third-class subject of the Tsar, or perhaps because of it, he had done very well for himself. He was in a substantial way of business in the timber industry, which was practically a Jewish monopoly in this corner of Russia.

Father would speak affectingly of his early days, and in listening I was stroked by the fierce winds whistling around him, and imagined I heard the distant bellowing of a wolf. He told me how together with Ossip he would sledge across snow and ice into the forests and negotiate a deal with the bailiffs of the great landowners. They would buy up hundreds of trees, paint their own sign on them and return in a week or two with their peasant labourers wielding log-saws and axes. Once felled, the trunks would be hauled to the riverside. The Svisloch River twisted through Minsk before it flowed into the Beresina to become a gushing tributary of the mighty Dnieper. In winter the rivers froze, so the logs would lie untouched until the spring thaw which brought great activity and noise. The logs were lashed together and sent floating downstream, to be received by the Dnieper and carried hundreds of miles to the Black Sea. Ossip Benenson conducted all his business by word of mouth. The gentile landowners trusted the Jews to pay up at the end of the season, and a transaction was never dishonoured. I was reminded of this years later, for father seemed to have inherited the practice and kept all the particulars of his giant international deals in his inside coat-pocket.

The Benensons, and many like them, had lived in these parts for three hundred years or more, surviving famine and pogrom and other cataclysms when the land was the cockpit of rival chieftains, the feared 'hetmans' who wielded their swords in search of booty and for love of Christ. Grandfather Ossip knew the terrain from the time before the Tsar Liberator Alexander II freed the serfs. He had every confidence that Russia would in due course be the finest country in all the world for the Jews to live in. He wasn't going to make tracks West. What was America but just another continent, where you still had to *schlep* the logs down-river, where there were long dark winters as here, except that it all happened in a different language?

Now, another side to Ossip Benenson's personality: I recall, at our home in Baku, a photograph with hundreds of bearded men ranged importantly in solemn pose, the front rank seated on the ground, then rising until they reached almost to the upper storey of a rough building that was the Jewish assembly hall of

Minsk. Ossip was among them. It was the Minsk Zionist Conference of 1902, attended by Jews from all over the empire who dared to believe the Messiah should be made to hurry along with his work. If the promised homeland was restored around the holy city of Jerusalem they could be a nation like any other.

It required courage in those days to be a Zionist, for the authorities frowned on separatist tendencies among the diverse races under the Tsar, and they suspected, rightly, that Zionism was not merely concerned with going away to live in Palestine, but was developing a consciousness of the Jews' own specific history, culture and civilization. The rabbis too frowned upon Zionism. They wished to keep their young lions in check just as the Orthodox priests did the Russian peasantry, for they had a vested interest in ignorance.

And about that photograph. A generation or so later I was shown the picture again, this time in London. There, another man pointed himself out to me, seated not far from Ossip Benenson. My path had crossed with Chaim Weizmann's. He too was a delegate, though younger than most, at the Minsk Conference. Weizmann was to achieve recognition as the world leader of Zionism, a real Jewish statesman and a household name among his people. I was to count him and his wife Vera among my dearest friends.

Being totally uninterested in Pinsk and all it connoted, I have never known much about my mother's background. She never spoke of it to me, though I suspect the Goldbergs were well-established, and big fish in their ghetto pond. My sister Fira was close to mother, and no doubt they confided in each other. The youngest of us, Manya, persistently curious as she was about everything, could well have been a mine of information on the Pinsk family. I have always lived in the present. This may account for what people have described as the hardness in my character. Or perhaps I was, in some strange way, dormant until maturity. When I woke up there was no-one to ask.

Shortly after marriage in the late 1880s father broke away from the Pale of Settlement, and parental bonds. He had his sights on faraway Caucasus, a realm which in the nineteenth century formed part of every young Russian's romantic dreams. Not yet thirty, he took his wife and settled in Baku, to become the owner of an oil-field. Grigori was no romantic; it was the gambler in his strain that sent him so remote from his roots.

Europeans could go mad in that torrid climate, but fortunes were to be made there, so he and Sophie began raising a family: first a son, Yasha, then us three girls.

The lore of the West ascribes the magic of oil, and the drama of prospecting for it, to that famous boring in the Pennsylvania of the 1850s. But the Russians, the Georgians and Armenians had been warring over oil since ancient times, from the moment they learnt to use it as a fuel. Some tribes worshipped oil as a divine element, the whole area being known as the Region of the Eternal Fire. Oil overflowed into the villages along the Caspian shore, submerging houses even in recent times. Oil was a curse and a blessing in those parts. It was said that because of its health-giving vapours Baku was spared the Black Death, but oil also poisoned the soil, sending Tatars and Georgians wandering across the plateau and into the hills in search of pasturage.

Russia conquered Baku in 1806 to take this distant frontier within the Romanov patrimony and inherit a population composed of suspicious gypsy races descended from peoples enslaved by Genghis Khan. Every effete Russian nobleman, veins bursting as he sat at the regimental card-tables, affected to yearn for spiritual deliverance in the mountains of the Caucasus. The writer Lermontov of course embraced death here, in an ironic ending to a life he had himself mapped out in *A Hero of our Time*. When father arrived, Batoum on the Black Sea was the busiest oil port on the globe, with Russia and her Persian dependencies producing half the world's supply.

Baku lies on the tip of a peninsula that dips into the Caspian like a tongue sampling the storm-tossed waters. I have memories of the flaming waves lighting up the night as the vapours exploded into a thousand fires on the surface of the lake. For most of the nineteenth century the oil was contained in huge ponds inside and beyond the straggling town. Armies of labourers, each distinguished by his national dress, would scoop at the heavy liquid with primitive implements, pour it crude into skins and transport it by camel caravan to Batoum for shipment overseas, or to Tiflis and Astrakhan, or Saratov on the Volga. Drilling was by hand, for the American system of steam drilling was unknown. In fact, until my father's generation, most of the oil used in western Russia came all the way from the United States. Over there it was being refined into a manageable kerosene fuel for lamps. Russia was even then dragging her feet, neglecting her riches, waiting for another emperor to work the miracles of another Peter the Great. We lived in a world that was half industrial revolution, half Byzantine.

Then the Nobel brothers of Sweden came, swiftly followed by the Rothschilds of Paris. They adopted American methods and divided Baku between them, the Rothschilds having the major interests in what was called the white town, with the Nobels in the black town. Grigori Benenson arrived in the white town; before many years elapsed he was among the leading prospectors.

We lived in a spacious apartment cooled by thick walls and closely draped curtains, on Marine Boulevard. In front of us lay the world's largest lake and its richest source of caviare, from the sturgeon which proliferated there. From our balcony, which stretched across the length of the windows of our home, we observed the smoke belching out of the wooden derricks of the oil-fields. One day father came home and beckoned us all to hurry to the balcony and see his newest gusher. The oil spouted forth, and to our consternation we saw it burst into flames. 'Don't worry,' he said, 'it often happens.'

I suppose we were not advanced enough to know how to cap the gushers promptly. Father said the workers dreaded them, preferring to cope with the stuff as it oozed naturally out of the ground. Father spoke of a visiting American oilman who told him: 'Back home when we release a gusher we regard it as another fortune. Here you look on it as a disaster.'

When that observation was made I do not know. Certainly, father gave no appearance of contending with disaster for he constantly impressed his wife with his achievements. He may not have been as rich as the Rothschilds (perhaps he was, I had no way of telling) but he was a giant nevertheless. My French governess was terrified of him. She explained his business to me, doubtless in girlish words of one syllable, and it penetrated my mind that he was master also of territories along the great new railroad that crossed the Urals. So much for Russia's Pale of Jewish Settlement.

Strangely, I barely remember my brother Yasha in Baku. Jewish families are supposed to be close, but the Benensons came together only on Fridays, when mother lit the candles to usher in the Sabbath and we would be served the evening meal. Yasha was several years my senior. I retain a vague picture of him in his school uniform with the glazed peaked cap, and can still feel the sting in my arm where he once slapped me for interfering with his possessions. When I was seven or eight he left the little world I inhabited to go off and study chemistry in Germany. I assumed he was gone forever.

Fira's birth in 1899 was attended, I recall, by considerable domestic upheaval, for we were joined at the same time by a *kormilitza*, her wet-nurse. She was a Tatar, and resplendent from her richly-embroidered bonnet to her slippers of red velvet. The wet-nurse occupied a position of supreme importance in our household. It was an iron rule never to disturb, offend, or annoy her in any way, lest she become upset and her milk dry up. Jealous of little Fira, I sulked a great deal. I seemed to have no one to talk to, except Mam'selle my governess. And her I must have led quite a dance with my wilfulness, though I quickly took to speaking a simple French. Mam'selle left us shortly before my departure from Baku at the age of ten. As our coachman drove her to the station, I caught a glimpse of father raising his hat in a farewell that revealed a gallantry I had never before associated with him.

My childhood pictures of that man are curiously mixed. I held him in remote adoration, as a tsar of sorts in his own right. But I search my memory for some intimacy, some gesture of affection or special interest in me, and I find nothing. Large homes can make for loneliness in children, and I must have felt many a pang at the sight, in the long cool evenings, of the Armenian and Khirgiz families seated at the sea-shore, the mother in her best long *sarafan* spreading the black bread and cheese, the father tinkering with the portable samovar, children at play around them.

Father never played with me, and neither did mother. My governess took me for short walks, and to school daily. Before bed mother used to brush my long reddish-brown hair; it was her one concession to maternal instinct. She wore lots of bracelets which jangled as she brushed, and if at times I emitted a cry of pain, she would say: 'Don't fuss! A mother can't hurt her child, it says so in the Talmud.' I knew better. She simply disliked me, and I could understand why. I was self-consciously plump, and when I was dressed in one of my long party frocks she heaved a sigh, and looked the other way. Father was too busy to notice me. I rarely approached him, taking my cue from mother. Whatever went on in the privacy of their bedroom, I found little sign of warmth between them during the day. And I have no recollection of father coming into my bedroom, or kissing me, or telling me a story. I am not sure that it ever occurred to me that he should. Nor mother, for that matter.

It seemed that being in the oil business involved huge problems, and only a man of my father's calibre could cope with them. Sometimes I overheard him speak of difficulties with his workmen, and if he referred to any person in particular it was always to specify: 'Of course, he's a mad Tatar', or 'Naturally, what can one expect from an Armenian!' or even 'That stupid goat of a Jew.' (The Jews of the Caucasus were a primitive mountain tribe, speaking a Georgian dialect.)

Had my brother remained with us in Baku a little longer I might perhaps have drawn from him a stronger family sense. In my last memory he was in grown-up attire, like a military student, and saying a brief goodbye.

I asked mother, 'Why is Yasha going off to Europe?'

'He must get a proper education. They don't allow many Jews into our universities,' she replied. 'If he doesn't leave they may send for him to join the army now there's trouble with Japan.' I may have missed him for a while, though I was not the girl to express an emotion. Nothing much was said about Yasha in my hearing after that.

Any loving thoughts I had were reserved for father, especially when Fira came, a lively little doll, to preoccupy mother. We kept the Sabbath, as far as I could detect. Mother went off to Baku's small synagogue, which was near our home in the palm-lined boulevard, not greatly different from the houses on either side. The Jews did not make an exhibition of their religion, unlike the Moslems who dressed in finery on their Sabbath to answer the muezzin's call, the men bunched together in sedate progress to the mosque, and a few women following dutifully behind. The Christians moved through the town in full marching order on saints' days, the priest leading in his tall Armenian hood, his white-robed choirboys bearing the cross from which the Jews averted their gaze, lest they be struck down by blindness or whatever.

Father spent the Sabbath morning at home with his papers, saving the afternoon of course for his siesta. Then he would be off to some meeting-place where the merchants of Baku came to discuss their important affairs. His sole concession to the Lord's day, I recall, was in going on foot rather than summoning his carriage. It would be out of deference to his friends, not through religious conviction. I would rush to the balcony to see him leave; the reward of a wave was enough to make me a happy girl.

Each morning I wore a brown tunic with a white apron, and walking me to school my governess was suddenly released of all restraint. The years separating us dissolved as she prattled in her poor Russian about her life at home in Bordeaux. A boy there loved her, she told me, and once he had swum across the river, which she said was very wide at Bordeaux, to greet her on the other side. Mam'selle spoke in great detail of the wonders of Paris, though now, as I think of it, I doubt whether she had ever been there, except perhaps to change trains on her journey to Baku. I knew that mother had been to Paris. How else would she have cultivated such grace, and learnt to wear fine clothes and jewellery! It couldn't have been from Pinsk.

Having deposited me at the school gate, I could see Mam'selle in full flood with the other governesses and servants, and hear their rich laughter. We were girls only at school, all European. We started the day with '*Shto za druga mi imeyem, Nas on k zhizni probudil*' – the hymn familiar as 'What a friend we have in Jesus'. Stories of the saints were then recounted, and how we were to follow their example of devotion and sacrifice in all we did. I was not bothered that this was Christian education, and evidently it did not trouble my parents, for they could easily have hired a *melamed*, a Hebrew teacher, to give me lessons at home. Father did not see the Jews as eternally a segregated sect, though he had his doubts about the Georgian labourers who called themselves Jews and prayed every evening. They would never be Europeanized.

During a recital of poetry one morning, it must have been 1903, our teacher suddenly fell off her chair and went sprawling. We all laughed. Then the floor trembled, and from our schoolroom window I saw a roof crash to the ground. The noise became deafening. Buildings toppled all round us, we began screaming, and were huddled into a corner. I remember little after this, except our coachman gathering me in his arms and bringing me home through streets filled with people running from their houses in terror.

The earthquake ended as suddenly as it began. But it seemed as if the anger that had sprung from the ground now infected the human race. A revolutionary mood was sweeping through Russia, as though the immense continent was being set ablaze. I heard for the first time of a city named Kishinev. It was in Bessarabia and there, in April 1903, a rebellion of sustained

25

savagery occurred; directed, one would have thought, against the Tsar and the aristocracy, who lived in degenerate splendour. No, this was Good Friday, and bands of hungry workers went out to hunt down the poorest Jews in their wretched ghettoes. Houses were burnt, shops looted, with hundreds left dead or wounded. Punishment was being meted out to the killers of Christ. Then other, less severe pogroms took place in more towns within the Pale.

Tension mounted in Baku, not so much against the Jews, who were hardly discernible here. The Georgians in their Oriental dress were barely regarded as Jews; more Cossack than the Cossacks, the men carried the sharp-edged *kingal* dagger and their women, swathed from head to foot in coarse garments decorated in filigree, were rarely seen. Baku's disorders started with the workers on strike against conditions in the oil-fields. Father looked flushed and distracted. It was now the autumn of 1904. War had been in progress against the Japanese for some months and, unbelievably, was bringing humiliating defeats upon Russia. The military garrison in Baku, generally large and watchful, had been depleted to a mere detachment. Demonstrations led to sabotage, and then to the wilful firing of the oil wells. The tribesmen, only lately released from serfdom, had been treated as though they had few rights, and no feelings. Nowhere in the Empire were the discrepancies of class as wide as here. A sheet of fire engulfed the black town. Then, brandishing their torches, men came to set the white town alight.

I was almost ten years of age, and can still hear my mother imploring my father: 'Let us leave this place. Soon they'll be after us!' Did this mean those wild people were going to burn our house down? 'No, silly child,' said my governess, who was still with us. 'Your good father will soon settle them. We have barbarians in France too.'

She was right. The all-powerful Grigori Benenson settled the trouble exactly as she foretold. I was sure he personally had imposed peace, and that all the workers were now back at their labours, happy at being allowed to help their master make his money, thankful to him for their daily pittance.

Perhaps the idea was not all that foolish. It was beyond my knowledge, and would never have entered my comprehension, but the Tatar near-slaves of the oil-fields did not hate their masters a tithe as much as they hated their better educated Armenian fellow-workers. The simmering volcano in Baku and its surroundings was the enmity between these two races living in juxtaposition since the dawn of Russia. It now erupted with such ferocity, rifle against *kingal*, man against man, woman against woman, that sometimes the army itself took flight. Russia's notorious hooligan gangs, the Black Hundreds, invaded the streets to terrorize Christians and Moslems alike. The Cossacks were called in by a fearful Governor. They charged through the riotous crowds, their horses trampling man and beast underfoot in an effort to restore order. By the time the slaughter stopped no one could agree how it had begun. But thousands perished.

Was the Empire itself dying? Many people thought so, because of the happenings at the very centre of authority. St Petersburg, in January 1905, had witnessed 'Bloody Sunday', a demonstration in front of the Winter Palace when the troops fired on starving workers and their families. They had come solely to appeal to Tsar Nicholas, more in loyalty than in revolt. A priest had been at their head, and since that day the Russians employ the name 'Father Gapon' as a synonym for *agent provocateur*.

The Tsar looked on in incredulity, just like the little tsars of Baku. Soldiers mutinied in their barracks. Sailors on the battleship *Potemkin* threw their officers overboard. New pogroms occurred in Odessa and Mogilev, though this time the Jews were fighting back, joining the revolutionaries in the streets. Russia was flailed by a punishment that could only be wrought by God. The brontosaurus, survivor of a political ice age, seemed at last to be shaking off the bonds of despotism and heaving into life. Fanaticism and inertia were earning their retribution.

Held in its fever of suspicion, Baku had a recrudescence of communal butchery in September.

We again felt beleaguered in our home. Father now made a decision. He had spent a large part of his manhood here in the oil-fields, turning a small fortune into a great one. Some of his Jewish friends had taken out the customary insurance policy – conversion to Christianity. Not Grigori Benenson. He had his own way of doing things. If Russia was changing, then he would be an active partner in that change. He felt as much a Russian as any *moujik*. He was now a merchant of the first guild, so he would go and live in St Petersburg. There was, for him, no better place to face the challenge of the twentieth century.

Search my memory as I do, I cannot reconstruct how it was

27

that I, my mother and Fira, next found ourselves, assisted by nurse-maid and lady's maid, in, of all places, Wiesbaden beside the Rhine. What precise activity organized mother and her bracelets and fine silks, me with my girly obsessions and coffee-coloured tunics, Fira and her dolls, away from the Caspian shore? What were the farewells? What trains took us the thousands of miles across Russia? It is a blank.

Mother suddenly said: 'Fenya' – it was the diminutive, used by the family, of my first name Feodosia – 'Fenya, you will be staying here for some time. I shall come and visit you in a little while.' She spoke with a rare tenderness, but barely offered me a glance. Then a quick embrace and she was off, Fira trailing at her skirts. Too stunned to break into tears, I was suddenly very cold.

'Here' was the establishment of Fräulein Wolff for nice Jewish girls. I was too shocked to speak. 'In a little while' would be one year later. There had been no consultation with me, no advance warning, no preparation, no indication even a week or so before when we had taken up quarters in our ornate hotel. Surrounded by flunkeys we had eaten our meals in a brilliantly lit dining-room, virtually in silence. Not a word that I was to be abandoned. I had never been away from home. I had not even taken leave properly from father. I had learnt French, but knew not a word of German.

Working back to the date retrospectively, I find that this was October 1905, and I was not yet eleven. Fräulein Wolff was to have me in her care for nearly five of the most impressionable years of my life. But why Wiesbaden? It took an age to reason that out: mother's favourite dressmaker was established there. It was a happy arrangement for her.

Three unmarried Wolff sisters conducted the school, a very superior establishment in the Kapellenstrasse. They based their instruction on three iron principles, inspired no doubt by Bismarck himself. The first was that the Germany of Kaiser Wilhelm was the greatest of all countries on the earth's surface. Well, I knew better – that position belonged to Russia. The second principle was that anyone born and raised east of the River Oder was in most respects sub-human, never having learnt to speak properly, write intelligibly, dress correctly, or perform an adequate curtsy. The third principle deemed food as the nearest thing to daily administered poison, so the less consumed the better. In our refectory a banner spread across the whole of one wall proclaimed 'True Nourishment comes from the Spirit'. And so we had to learn to love the Kaiser, keep clinically clean, show extreme deference towards our elders, and allow ourselves to be transformed into proud *Mädchen* by a process of starvation. I was subsequently told by Fira that in my case it hadn't worked.

The better part of twelve months must have elapsed before I became reconciled to this outpost of Sparta on the Rhine. We identified the three sisters as *old* Fräulein Wolff, *young* Fräulein Wolff, and simply Fräulein Wolff (the one in the middle). I wrote letters complaining bitterly about the hunger and the discipline, begging to be returned home. All to no avail. I did not make a single close friend, though this was probably my fault, not the school's. I was embarrassed at seemingly having no real family. In holiday periods and even at weekends the parents of the other girls arrived and took their children out on trips, no doubt also to eat, while I wandered through the school alone. When those sharing my dormitory made great play of getting ready to go off to the mountains I would demonstrate my displeasure by poking out my tongue to its fullest extent.

Father and mother eventually turned up. I was informed I had a new baby sister – just like that, without prior warning. We travelled. A few days were spent in Paris and Monte Carlo, then weeks in Carlsbad, where mother took her 'cure'. Evidently St Petersburg was out of bounds to me. Father's stay was brief, and this I understood to be because of his pressing affairs of business. Then mother had me measured up for new clothes. I was not allowed to choose colours or style, there were quarrels and tears, so by the time she deposited me back with Fräulein Wolff I breathed a sigh almost of relief.

During the second year the situation improved somewhat. I now spoke and read German fluently, and was familiar with long passages of Goethe. His poem 'The Singer' struck me as reflecting such noble spiritual sentiments. When young Fräulein Wolff beat out Heine's 'Lorelei' on the piano and together we warbled the siren's legend, I found my eyes brimming. I too had long tresses, and was quite pleased with them, but would they ever captivate a man?

In Baku I had been making a beginning with Pushkin's lyrics, but now all that receded. In five years at Fräulein Wolff's I never picked up a Russian book. I don't recall even seeing one.

On Saturday afternoons we were paraded through the town and shown off to the local population. It was our reward for being good girls that Sabbath morning, when the refectory received its weekly conversion into a genteel synagogue. There we intoned the twenty-third psalm, and the 'Hear, O Israel' in such a manner that only the most attentive listener could have discerned that in our German version some of the words were swopped for a more interesting though mildly rude phraseology. I was beginning to enjoy Wiesbaden, especially as it was now my privilege to be among those who cleared the dishes when the Wolffs took their meals in their private dining-room, and I could devour their leavings.

As Fira grew older she accompanied mother on her annual visits. They were both attired in such finery as to leave me wondering whether the day could arrive when I might dress up in delicate fabrics without the skirt straining across my all-too-pronounced hips. Father seemed to be with us just long enough in Carlsbad to see our luggage stored in the Nassauer Hof Hotel, porters tipped, an evening or two passed stoically in this female company as though in a dentist's chair, and he would be off again, back to St Petersburg.

This I found completely natural. Mother, Fira and I spent long hours seated at the windows of our hotel suite facing the Kurhaus, waiting for meal-times (or at least I was!). This gave us a ringside view of the ladies and gentlemen whose regular visits to the spa for the treatment of their maladies were the nearest thing they had to a religion. Time to dress, time to walk, time to be recognized – all was geared to the life-style of the fashionable lady, or rather, to the life-style of the fashionable neglected lady. No doubt more mannish diversions existed too, but these did not feature in Baedeker and were well concealed from the public gaze. I believed the entire world spent the season as we did.

Fira once interrogated me about Fräulein Wolff's.

'What do you do there?'

'What do you think! We read books, do painting and embroidery, go out to art galleries.'

'Are the teachers good to you?'

'Sometimes.'

'What about the other times, Fenya? Do they scold you, or beat you? Mother says they are going to bring you up properly, because you're beyond her.'

'Does she now!'

'Yes. She says you are so moody, you hardly ever open your mouth. And you wear your clothes sloppily. She says she won't know what to do with you when you come home.'

'She won't be doing anything with me. I'll manage.'

'Do you take your clothes off in front of the other girls in your dormitory?'

'Of course.'

'I wouldn't. They would see that birth-mark on my bottom.'

Oh, if only I had such a birth-mark as my only defective feature! I would have proudly displayed it to the entire world. I had a large nose, and tiny, beady eyes.

Fira joined me at Fräulein Wolff's when she was about nine. It was a disaster. She refused to speak even the little bits of German she learned, and I hated being caught out talking Russian with her. She wept every night, so I was made to sleep with her in her dorm with three others of her age. It was humiliating.

One day old Fräulein Wolff said: 'Your sister is returning home. We can do nothing with Russian children like that. She doesn't belong here.' Mother arrived and Fira clung to her, bawling as though she had just been rescued from drowning, or a lion's den.

It was a relief. I was not myself looking forward to the day of my return to the family circle. Manya was a toddler by then, though I had not yet seen her. She would be too old for a wet-nurse, thank goodness, but still I couldn't face daily life encumbered with a chattering infant. Manya's very existence struck me as arising from some unwholesome contract between father and mother. I drove the thought from my head.

Were all civilized families like mine, I wondered? Did all girls in their teens quarrel with their mothers, and did all mothers spend their days changing their gowns and selecting their necklaces, and switching on their warmest smiles for their friends only to reserve their ugliest frown for their eldest daughters? In Baku I had seen great broods of children with their parents, a boy playing the balalaika, and a girl too sometimes. But they didn't count in the way we did. They had no proper homes, with servants and governesses. What happened to these children while their mothers were away wet-nursing the babies of the Europeans I could not imagine.

When I turned fifteen I knew the dreaded day was near for me to be sent off to St Petersburg. Wiesbaden was now the only place I felt I could ever love, and Fräulein Wolff's Academy for Young Girls in this rambling old building on the Kapellenstrasse the only home I desired. Even now, I had never taken a promenade unaccompanied through the Kur-Park, with its great limes and the statue of Gustav Freitag. I had never attended a performance at the Opera except in the company of a bunch of screaming females, never had the courage to ask anyone why, once a month, my woollen knickers should be stained with blood. I was unmoved when a letter arrived from mother informing me that we now had one of the finest apartments in St Petersburg, and so near to the Winter Palace that you could say we were neighbours of the Imperial family, the Romanovs. She said that from the room being prepared for me I could look down upon the Moika, the canal into which Pierre, that crazy aristocrat, was supposed to have flung a policeman tied to the back of a bear. 'You remember, it's in *War and Peace*,' mother had written.

I had never read *War and Peace*, but it struck me that a civilized German writer like Schiller would not have invented anything so ridiculous. It was so typical of barbaric Russia. What would I do with myself in that house, and in that city? Perhaps throw myself into the Moika.

In the Greek Chapel at Wiesbaden we used to visit the tomb of a Russian princess who had died there many years before. It was a beautiful monument, and I would linger a while there alone, thinking of myself as this Elizabeth Michailovna. In my imagination she had killed herself because of an unhappy romance; her lover had gone off to the wars, I decided, never to return. I too could die in Wiesbaden, readily. But who would grieve? I did not dare dream of such a lover for myself – it would be obscene, a sin for a Jewish girl at Fräulein Wolff's to admit to those thoughts.

My mind ranged over the men I had encountered, and what they meant to me. Herr Wolpart came each Monday to teach us the violin, and I considered with revulsion his great feet and the buttons bursting off his dusty boots. And Heinrich, in charge of all the odd jobs around the school; he was shaped like a bow, with a copious grizzled moustache so that when he spoke the words came through absurd whistles. Once, at the Opera, my eyes rested on the handsome young tenor in the throes of 'Der Rosenkavalier', but he belonged to an exalted world where my imagination could not roam.

And father. Now there was a man I could truly love, if it was allowed – erect, handsome and pure of spirit. I wondered, did he ever press mother in his arms, wipe her tears away, confess his undying devotion before departing for that other realm he inhabited, and which revolved around him? And would I ever know?

I caught myself conjecturing long, significant conversations with him. Now that I was an adult we could grow closer together. He would find me eager to hear of his problems and successes. Who could say, but one day he might well seek my advice on some important business decision that brooked no delay! I knew he would find me a great help.

When he came to take me back to Russia, early in 1910, we exchanged a swift awkward greeting. I yearned to weep out of affection for him, but the cold kiss I received stemmed all emotion. It was only when old Fräulein Wolff came to say goodbye, dear Fräulein Wolff, clothed as always like a clergyman and marching like a grenadier, that my composure disintegrated and I rushed to her, arms outstretched. Not one of my friends was there to see me off. Who really claimed me as a friend?

We travelled in one of the new motor taxis to Wiesbaden's red-bricked railway station, surely the proudest structure in the city of those days. Momentarily, I stood stock still before mounting the steps into the palatial entrance hall. I knew I was about to be swallowed up and made into someone else. A porter went ahead with my luggage.

Gently, as though guiltily, father spoke: '*Idyom skoraye*, Fenya, we'd better hurry, or we'll miss the train.'

Mechanically, I followed. We entered our reserved carriage. Taking my place in the corner by the window, I read a newspaper placard which has fixed into my memory to this day. It was the Berlin *Illustrirte Zeitung*, and announced: Pictures of the Funeral of King Edward of England.

As the train steamed away father leaned across to me. He pressed something in my hand, a string of pearls with a diamond-clip in a butterfly shape. My eyes spoke a demure 'thank you'.

Twenty years later I took the pearls to a Bond Street dealer and received a cheque for three hundred pounds. At that time an unemployed British working man was being paid a weekly dole of fourteen shillings.

2 The View from St Petersburg

All was quiet when we arrived at the Varshavsky Station in St Petersburg. It was late, and a cold Baltic blast moaned through the ironwork of the deserted platform. I shivered, shielding my throat as we descended from the train. A man fell upon our luggage. Silently we walked to our carriage. Perched at the ready on his box was the fattest coachman I ever saw, in full livery.

It was not long before we reached the Moika. As we approached Number 16 by the waterside the great double doors opened, as if miraculously, on to a courtyard – the expectancy of our arrival resounding louder than bells. Passive to the last, I was shepherded into our flat. A parlourmaid showed me to my room. As I closed the door behind her, I decided that I would never leave it. The best way to face my future, I told myself, was to remain unnoticed in here and starve peacefully to death.

I had overlooked one significant fact: the existence of Manya. A tiny stranger was already seated in a corner chair when I awoke in the morning. How long she had been there gazing at me I could not imagine. But the first words she spoke would be memorable.

'We don't sleep in our chemises,' she lisped. 'We put on night-dresses. That cupboard over there is full of them. Choose any colour you like.'

Starving to death in this house was not going to be easy. Anyway, I was ravenous.

To be thus introduced to a presence who intended no delay in establishing our relationship roused my foreboding of the night before. Clearly, little Manya regarded me as one of her belongings, long promised and at last delivered and possessed. Further assertions of her position followed in quick succession.

'You are to have Dounyasha to do things for you. You'll be sharing her with Fira. I have Rikarna, all to myself. They're asleep. But not Miss Lympany, she gets up first and is already out on her walk. She crosses the bridge every morning, then goes along the canal past the Royal Palace. She comes back after taking her deep-breathing exercises beside the Neva.' Was there nothing this child didn't know about anybody!

'Who is Rikarna?'

'My own servant. She gives me lessons too. But she can't speak French. Father brought her from Hellthinkforth. That's in Finland. May I kiss you, Fenya?'

A supreme act of resignation was called for. I allowed her to approach, and she brushed her lips on my cheek. I took this to be my initiation ceremony. Henceforward there would be no escape. Well and truly, I had to take my place that day as a Benenson.

Manya had brown hair and eyes, tiny features, and a disconcerting way of searching you up and down while her head seemed to point in another direction. Fira, I soon discovered, was the jewel in the Benenson diadem. She had grown tall since I last saw her in Wiesbaden, almost my height. She was a proper miss, attending school every day and shoo-ing Manya from her heels so that she could get on with the business of making her important presence felt. Fira wore her hair in tight curls, and one day as I observed Dounyasha helping her on with her boots I noticed her hands firmly clutching the arms of her chair. She had the most finely sculptured hands I had ever seen. Fira was self-contained, penetrating, decisive – all that at eleven. And here I was at fifteen, a hopeless, dumpy creature about as welcome in this ménage, I thought, as a hippopotamus. And a hippopotamus who had spent the most important years of her life sleeping in her chemise.

It came to me as a matter of no great import that mother had been right. We *were* neighbours of the Romanovs, almost. Our house stood at the end of the quay lining the narrow Moika, and there on the opposite side of the waterway rose the Hermitage, where Potemkin had started his career as lover number umpteen to Catherine the Great. From our drawing-room, a little Hermitage in itself, you might catch a glimpse of the guards parading in front of the Winter Palace. At an angle from our furthest window was the square into which the *agent provocateur* Father Gapon had, while we were still in Baku, led the innocents to their slaughter. On rainy evenings it shimmered with the reflection of a thousand lights from the Imperial residence. The Yussoupov Palace, in which Rasputin would one day emit a last agonized breath, was situated on our side of the canal, perhaps a fifteen-minute stroll away, at Number 94.

Thus had my father, of the accursed race, descended as all good Russians believed from the murderers of their Saviour, planted his roots: in the heart of the most august square mile of this holy empire, beside the huge cathedrals of its imposing religious authority, and just beyond the gates of the palace where Nicholas slept with Alexandra. Father slipped easily into ghetto self-parody, and once I heard him boast, 'Not bad, not bad, eh, for a little Jew from Minsk? On a quiet night, with the wind blowing in the right direction, you can hear the Tsar sneeze, and out will come Prime Minister Stolypin with a *Gesundheit!*' It did not immediately occur to me that this was his masculine humour, and once, when conditions were propitious, I was curious enough to strain my ears so as to catch His Imperial Majesty in the act, and wait for the echoing blessing. Without success, I might add.

I was generally determined not to be inquisitive about all our grandeur, as though I had seen it all before, from my worldliness cultivated in Germany. But before long, enough scraps of business conversation reached my apathetic ears to tell me that half of Russia must be in Grigori Benenson's pocket – a stretch of the Nevsky Prospekt as far as the Fontanka equivalent to Regent Street from Piccadilly to Oxford Circus, great forests along the Dnieper, and regions deep in the Urals concealing gold, platinum, and heaven alone knew what else. Naturally, he spent long periods away controlling it all, a matter which it seemed to me mother was taking rather ungraciously. She would counter father's exuberant greetings on his return with a cold silence.

I felt empty inside, a shadow moving across the façade formed by this family, this home, and its possessions. They were no more real than the scenery at the Mariinsky Theatre, particularly on the evening when Miss Lympany (who transpired to be our governess from England, and who escaped from us at every opportunity to lock herself in her room with her piano) took Fira and me to the Opera; for there on the stage was the bridge I could see from my bedroom, but in cardboard reproduction to illustrate an episode in the fatuous three-card-trick parody which alone remained of Pushkin's subtle *Queen of Spades* after Tchaikovsky had done with it.

We occupied a score of rooms, the upper part of Prince Volkonsky's granite mansion. He used the ground floor only, and I found myself thinking of the French Revolution – one of Fräulein Wolff's keenest subjects – as the carriages of his aristo friends clattered like tumbrils into our shared courtyard. Volkonsky was descended from a Decembrist hero of the last century, when a group of army officers tried to liberalize the Empire and paid for the conspiracy with long years of exile.

Of course, I knew nothing of the Decembrists at that time. It was my bookish cousin Leopold who told me of them, and much else about which I was professing total ignorance. Leopold and his brother Grigori had come from Minsk to live with us, for they had secured entry into the university. As befitted poor relations they shared an upstairs room, and from them I learned that many Russians lived somewhat less splendidly than we, and that father was probably regarded as an enemy by the mass of people beyond our exclusive Admiralty quarter of Petersburg. Here in the capital lived Russians who enjoyed greater legal rights under the Tsar than did the Benensons and yet did not have enough to eat.

Leopold could be rather boring about the Duma, and what a hoax the Russian parliament had become. When I got a word in, I asked him about his girl-friends. Didn't he meet them in secret rendezvous by the Bronze Horseman, which I understood was the general idea? He would quickly change the subject and fill me in on the Constitutional Democrats and the Social Revolutionaries, and the close-cropped firebrand Alexander Kerensky, whose voice was said to be like the bells of the Kremlin.

These were subjects in which I displayed not the slightest interest. What mattered to me, was me. I was a stranger, even an interloper, in this country, in this culture, in this household. The tip-toeing lackeys who hovered around the family, almost proclaiming that we had their subservience not because we deserved it but because we bought it, began to infuriate me.

At Fräulein Wolff's every industrious minute was accounted for, but here I was idle. Each morning, as Dounyasha tapped on my door to announce breakfast with the customary formula, 'Barishnya Flora, the tea is ready,' I dreaded the new day. Where was I going? If I was nothing, who would want me, who would marry me? I warned mother of the dreadful consequences. If I didn't marry when the time came, neither could Fira, or little Manya. It was inscribed, with letters of deep passion as though part of the Ten Commandments, that in a Jewish family the eldest daughter had to be the first.

Mother hated being troubled by long discussions with me. Her programme was fully mapped out, what with visits to her Petersburg dressmaker Mme Berthe, her social round, her charities and her preparations for her Wednesday *jours fixes*.

'Have a little patience, Fenya,' she said. 'Any boy in this city will be thrilled to marry you. You're not yet sixteen.'

'I don't know anybody,' I wailed. 'I wouldn't know what to say to them if I did.'

'First you will finish your education. You're having a teacher to polish up your Russian so that you can take your matriculation. I've discussed it with father.'

'Then what?'

'For you, Fenya, we'll find a prince.' Perhaps she was joking. I didn't think so.

'There aren't any Jewish princes.'

'No? The Gunzburgs are barons, aren't they?' She was referring to the pride of Russian Jewry. They were at the top of the social scale and it was said they were friendly with the Romanovs. One of them was father's lawyer.

'Mother, you know perfectly well none of the Gunzburgs would look at me!'

Her chin turned perceptibly upward. 'Wouldn't they? We've more money than they have.'

'Why don't you put me up for sale with an advertisement in *Razsvyet*?'

'Go away, I'm busy. And change that dress, you look awful!'

However, under the guidance of the teacher whom I recall as barely reaching my shoulder, by name Andreyeva, I started on Russian history and literature. We worked in my room, undisturbed by the others. Miss Lympany appeared displeased. She adored Russia, but nothing, in her view, should distract my attention from English. I was now familiar with four languages, including a good French, without which you were branded a cannibal in St Petersburg (once at the Michaelovsky Theatre the young Sacha Guitry and Yvonne Arnaud were performing Molière, and I watched with scorn as the audience roared with laughter in the wrong places). Yet, to this day I have never been completely proficient in any language. I was to develop a theory of my own about education, to compensate for my lack of it: a partially educated person, like the partially disabled, will cultivate skills that exceed the accomplishments of normal people.

Andreyeva's methods were not Fräulein Wolff's. In Wiesbaden all went at the majestic pace of a Catholic procession. Endless weeks were devoted to Kleist, for example, and every syllable he breathed. Andreyeva skimmed through Pushkin and Lermontov, took Gogol at a gallop, slapped Turgenev on the table instructing me to read him in my spare time and came to rest with Tolstoy's *Anna Karenina*, the only literary character she really liked. I panted to keep up, holding the external matriculation test in front of my mind as though it were life's great passing-out parade. Suddenly, after about a year, Andreyeva departed. She was to be married.

Shaking off a fantasy of my little teacher coupling with a bear of a man while they had a good laugh at the expense of the Benenson girl suffocating beneath a mountain of books, I finished the matriculation course entirely on my own, not too badly as it happened, early in 1912. By this time my horizon was expanding somewhat, for we were spending our summers in a different world, our country estate on the River Luga close by the Gulf of Finland at Redkino. Eyeing my fully-rounded limbs, mother emphasized that wolves lurked in the neighbourhood and I was not to venture from the house unescorted.

'Father says the wolves are very fond of Jewish girls,' Manya informed me helpfully.

There are two Redkinos in Russia. Ours was some forty miles south-west of Petersburg, near enough for father to make frequent trips to the capital, but still frontier territory, harsh and mysterious. A score of villages were situated on our lands. The rambling old colonnaded house, its peeling white exterior fronting a large English-style park, had a tang of dried fish and decaying corn emanating from the deep cellars where massive blocks of ice stayed unmelted from year to year. You knew here that you were treading the byways of history: the house was a former hunting-lodge originally built for Prince Orlov when Catherine presented that favourite of hers with the Gatchino lands, complete with a fabulous palace and ten thousand serfs. An old retainer who came with the house, the gruff kitchen-maid Natasha, had in fact been a serf in her young days, half a century earlier. The park's flower-beds and lilacs and oleander bushes were divided by a long driveway, though when Manya returned after the Second World War she found they had all been uprooted, and the house itself, converted into the district high school, had been done over in terra-cotta.

Father had acquired Redkino while I was still at Wiesbaden,

when the nobility, unable to sustain the feudal estates, were disposing of portions of their patrimony. At first the family travelled down in the carriage, our servants having gone on previously by train to the sleepy little Moloskovitsky Station. In my time we were chauffeured in our new Benz, Miss Lympany seated with us girls in the back wearing the neat yellow bonnet she reserved for excursions out of town. The first time the motor-car rumbled through the countryside the peasants gaped in wonder and made the sign of the cross.

Redkino exerted its magic over us all. I was much calmer, for mother was able to put up with me more easily when I wore country clothes. It was as though we had left the diffidence, the stilted, monotonous style of our life, under the dust-sheets of our Moika residence. My parents were closer here, and we seemed to become a real family as together we strode through heavily overgrown glades, or halted to chat with the peasants scything away in their tiny holdings. Once I glimpsed father taking mother's hand to help her across a stream. It was a slight gesture, but one to lift my heart.

Dressed by his tailor to look every inch a baron, father recovered his youth, riding and fishing (he would not shoot) in the country. It was a joy to observe how that normally finicky man disregarded the Redkino mud bespattering his clothes, or lost a little of his dignity as he danced a clumsy mazurka to the music of an ill-tuned balalaika. He ordered a gramophone from Meltzer's emporium in Petersburg, which Fira and I promptly commandeered to practise the new craze, the tango, with Manya studying our feet from her floor's eye view.

Despite mother's protests, father insisted that Fira and I ride with him in the forest. We put on our daring knickerbockers and mounted our horses bare-back. Mother had a quite neurotic fear that some harm would befall us, that one of her girls would be brought back on a stretcher. In retrospect I think this was her way of reminding father that, now that Yasha was away in Germany, he yearned for a son. We rode round the villages and paid our respects to the peasant-priests, to be told of a poor widow or an orphan needing help. It was the cue for father to make his contribution, after which he would be invited to share a glass of vodka with the priest and, this being Russia, the priest's wife.

Of course, they knew we were Jews, and if there was an undercurrent of mutual hostility it never showed. In St Peters-

40

burg it could be different. I had had a never-to-be-forgotten experience the year before, when Manya contracted scarlet fever and we older girls, with Miss Lympany, had to leave the house for a while and stay with one of father's employees. All was prepared for the important guests so that we should not suffer the least discomfort. However, the concierge appeared – doubtless, like so many petty officials in the city, he drew a second income as an agent of the secret police – declaring that the Englishwoman could stay but not the Benenson girls. The Jewesses had no independent right of residence in the capital and therefore could only be accommodated in their own home, where they were covered by their father's permit.

The situation was quickly rectified with a bribe, but the humiliating experience opened my eyes to the true meaning of a doctrine I had only been faintly aware of – Zionism. So that pompous journalist Mr Sokolow, who was our frequent guest and the recipient of a regular subsidy for his Warsaw newspaper, was right after all!

Now, at Redkino, father opened up to me and I learnt of some of the problems encountered by a Jew living in Russia: why, for example, his friend Libermann had been sent for a three-month incarceration in a remote monastery. A banker and convert to the church, Libermann had been spied upon while secretly celebrating the Jewish Passover with his family.

To my surprise, I discovered that father was himself deeply involved in a *cause célèbre*. A Jewish odd-job man in Kiev had been charged with the ritual murder of a Christian child, and was rotting in some prison awaiting trial. We were seated in the loggia in front of the house, the samovar bubbling away on the ancient oak table, and Manya lolling herself to sleep in the hammock suspended above the dust.

Father lit a long cigarette. 'The man's name is Mendel Beilis,' he said, 'a dim-wit. They say he took the child's blood to make the Passover *matzos*.'

I shivered. 'Can anybody really believe that!'

'This is Russia, Fenya, not Germany. Any excuse will bring the rabble on to the streets for a pogrom. Not only in Baku, but in Odessa, Mogilev, Zhitomir. You've heard of the Black Hundreds?'

'Of course.'

'They get paid by the police, and I wouldn't be surprised if Sheglovitov, the Minister of Justice, has something to do with them. I know that anti-Semitic rascal well. We won't let him execute Beilis, though.'

So this was why our house was so frequently filled with important visitors of late: Max Vinaver, who was a leader of the Cadet party (Constitutional Democrats) in the Duma, Oscar Grusenberg, the lawyer who won his fame in the Maxim Gorki trial, and of course Nahum Sokolow, the journalistic champion of the Jews. Stuck away in my room ploughing through Turgenev I had been almost oblivious of it all.

'No, they won't get away with it,' father repeated. 'We've got the best Russian liberals on our side. The pity is, Tolstoy is dead. But we have Gorki, and Kerensky. I don't like that fellow, with his wild ideas, but he's a genuine friend of the Jews.'

Old Natasha came out to replenish the charcoal in the samovar. I felt a little sick, and disgusted with myself. I had actually been feeling hard done by! Here was an old peasant woman, once a serf, and here were we. She was honoured as a Russian, her place in heaven already booked among the angels; and we were suspected of descent from the devil. Did she think so too, I wondered?

'If they find Mendel Beilis guilty there will be no hope for Russia,' father said.

I must interpose here a story to indicate how the Beilis affair came to spread its poison, even within our home, the following year, before the trial came up. We were not strictly observant Jews, but the first evening of Passover, the *Seder* feast, was always an occasion in our family. An elaborate table was spread, and we began with an amusing traditional ceremony, loved by my young sisters, of going round the house while father pretended to search for any scraps of bread that had to be removed. He liked to act it up, and it was hilarious.

Preparations for the *Seder* took hours and hours. Cousins and aunts and uncles joined us that night, as well as some of father's business friends, Jewish and gentile. Special items of food were intended to symbolize our slavery in Egypt, the Paschal lamb and the Exodus with, in the centre of the table, a goblet of wine for the prophet Elijah, should he choose to arrive unexpectedly.

The meal was in fact a religious service. It was interspersed with Bible readings and terminated with the singing of Passover songs. At given signals from the head of the family we would each take a portion of *matzo*, the 'bread of affliction'.

That year, just as all was ready, our butler led a delegation of servants to mother's boudoir. They had done all their work, he said, and were now leaving the house. 'We cannot serve a meal while you consume the blood of a Christian child,' the butler informed mother. 'We shall return tomorrow.'

Mother took it calmly, without a word of reproof. She then came to us girls, distributed aprons, and we served the meal ourselves. Religion has meant less than ever to me since that Passover of 1913. As it happened, Mendel Beilis was acquitted in the end, to Russia's credit.

Father had sounded unusually pessimistic for Russia when he recounted the case to me at Redkino. But he was really full of hope for the country. The Benenson interests had taken a tremendous stride in 1911 with the introduction of fresh capital from the City of London. The seeds of his scheme were planted in 1909, when Tsar Nicholas sailed to Cowes on the Isle of Wight for a state visit to his Uncle Bertie – the name by which every Russian who followed the fortunes of royalty knew King Edward VII.

Russia was until then a terra incognita to the British. Not only backward and despotic, she was inward-looking, with a concealed history that breathed great age but suspect legitimacy. Under popular pressure, and in fear for the extinction of his dynasty, the Tsar had convened the Duma in 1905. This brought to St Petersburg representatives from the four corners of the sprawling Empire, yet as a parliament it was purely a symbol, mocked by all Europe. The war with Japan had demonstrated Russia's capacity for self-mutilation; in fact Nicky was almost at war with his Uncle Bertie too during that fiasco, one of his admirals firing on some English fishing boats in the North Sea because, from the end of his telescope, he thought he had encountered the entire Japanese ocean-going fleet!

Now Britain and Russia were friends again. It was a signal the London financiers could not resist, and they began gently enough with a small merchant bank, Boulton and Company. It nailed up its brass plate on Admiralty Quay, no further from the Benenson residence than the Winter Palace, though in the opposite direction. A young Englishman named F. R. Cripps, attired in black jacket, winged collar and striped trousers, still in his twenties, passed our home every morning as he walked his dog. He was the local representative of Boulton's, and in the cosy Edwardian fashion he lived above the shop.

Mr Cripps came to dinner. 'Call me Freddie,' he said, eyeing our drawing-room as if he had suddenly found himself facing an audience from a cluttered-up vaudeville stage. Fira rushed away unable to suppress her mirth at his efforts to speak Russian. Before long Boulton and Benenson were partners in a great enterprise: exploitation of new goldfields on the banks of the Lena in the virgin wastes of Siberia. The nearest railway station was at Irkutsk, over a thousand miles from the region, and you could get a day's work out of the tribesmen for a dish of *borcht*. Once again, as in Baku, that shocking contrast with America: there, when gold was discovered, the workingman trekked west with dreams of washing a fortune into his pan; here in Russia the miners brought wealth to their masters in return for a regular ration of bread, meat and cabbage soup.

It therefore came about that father had returned in 1910 from a visit to London with a passion for things English, while Freddie Cripps, now one of our regulars, sat at the piano to sing a ditty about a certain Dr Crippen. Not then understanding that in the English language proper nouns have no inflected endings, I thought perhaps the two might be related. On enquiry from father I was told that Freddie had more august connections. He was in fact the son of a future nobleman (a younger brother would one day come into prominence as the socialist politician Sir Stafford Cripps).

Freddie struck me as a clown, nothing more. But not for the first time in my encounters with a member of the opposite sex, I discovered I had underestimated him. Not father. He made Freddie a director of his bank, which became the principal agent of trade between the two countries, with supplies to revitalize and modernize the Russian armed forces looming large. The government paid in gold, provided as it chanced from father's own sources at Lena – for Grigori Benenson it was literally the Midas touch.

As father ascended to the commanding heights of international commerce, his wife's attitude grew increasingly detached. Of course, she loved the affluence and proved the perfect hostess when business associates had to be entertained. Her formal dinners entailed her in feats of organization – 'Not a meal, Sophia Borisovna, but a symphony,' one of her guests told her as he kissed her hand in a fulsome farewell. Her Wednesday afternoons, I learnt from my friend Anna Becker, whose father had likewise made his money in the Baku oil-fields, were the talk of Jewish Petersburg. Anna assured me that my prospects for an excellent marriage were rated as the very highest. Still, ours was not a happy household. I blamed mother; she did not appear to work at making it one! And to my dismay, she would not permit any of the boys I met to call on me at home.

Russian middle-class girls were then winning their independence. Some had parental blessing to enrol in West European universities, mainly as medical students. The over-ripe seventeen-year-old Flora Benenson was not allowed to leave the house unchaperoned. Not once had I visited a restaurant, or travelled on the tramway. Neither did I carry money; though I could have anything I desired it did not occur to my parents to make me an allowance, and I am not sure now that I ever discovered how many kopeks made a rouble. The suspicion came to me that a cunning plot existed to keep me in a state of subjection. Perhaps they thought me a simpleton. Perhaps I suffered from some terrible illness, or abnormality, that made me different from other girls! Under the rules of our household (rules! the absence of them, rather) I was not being allowed to grow up. Five years banished to my personal Siberia of Wiesbaden, and now they would not let me out of their control.

Apart from our family socializing, when we travelled as a herd to charity suppers and the like, I received my own personal invitations to dance with the younger set. These led to pretty sombre occasions during the winter season, for instead of a boy friend I had to trail Dounyasha along. Mother's repeated admonishments rang in my ears: don't stay out too late, be sure not to eat too much, remember to be polite to your hostess. The instructions pursued me till the carriage – we still retained it despite having acquired a motor-car – with Dounyasha clutching my evening shoes to her heart as if they were a hymn book and she was on her way to church. She waited outside, no doubt cuddling up to one of the coachmen for warmth, till the evening's end.

By some implicit and unquestioned convention neither of my cousins was invited to the balls and parties I attended (Leopold had graduated and worked in our bank, while Grigori studied forestry science). Perhaps for the other girls they were enjoyable affairs, much anticipated. I rarely found them so. I was convinced, picturing Sonya the cousin of Natasha Rostov in *War and Peace*, who also had light auburn hair as her most pleasing feature, that I was there purely on sufferance. I would sit like a

45

dummy until summoned to the floor by some impeccably attired youth in dress clothes or student uniform.

It would mostly be that old mazurka or a Viennese waltz, danced to an orchestra in peasant costume. Late in the evening when the atmosphere flagged, we would try our sedate, Arctic version of the tango. And I groaned to myself: What am I doing here, who is this oaf? Sometimes he might try some pallid story to overwhelm me with his sophistication: 'Mademoiselle Benenson, have you heard the latest about Rasputin and the prioress from Luchina?' Or, to draw me out on our family doings, 'Mademoiselle Benenson, I hear that you are shortly leaving for a visit to England.' A desultory conversation would then ensue, while my imagination roamed to a disturbing vision of a captain of the guards plunging his lips into my breast.

They weren't much to me, these young men, but they could have been a start. So I was deeply ashamed when my dancing partners called the following day, as was the custom, and mother gave orders that they were not to be admitted. 'They're only after your money.' The categoric assertion offended me.

'I haven't any money!'

'You're not going to throw yourself away on anybody. Those boys will finish up as lawyer's clerks and shopkeepers,' she scoffed. I had heard it all so often! This Sophie Goldberg from Pinsk had done very well for herself, and now her eyes were set on Mount Olympus. By her lights money must go to money, Jew fuse with Jew.

In Fira's eyes I was unfair to mother. 'Don't call mother a snob,' she charged me, judging the situation quite differently in her precocious twelve-year-old mind. 'She's dreading the day you get married.'

'There's little chance of that.'

'She needs you, because she's not happy with father. Look at Yasha.'

'What about Yasha?'

'We never hear from him since he married that music student in Berlin. There was an awful row while you were away. Vera was without a penny, and mother didn't like her anyway.' I groaned to myself. Money again! Did this have any connection with the fact that Yasha did not once visit me in Wiesbaden? My God, what a family!

'Father looks after them. But mother says Yasha doesn't think of himself as her son any more. So she's holding on to you. After all,' she said gravely, 'Manya and I are just children.'

'Mother's not fair to father. He loves her! She should be very proud of him. And so should we.'

'I *am* proud of him,' Fira protested, 'but he's always too busy to spend time with us.'

My outbursts were not frequent, nor was I in a condition of permanent misery – just suspension. A time would come when my father would lead me out of this trap, of that I was convinced. In my calculation an eldest daughter was surely entitled to a role, a sort of recognition. Her life had to be assessed, her future planned. Father would know what to do. Wasn't he a leader in this great country, and totally fearless? I saw him lifting me with an encouraging smile on to a swiftly moving train, and I would be carried towards a horizon of wonderful fulfilment arranged according to his instructions.

In the meantime we would be going, all of us, to London where he was to review the state of his business in the hub of the Western world. I knew he would be spending much of his time in a street there called Moorgate, where he had his bank. We would be staying in a hotel called Claridge's.

Our governess helped to feed some excitement into the prospect. 'It's a city of gardens,' she explained. 'The traffic is on the move night and day, taking people to their pleasure in music halls, and for trips to the seaside – not like chilly Lake Ladoga, but where it is warm enough to bathe.' And, in her attractive, low voice, face smiling, she sang:

> Oh, Mr Porter, what shall I do,
> I want to go to Birmingham, they've put me out at Crewe.
> Oh, take me back to London as quickly as you can,
> Oh, Mr Porter, what a silly girl I am!

I could barely visualize it. We had been reading Dickens, which revealed the English as funny men with untidy bodies and unfortunate habits, and women of a most bizarre character. She would have none of it. 'Those are old stories of long ago. You should see the people in their Sunday best in Richmond Park, you will love it, Flora. And our soldiers and sailors are so smart, with bright brass buttons, not like here. You would think every one was a colonel at least.' Well, I was more than ready.

47

For a foretaste of this England, I must return to another occasion in 1912. First, the man from Cartier called, on one of his regular visits from Paris. Mother selected an emerald necklace and ear-rings for herself and allowed me to choose a row of pearls that fell low, as I had seen in an Isadora Duncan portrait, almost to my waist. Fira received a delicate locket from Fabergé's workshop. I was fitted by Mme Berthe, mother closely supervising, with a maroon lace and georgette dinner-gown (quite the wrong thing for a girl of my age and shape).

The British ambassador, Sir George Buchanan, was coming to dinner. We had frequent dinner-parties, but this was to be a ceremonial affair, in our ballroom. Count Alexis Bobrinsky would be among the guests; he was a descendant of Catherine the Great's 'little Bo', her child by Orlov, and President of the Council of father's Russian and English Bank.

Freddie Cripps turned up early and greeted me with a theatrical schoolboy flourish. 'Flora Grigorievna, you look radiant,' he called from across the room, then minced forward to assume an expression of sublime approval.

'So do you, honourable Mr Cripps, like the Prince of Wales.' And I treated him to an elaborate curtsy. I suspected he was enjoying a private joke at the expense of the ghetto. A pity he wasn't of our tribe, I might have worked more seriously on him. (When he did marry it was to a Duchess of Westminster.)

As they all trooped in and formed little groups around the room I thought of the opening scene of *Die Fledermaus*. The ambassador introduced Lord Balfour of Burleigh – nothing to do with the famous statesman – who was chairman of the London branch of the bank. Next I encountered my first monocle. It was affixed to the eye of Austen Chamberlain, and Freddie whispered a thumbnail sketch of its owner to me: 'Top man in the Conservative Party, but he's lost his job. Used to be Chancellor of the Exchequer, our finance minister.'

I remember that evening most as an extended exchange of pleasantries and compliments, and my discovery that Englishmen (or were these Scotsmen?) have a peculiar mirthless laugh, almost their own patent. I do not recall any mention of so prosaic a subject as money. The bank's object was to foster closer relations between two empires already linked in the descendants of Queen Victoria. England had neglected Russia too long. Grigori Benenson was an outstanding figure in the revival of his country's fortunes, and so on. It was interminable. Mr Chamberlain made a joke I failed to understand about Mr Asquith, whom he evidently did not much like.

It was really mother's evening. We caught ourselves throwing each other quick glances, almost conspiratorially, as if the front we each had to maintain required mutual encouragement. Elegance she wore naturally, but I detected a kind of desperation in her over-eager responses to the most casual remarks addressed to her. What role, I kept wondering, did she actually play in father's living pattern? And what was lacking? Would I one day have to sustain an occasion like this, strike up her pose of studied ease within a small-sized palace while my husband plucked riches from the world's geography?

Manya, her large white bow billowing in her hair, tip-toed over to mother for a good-night kiss, and I noticed to my envy how she could make that expression yield, soften. Theirs was truly a relationship of parent and daughter. Had it ever been like that in my childhood years in Baku? Life's unanswered questions hung heavily on me that night. I slept restlessly.

The next day's *Journal de St Pétersbourg*, the banker's French-language paper, carried a long report on the front page, and father was sent a message requesting him to save the Russian Empire from collapse.

Well, not exactly. That's just the way he sardonically put it. But that morning he had to change his usual routine. Instead of walking over to his office he was taken in the coach across the Fontanka and deposited outside a block of flats in shabby Gorokhovaya Street. He mounted the stairs to the third floor. Father had been summoned to a meeting with Rasputin.

All Petersburg knew the monk's address, how he lived in near-squalor, and what went on between the sheets at his apartment. He kept virtually open house, like the wonder-rabbis of the Pale, for any petitioner. But there was much more to the earthy priest than his mysterious influence over the women of the Court. He was one of the common people and deeply concerned with their lot. He spoke frequently about the injustices of Russia, and he knew that his enemies wished him in the grave, or at least back in his old village in Siberia. So what could he want with father?

Of course, money. Father related how Rasputin received him in a white-walled room crowded with his hangers-on. The odour of stale incense was all-pervading. Rasputin had proffered him a glass of tea. A half-empty vodka bottle stood on the mantel-shelf

49

over the fireplace. There was not an ikon to be seen. Mother asked whether he had fixed father with that famous stare. I laughed a little, recalling an endless English poem about an Ancient Mariner.

'He didn't look directly at me once,' said father. 'He told me that all the newspapers are corrupt, and the peasants are not being fairly treated in them. They had nowhere to express their point of view. He wasn't thinking of the illegal revolutionary papers. He's against those. So he's going to fill the breach. He has writers, printers, everything ready. And I've been given the privilege of paying for it.'

'How much does he want?' asked mother.

'Does it matter? A lot.'

'And you're going to give it to him!'

Father looked at his wife piteously. 'What else? Could I turn my back and tell him to go to hell? I am a Jew, the man could finish me.'

And so a newspaper was born. Rasputin called it *Golos Semlii*, 'Voice of the Soil'. How long it survived I do not know. Perhaps it appeared until the Youssoupov conspiracy that killed the *staretz* off. Perhaps Rasputin used the money for demonic purposes of his own. Father was not interested. It merely proved that no matter how powerful a Jew might become in this country he would always be used, in the traditional way, for someone else's convenience. You either paid up or you went under. For the interested reader, one copy of Rasputin's paper reposes in the files of the London newspaper library at Colindale. It is issue Number Four.

As far as I know, father never himself travelled to Siberia to inspect his mining interests. Though the Lena flows swift and broad there, it is moonscape terrain. A journey across the frozen wilderness from the railhead at Irkutsk was an expedition in those days. Father was the anonymous absentee proprietor with faithful local agents to control operations. The miners were also watched over by government officials and detachments of police. It was almost a secret operation, part of the great silence in which so much of Russia was entombed.

Until the massacre. My cousin Leopold, ashen-faced, spoke to me about it that terrible day in 1912 when he returned from the bank. He liked coming to my room, hoping to instruct me in his revolutionary politics as we observed the barges inching their way along the Moika. Now a hint of I-told-you-so tinged his voice.

It had been tense in the goldfields for weeks, he said. The workers were treated like slaves, and their families had to endure winter nine months long in hovels that were little better than caves. Murmurings of protest over the meat ration had turned into a riot, and then hundreds of miners went out on strike.

'People out there have no shops, no hospitals. They rely on the company for everything.'

'And the company doesn't give them enough to eat?' I thought of all the food discarded in this house, the immense stores on ice at Redkino. Surely father would want his employees to have sufficient food!

'The company always maintains there's enough. Or should be. But it gets stolen. The foremen hide quantities of it to sell off. It's an old story.'

That evening I surveyed our rich dining-table with guilt and distaste. Father told a shocking story, though we could only have been given part of it. The workers had brought their families with them to march on the administration. Then the demonstration got out of hand, the police commander lost his head and gave the order to fire. Two hundred died. It was a repeat of Bloody Sunday in front of the Winter Palace.

The Lena massacre produced disorders throughout the country, and a storm in the Duma. Fira and I were miserable. The agitation was directed against this man, our father, who reaped wealth and influence on the backs of the workers. And we reaped it too. We had to do something!

'You must tell him, Fenya. He has to help the poor people,' Fira wept. 'I'd rather we were poor ourselves.'

I confronted father with all the severity I could muster, feeling ridiculous. 'You ought to go to Lena and explain to the workers that you knew nothing about their conditions. Let them understand that everything will be better from now on. You cannot be blamed.'

'Fenya, don't worry about it. It's out of my hands anyway. The liberals in the Duma have started an inquiry of their own, apart from the government investigation. They're sending Kerensky, and if I know that man he'll pile up the case against the company, and we shall be the villains. Of course I'll make sure that conditions are better at Lena. We had the wrong people in charge. These things happen all the time in Russia.'

The Kerensky inquiry revealed the horrors of the Lena Goldfields: how sick miners had expired from exposure, their boots frozen to their feet; how children grew up illiterate, and women were subjected to the grossest treatment devised by man. The inquiry had the desired effect. The situation improved radically. The lawyer Alexander Kerensky became the people's hero and entered the Duma as a leader of the Socialist Revolutionaries. It had been a nightmare for the Benensons.

Lena was to work its way through my system. I knew nothing of the labouring classes, of course, but something told me I would one day be allied to them. I felt I owed them a debt.

However, for a young person of privilege, a solution to discontent, even if only temporary, can be found in travel. One foggy afternoon early in 1913 our entire family, accompanied by a retinue of servants, arrived like nesting starlings on the platform of Victoria Station in London. We were met by a gentleman who declared himself to be Mr Herbert Guedalla.

Mr Guedalla was living proof that the London half of the Russian and English Bank was flourishing no less than the Petersburg branch. He was its managing director in Moorgate, and he spread a welcome to us that would have been more appropriate to visiting royalty about to seal a pact of eternal friendship with the British Empire.

Was our suite at Claridge's insufficient for so large a party? A door was unlocked and behold! the space was doubled, with connecting bells to our staff in their attic quarters. Fira and Manya tried all the window balconies looking out to London on three sides, only to retreat in disorder, coughing and sneezing. They tried the grand staircase and then scattered over the restaurant, returning with the glad tidings of the presence of a large orchestra got up, in the words of Fira, 'like Hungarian admirals'. That girl certainly knew about clothes.

Did we enjoy the theatre? Mr Guedalla had our tickets for the latest Marie Tempest drama *Esther Castways*, with Arthur Wontner (whose little son would one day inherit our suite at Claridge's and indeed the entire hotel) as the poor victim enticed away by Another Woman. What about the opera? It was Thomas Beecham's season of Richard Strauss, alternating with Nijinsky and our own beloved Karsavina dancing the new Stravinsky ballets.

While father sat in Moorgate, counting all his English money no doubt, mother and I were transported to a feast of corsetry at Dickens and Jones. I was fitted with several 'specialities' as they

52

called them, boned down to the hips; the magazine I had leafed through assured me they would endow my figure with an alluring suggestion of unrestricted suppleness. They tried. We summoned Mr David the posticheur from Maison Nicol in Haymarket to dress our hair. This entailed more excitement with what the British called a 'court' milliner (I wondered which court). The rage in London was for broad-brimmed hats in velour felt, out of which rose a gull's wing at a rakish angle.

What about a trip to the countryside? This we did as a complete family. We were received by Freddie Cripps's father at Parmoor, his estate fronting the Thames at Henley and climbing through farmland into the Chilterns. I was rather surprised to find such a house in England lit entirely by oil-lamps, as electricity did not seem as yet to have reached the district. Freddie's forbidding aunt, when we were introduced to her, transpired to be Mrs Beatrice Webb. The visit went off quite well on the whole, though I received a jolt when the old man, his eye twinkling, asked me whether I had met the American actress Freddie had with him in Petersburg. Thus I learned that no Englishman is as he seems. But I too had a secret before I left, that perhaps Freddie didn't share. Sir Charles had been promised a new title. 'I shall call myself Lord Parmoor, after this place,' he confided to me. 'But please don't breathe a word.'

Naturally, England proved an enthralling experience for us all, though we had tears too. Miss Lympany would not be returning home with us. 'I've been warning you long enough,' she said with her self-conscious little smile. 'I'm going to marry Mr Johnstone.' We had never really absorbed the information.

'But how can you go now?' pleaded Fira. 'There's so much you promised to show us. You said Buckingham Palace and the Tower of London and those things. We've seen *nothing*!'

'You will, my dear. You have lots of people helping you. I shall never forget my darling Benenson girls. And I'll never forget Russia. If I have a daughter of my own I shall give her a Russian name, as a reminder. That I promise you.'

Her daughter Moura (a Slavic form of Mary) was born in 1916. She began her career as a concert pianist at the age of twelve, and we observed her fame spread with all the pride of ownership.

Mother was dubious about replacing Miss Lympany. 'You and Fira know English so well,' she said, 'and Manya loves Rikarna. I don't see the point of bringing another governess to Petersburg.'

53

I would not have it. I spoke English abominably. And I wanted more of everything England represented.

'All right, if you insist, Fenya. But you will have to make the arrangements yourself. I haven't the time.'

It was quite a victory, the first occasion I had made a family decision of any import. So, rather pleased with myself, I took a taxi to Madame Aubert's agency in Regent Street.

'I think I have the very girl. Miss Cook. Would £45 be satisfactory?' Madame Aubert had no qualms about doing business with a young foreigner who lived at Claridge's, even though it meant dispatching one of her charges into the unknown without first verifying my credentials. Weren't those the days of the white slave traffic? Couldn't I have been an agent with an innocent-looking face?

I hadn't the slightest idea whether the £45 would be Miss Cook's pay for a week, or a month, or a year, or indeed whether I had purchased the governess outright. At any rate I agreed. Miss Cook promptly turned up. She was thin as a broomstick but very easy-going, not like Miss Lympany. 'You can call me Cookie,' she declared. Her predecessor would never have tolerated such familiarity.

Mother explained that the £45 was the usual annual salary for an English governess. 'I suppose you know what you're doing, Fenya. I see you want to run the family. Like a Sultana.' She often had cause to call me that in the years to come.

Herbert Guedalla was of old Sephardic stock, originating from Spain. The Sephardic Jews affected to think themselves a cut above us Ashkenazim with our East European background. But if Herbert harboured such prejudices they were quickly overcome in the case of his chief and his family, though I doubt if he was guilty of them in the first place. He belonged to the higher Anglo-Jewish coterie that welded Ashkenazim to Sephardim through the right school, the right university, the right marriage. He was generous, imaginative and well-connected. He brought us to his home in Bedford Court Mansions, and his country house in Berkshire, where he entertained in style.

One evening I came to his Bloomsbury flat and barely had I time to remove my coat than he took me into his library, where innumerable portraits of his wife greeted my eyes: as Portia in the *Merchant of Venice*, Ophelia in *Hamlet*, Julia in *The Rivals*. He went from picture to picture, explaining that as Lily Hanbury she had been the toast of London. They had only been married

54

three years when she died, in 1908. Obviously he had not yet recovered from the blow.

'When I first saw her, at the Savoy Theatre, I knew she'd be mine. But she waited sixteen years before saying yes. Lily gave me the most wonderful years of my life. Her last performance was the feminine lead in *The Prisoner of Zenda*.' I felt his closeness, and the room grew oppressive.

Herbert had a life in the theatre entirely separate from his City existence. At his parties I met Beerbohm Tree and his actress wife Maud. Once there was a great rustling of skirt heralding the entry of Mrs Patrick Campbell. I never came to Bloomsbury without encountering Philip Guedalla, Herbert's nephew, holding forth on some aspect of literature or politics. Not yet the celebrated biographer, Philip had been an amateur actor at Oxford. He stood out as the most theatrical of any in his uncle's circle. Swarthy, rather handsome, he dressed flamboyantly, like a latter-day Disraeli. It was plain to everyone that Herbert was trying to bring me and his nephew, then an impecunious young lawyer, together.

I was flattered, of course, and allowed it all to proceed. Philip Guedalla introduced me to his friends, privileged sophisticates who assembled freely, without plan or forewarning, at all hours of the day and night. They were at the same time earnest and frivolous, very English in their love of sport and dining out, but a closed circle nevertheless. Among Philip's friends were the brothers Henry and Gerald Reitlinger, both of whom were very knowledgeable about art. Their father had some business dealings with the Russian and English Bank, while they consumed their days looking at pictures and their nights at the Café Royal. (Later Gerald was to atone for these lotus years by immuring himself in important research on the destruction of European Jewry under Hitler, producing a classic study *The Final Solution*.)

It so happened, therefore, that my London experience became distilled into a series of flirtations. Mother naturally assumed my new friends were after my money. If so, it was worth it, in the confidence I gained through knowing them. It demonstrated at least that my over-protected era was approaching its end.

Both Philip Guedalla and Henry Reitlinger sustained their attentions during that month in London. Perhaps it was all just a game of which I didn't understand the rules. But it was now time to leave, for we were to return to Russia via another little tour that took us to Monte Carlo and similar centres of elegance and indulgence. The real triumph of my London visit was Cookie. I saw her as my creation, my gesture of independence, acquired for £45.

An all-infecting patriotic fever greeted our homecoming. In 1913 the Romanovs celebrated the three-hundredth anniversary of the dynasty, and few could resist the emotion generated by such a landmark. Church bells pealed continuously, it seemed, to augur Petersburg's most brilliant season for the rich, and the miraculous appearance of food in plenty to nourish those less fortunate. I fell in love with my native heath afresh. Or was it for the first time?

The square in front of the Winter Palace became a stage for endless scenes of pageantry as the Cossack Horse Artillery formed and re-formed along the Neva to demonstrate the might and glory of this nation; though the might was really a deceit and the nation barely a nation. Daylight hung from the skies and the Russians seemed never to go to bed, turning the famous national insomnia from our white nights to advantage at last.

Out of all this the imagination wove an aureole about the Tsar and his consort that gave him descent from the gods. Their very impression of innocence became exalted in the public mind. I shall never forget the picture in the Nevsky Prospekt as the Romanovs arrived for the service of thanksgiving at the Kazan Cathedral. We gathered at the bank, in the building of the Singer Sewing Machine Company and directly opposite the huge church. Mother had long planned for this day, with enough *zakuski* and vodka to ensure that our guests would not die of starvation as they observed the arrival of the royal carriages. Faintly, echoes of the Te Deum emerged from the Cathedral, reached over the concourse and caught our ears. And when they trooped out in procession we joined millions in a moment of collective awe. Who could imagine how soon it would end, in the tragic fate of the Romanovs at Ekaterinburg!

At Redkino that year we were a first family too, in our own little kingdom. How father relished his role that summer! The peasants were bringing in the corn harvest and we crossed the estate four ways to pay our respects at each village. Busy were the days, jolly the nights, for we were followed by servants driving carts and bearing vodka by the bucketful, which they ladled out to all and sundry. Is it just a touch of imagination for me to recall 1913 at Redkino as a time when it seemed the entire Russian Army was on manoeuvres in the vicinity? Perhaps it was so in fact, for handsome officers really were stabling their horses beside ours while I blinked at the sight as though at forbidden fruit.

Some evenings, after their days in the fields, the peasants congregated with their balalaikas in our park, more vodka would be distributed and the revels continued till dawn. Mother would peek warily from a window and then, reluctantly, permit Fira and me to help Natasha and the other servants bring out trays of *zakuski* and steaming *piroschki*. We would be received with a cheer, and the hammering of a Boyar dance, occasionally accompanied by a gesture from peasant loins to make me blush. Night brought me little sleep that season, only the mingling of confused scraps of half-caught memories in which Bloomsbury spread over to Minsk and I ached from a pain that wasn't there. Soon I would be eighteen, older than Anna Becker, older than Methuselah, and still with the name I was born to. It would be a long Russian winter.

I waited for a sign that father realized something had to be done about my future – let him sell me into slavery if he wished, but *something*. He made no sign. Fira was growing into a sylph, though with a suggestion of the family nose, and remained close to mother.

The new year dawned to all the frivolities with which plutocrats like us deceived themselves into thinking they were aristocrats. Expensively adorned, we skated along the frozen Neva, danced the evenings away, read the new Arnold Bennett and Somerset Maugham novels as they arrived from London. Cookie was good fun, and cheerfully accepted my moods. 'Flora,' she would say, 'what a wedding yours will be!' But as I studied myself in the mirror I saw I was not growing more beautiful. We travelled again to Monte Carlo. We returned. Soon it would be spring, then summer, and father would be trout-fishing again at Redkino.

I was out for the afternoon with Fira and Cookie one bright day in 1914. The carriage was ours for as long as we wanted it, and the fat coachman lunged with his whip and jollied up the horses, to impress upon his passengers that here he was in charge, St Petersburg belonged to him. I recall the excursion particularly because Fira acquired, to my disbelief, a measure of pale blue shantung silk, declaring that she was going to make it up into a party frock for herself. She knew exactly what to buy for trimmings, and this entailed wandering from shop to shop in the Gostiny Dvor until she found exactly the items she needed. What a child!

The carriage brought us home towards five o'clock. The concierge, I thought, greeted us slightly more deferentially than was his custom. Upstairs in our flat all was quiet. Strangely, the blinds were drawn. Was anything amiss?

Yes. Father was in his darkened bedroom, surrounded by doctors and nurses. His head and face were completely covered in bandages. The devil had entered our lives, in the dainty person of one Tamara Kolinskaya armed with a bottle of vitriol. I was never to meet her in the flesh, but she would haunt my existence for decades to come.

3 A Londoner à la Russe

All I knew in those days of the intimate relations between men and women came from books. In the Russian novels I read a mistress would often be hovering in the background, curtained from the main events in the story but representing a mysterious force drawing men to acts of sublime altruism or foolish pride. Real love to me meant romance. The rest was shunned, unthinkable and certainly unutterable.

Once at the theatre we watched some trite frivolity about a man bewitched. Mother whispered reassurance to Fira and me: 'Don't think about it, girls. He's a silly old man, but a gentleman.'

Could it be that father, all these years, had been living a second life? Did this explain the desiccated atmosphere generated in our home, the coldness of my parents towards each other, the protracted absences of the man I worshipped? Did he have another ménage in this city, its bedroom alternating with the one he shared with his wife? Whom did he embrace? Did the parents of grown children need to love each other? And if not . . .?

Answers to these questions, and much else, were revealed in mother's expression that cruel day as she emerged from father's room to fetch and carry for the doctors. I don't think I felt sorry for her, but I understood her at last. A marriage that had mocked at love for more years than I could calculate had exposed its true nature in the space of minutes. Her look told all.

'I dare you to go in there,' she seemed to be saying to me, 'for you will find not a father, not a husband, but a toppled monument.'

Kolinskaya had, it transpired, been pressing father for years to divorce his wife. He had refused, to spare his family the humiliation. Mother had finally held on to what was rightfully hers, and to keep her children unblemished: in our society hypocrisy might be excused, but scandal would neither be forgiven nor forgotten.

Father and his mistress were apparently already estranged, but she had pressed him (lured him?) to a final meeting. It had taken place on a train on the outskirts of St Petersburg. She had demanded money, half his fortune, for herself and the child she said she was expecting. Father could not be moved. What happened next might have come out of a story by Dostoevsky. Kolinskaya held a box of chocolates which she proffered to father. As he bent to choose one she withdrew the acid concealed in her muff and flung it in his face. His cries of agony were heard in another carriage, the train was stopped and a doctor who happened to be a passenger administered first-aid, perhaps preventing blindness. We did not yet know. The woman was apprehended and taken away. Nearly seventy years have now elapsed since that day, yet the recollection still suffuses me with the sensation which tells a girl she has reached womanhood.

Father's millions could not command a Russian specialist to save his sight. Only in Germany, we were informed, had surgery advanced sufficiently to treat such a case. Mother acted. A telegram went off to No 3 Hectorstrasse, in the Charlottenburg district of Berlin. The address came straight from her head, as though locked there in a secret compartment against some crisis as this. It was the home of her son, my unknown elder brother Yasha.

Yasha, then a research chemist in his late twenties, replied at once. He named the one man who might help father as Dr Erich Lexner, of the University of Jena. Yasha had contacted him, and he would accept father as his patient. Dr Lexner's advances in the grafting of human tissue had made him an eminent pioneer in the world of surgery. He wanted father's removal to his clinic without delay.

At this juncture something turned my mother into a mere onlooker of the drama. Doubtless she was in a state of delayed shock. It may have been the onset of an emotional fatigue – an inability to fight any more to keep an unwilling partner at her side. I find it difficult to voice the thought, but perhaps she received grim consolation in observing this man to whom she belonged not as a Colossus bestriding all the world she knew, but prostrate, a victim of his own reckless ego. She must have quailed from the prospect of closing up our home not for a victorious pageant across the spas of Europe as previously, but to shepherd a mutilated husband through endless hospital wards to have him, in the end, a blinded, disfigured charge upon her life.

The task fell to me. I felt no less love for my father than before. I think I would willingly have died in his place, if that should be decreed. A daughter understood better, or could draw upon a different reservoir of feeling, than could an aggrieved wife, and it must have been this that made me take command. How sudden was that reversal of roles! I had never of course read a train time-table in my life, or reserved a railway carriage. Now I did this, and all that followed. Mother clung to Fira, Manya sat passive and perplexed, quiet for once. This residence, with its endless rooms and stupid chandeliers, its servants, lackeys and hangers-on, was reduced to an echoing-chamber.

And while a constant vigil was kept over my father I moved through the silence of the place making the arrangements. It was May 1914, and I was not yet nineteen. More days of anguished waiting were required as we took up our family dispositions. Mother did not demur when I suggested taking little Manya with me to Jena. We would bring Rikarna (she of Hellthinkforth) whom Manya obviously loved more than any person in the world. Cookie was mine, and something of an irrelevance now in Petersburg: she would return to England. Being still at school, Fira was to remain to console mother and assist her in protecting the family territory.

The Benenson scandal was a morsel some St Petersburg newspapers could not resist. They scavenged through Tamara Kolinskaya's past for more and yet more choice gossip, anticipating a long trial of the accused. This additional torment stirred mother to a momentary renewal of her strength.

She recalled the help father had once extended to Rasputin. Wasn't it time to repay that service? Deliberately, she made the preparations, dressing with careful modesty. From her store of jewellery she selected a magnificent brooch. If anyone in the city could stem the daily flow of titillation it was surely the priest of Gorokhovaya Street. The meeting was brief. She left her present and the newspaper stories promptly ceased. There was no trial. Kolinskaya departed from St Petersburg. So did I, never to see Russia again.

The train throbbed in unison with my heart-beat on that journey, and the sight of the ambulance waiting at Jena to take father to the clinic brought me the relief that must come to a drowning man on his rescue.

61

'We shall be able to rebuild his features,' the doctor said, 'but it will take many weeks.'

'And his eyes?'

'We are in time.'

I found it effortless to converse again in German. The surgeon was a short man, with a correct, diffident manner, like a civil servant from a Russian inspectorate. I stood at father's bed, barely able to discern in the gloom that a man lay there. His voice came through the swathes of bandages enclosing his head.

'Don't worry, Fenya. It will be all right.' He had always been like that. 'Don't worry' was his formula for every catastrophe, as though whatever might befall us, as a family or as individuals, the Benensons possessed attributes enough to ride the tempest. I lacked his confidence, but shared his stoicism.

When my brother and his wife Vera arrived from Berlin I struggled without success to connect this person with the youth I had last seen as a child in Baku. It was clearly evident he wanted it that way, indicating by his manner that our meeting marked no reconciliation with the family. He would do his duty as a son but no more. Vera was almost as tall as Yasha; she might have had a personality at the piano, she revealed none as she sat taciturn beside her handsome though awkward husband. Germany was a country of camping, youth movements and wanderlust camaraderie; I recollect Yasha at some time speaking to me of a Jewish fellowship he belonged to, called *Blau-Weiss*. He hoped one day to settle with Vera in Palestine, so beneath that frigid exterior a zest for experience must have been at work.

May became June, with father lying expressionless behind his charred skin as one operation followed another. Little else interested me, though I felt it unwise to leave Manya in the exclusive care of Rikarna, her nurse and governess. Rikarna was afflicted with a neurosis dating from some sad experience in love many years before. Her Swedish-Finnish background shrouded her in a close religiosity and I had the unhappy suspicion that Manya was coming under the influence (a surmise that was to prove justified, as Manya later revealed). So I tried to bring my sister nearer to me – how successfully I do not know. I have never been very good with children, not even with my own son. And Manya was withdrawn.

However, my education was turned to fair use as together we

filled the days by walking round the attractive little city, inspecting the host of shrines marking the sojourn in Jena of Germany's cultural heroes – Goethe, Schiller, Hegel, Fichte. Manya was hardly of the age or disposition to be interested. She missed Petersburg and pined for Redkino, forever recalling the angels decorating the ceilings of the great rooms there. But she was not otherwise suffering, as far as one could tell, from the family catastrophe.

June turned into July, and ever so slowly father's wounds began to heal, though he knew he would be permanently disfigured. He was allowed out for brief walks to test his eyes against the light. I was oblivious of everything beyond the clinic and had been unaware of the assassination of an Austrian prince at Sarajevo, starting Europe on its slide towards Armageddon. When Yasha mentioned such things he dismissed any danger of war.

Late in the month the signals grew unmistakable. What would happen to the Benensons should Russia and Germany find themselves on opposite sides? Father of course said 'Don't worry', but one day, returning with him from a promenade among the crowds in Jena's lovely Paradise Park, Dr Lexner, his brow furrowed, told us the worst. He was a naval officer in reserve, and had been summoned to the colours. Russia mobilized on 31 July, and the two countries were at war.

The surgeon said: 'I am to take over the naval hospital in Hamburg. My work with Herr Benenson has reached a delicate stage, and it would be dangerous to stop it now. So I suggest you bring your father to Hamburg and I shall continue to treat him there. He still needs to undergo a further series of skin grafts.'

Within hours we seemed to be on a soil melting under our feet as young men in greenish uniform filled the streets. Each move we made became a harassing exercise. Suddenly everybody began to chase after taxis, long queues formed outside the banks, the railway platforms thronged with jostling humanity. To be a Russian was to be regarded with loathing: we were being accused of assassinating all Germany's political leaders and throwing bombs in the market-place. And worst for us, our regular flow of funds from Russia dried up, frozen at its source.

It was unthinkable that the Benensons should actually be short of ready cash. We were booked to take up residence at the Atlantic Hotel, a flamboyant edifice beside the Alster. Dr Lexner's fees had to be paid, a nurse retained, and of course we girls could not be expected to live beneath the standard to which we were accustomed. Many Russian citizens found themselves stranded in Germany, students and others, without means of subsistence. They clamoured at the makeshift offices set up by the relief agencies. It was unlikely that the Benensons would be joining them.

Father, whose every hesitant step had to be carefully guided, now considered himself restored enough to re-assert his dominance over all the money in the family exchequer, not excluding the petty cash. I was left once again without a penny of my own, just as it had been in Petersburg. Before leaving Jena he felt in his pocket for a note. 'My last hundred marks,' he said. 'Send mother a telegram to join us in Hamburg. Be sure and bring back the change.' Small change was a fast-disappearing commodity in the war's early days.

I went off as instructed, but in the crush at the telegraph office somehow lost the note. Devastated, I returned to father with the news that we were now stony broke.

'Never mind, Fenya. Let me see.' He fished once more in his coat. 'Ah, yes. I have another hundred marks here – my very last note.' The old ghetto humour was rising to the surface again. He never failed to catch me out with that one.

At the Saale-Bahnhof we had a moment of terror when father was required to produce his identification. He showed his passport (both Manya and I were on it) and the sight of the Russian crest sent a policeman into a frenzy. He tore away my father's dressings, exposing the raw flesh. Father remained stock still, his pustulated face revealing no emotion as his nurse quickly replaced the bandages.

Somehow, by the time we reached Hamburg the pressure of being Russian seemed to decrease. England, to the incredulity of the Germans, had entered the fray on the side of the Slavs. As a result, the torrent of anger was diverted away from us and on to everything British. Hamburg, Germany's window on the world, was filled with foreigners. Many of them, speaking English, wore little American flags in their lapels for fear of molestation. The world, I saw, was going mad.

Not that I responded with a surge of patriotism for my own country. I felt no necessity to comprehend the issues at stake, and it amused rather than disturbed me that people saluted each other in the streets with the new war-time greeting 'Gott strafe England'. I had no opinions on Belgian neutrality, or Austria's

My father

*My mother with
my younger sister Manya*

Our family house on the Moika in St. Petersburg

Myself as a teenager

*Myself shortly after I arrived
in England*

Marriage to Harold Solomon.
On my right, Fira. Manya
kneeling in the centre.

Alexander Kerensky in 1917.

*Chaim and Vera Weizmann
in their early married life*

*Wystan Auden with my son Peter –
'His Tartaric Majesty and his Royal
Umbrella Holder'. (See p. 146.)*

Myself with Mrs Roosevelt

With Mrs Churchill   *And Simon Marks*

*Manya Harari and
Fira, Countess Ilinska.*

problems with the Serbs. All I knew was that anywhere I had previously been with my father the path had been cleared for him, like the waters of the Nile opening up before the Israelites. Now he was an ordinary man. Perhaps his wounds were rendering him incognito; when they healed all would be right again, with Grigori Benenson recognized for what he was, in my mind one of the world's most important men. And indeed, within the portals of the Atlantic Hotel the magic worked once more. Our suite overlooking the lake measured up to our customary standard. The world knew its place, even though the porters carrying our bags thanked father for his tips with the invocation that the Almighty punish England.

Despite the dislocation around us my dear father had not been at a loss. Dr Lexner had arranged for him to be received with all propriety. Further, my father knew a man in Hamburg, Max Warburg, whose whispers in any direction were almost commands. He presided over the powerful Warburg bank, with its ramifications in New York, its stake in the Hamburg-Amerika Line, its connections in government. This distinguished burgher, having learnt of our predicament, arranged for father to keep his lines of communication open, rendering the Benenson funds accessible. How this was arranged I do not exactly know, but throughout our stay in Hamburg father was in correspondence with his people both in London and St Petersburg. Probably the route lay via the Warburg's New York branch. So there was always another last hundred-mark note in that cavernous pocket.

(Years later, Max Warburg's daughter, the beautiful, spirited Lola Hahn, was to become one of my dearest friends. It was after Max had been broken on the wheel of Hitlerism and she arrived in England a refugee – one of those ironic reversals of role to which my destiny has so frequently been subjected. Lola's brother-in-law Kurt Hahn came too, re-establishing in Scotland the school to which he had devoted his life, and which achieved new fame as Gordonstoun.)

What a strange place this Hamburg was at the onset of war! Bismarck, guarding the harbour from his tall pedestal, surely did not recognize it. All shipping had been commandeered, leaving thousands of would-be travellers with little to do but sit around in the cafés – I can see their blank faces to this day – or while away the hours window-shopping on the Jungfernstieg with its inviting boutiques. You could not venture out into that iridescent autumn sunshine without encountering detachments of troops marching off somewhere, arms swinging to their robust anthem:

Lieb Vaterland, magst ruhig sein,
Fest steht und treu die Wacht am Rhein.

whereupon every German mother would cease her chores, open her window wide and join the chorus. I observed that the soldiers' belt-buckles carried the slogan *Gott mit uns*, lest anyone be in doubt as to how the war was to end.

Mother and Fira had been caught by the war in Carlsbad. On their arrival in Hamburg we paraded as a harmonious family, father impatiently testing his skin against the weather. We sipped coffee at the Alster Pavilion, we strolled along the Collonaden, we began to laugh a little. Father's nurse, a Brunhild to the core, never missed an opportunity to notify us that by Christmas all her country's enemies would be vanquished. With the early Russian reverses and the swift German advance towards Paris she would taunt us with a shake of her imperious shoulders and, I thought, forget her professional gentleness as she tended her patient's wounds. Towards this he reacted like a stone, accepting the pain without demur. But it drove mother into hysterics.

A great Russian army was defeated in the swamps around Tannenberg. A month later Antwerp fell. Yasha was interned. Fira and I had to report to the police twice daily, and this grew into a welcome distraction, for we struck up friendships with other young Russians who likewise had little in which to employ themselves. We sampled the places of amusement that livened the field-grey atmosphere of Hamburg, though never daring to speak Russian in public. Biting our lips at the newspaper reports of the impending collapse of our country, we grimaced when the Kaiserin appeared on the cinema screens as a sort of goddess mother-figure: her six handsome sons were at the front.

I think the Germans had no doubt even in those days, well before the advent of Hitler, that their destiny was to control the entire continent. You could buy an illustrated magazine in Hamburg filled with war pictures captioned in virtually every European language, including such obscure tongues as Flemish and Serbo-Croat.

Christmas-time, and the promised victory had not yet materialized. The stalemate left us on the northern shore of the bleeding continent as though we had ceased to find an excuse for surviving our days. The Allied blockade placed a steel girdle round Germany, and for the average citizen food began disappearing from the shops. This we gathered from the newspapers, not from the lavish table regularly set for us in the restaurant at the Atlantic. Only when I passed the crowds silently scrutinizing the casualty lists posted around the city did I begin to perceive the real tragedy of the war.

Dr Lexner's responsibilities extended out of Hamburg to Ostend and Bruges, wherever naval hospitals were established in the wake of Germany's westward conquests. He held the rank of surgeon-admiral now, with less and less time for his Russian patient. Father did not object. He considered himself cured anyway by the end of the year and now spoke only of escape from Hamburg. The inertia imposed upon us as enemy aliens irked him more than it did the rest of us – idleness was a kind of norm to which the female side of the family was well adapted, though naturally mother yearned for her old life in Petersburg.

'It won't be as it was before,' I emphasized to her. 'They have now named it Petrograd, and much else has changed.' She remained unforgiving towards father, and a negative quantity. I was troubled by the prospect of our future as a family. It was not discussed, as far as I could tell, by my parents. But frightening decisions would have to be made.

I recalled mother's old reproach, or taunt, and realized that I was truly 'the Sultana' now. As our most qualified German speaker, and with father still unsure on his feet, I rushed hither and thither, edging to the front of the queue to find the right people with whom to register our request for repatriation. I must have made quite a spectacle in my black-striped woollen outfit complete with sealskin muff and hat – a model sent from Strohbach in Berlin – as I impressed the priority of our case upon one official after another. I had no idea that an established procedure for repatriation might exist and probably drew a picture of unfortunate orphans marooned in the storm, with connections that only coincidentally included a surgeon-admiral and the head of the Warburg bank.

Thankfully, we found ourselves on a steamer at last, bound for Stockholm. This was nearly one year after the outbreak of hostilities. Something additional to my own powerful advocacy had apparently been at work: two Turkish consuls in Russia, with their families, were counted a fair exchange for Grigori Benenson and his appendages. We left the Atlantic with heads held high, father distributing gratuities in gold coin to any and everyone in the lobby who looked like an employee, probably tipping a few other guests in the process. With a combination of relief and foreboding we turned our backs to the gimlet gaze of Bismarck and sailed out of the Elbe to entrust our fate to other captains, other kings. Mother spent the voyage in her cabin weeping.

In Stockholm we divided forces once more. There was no other way. Father intended to be in London; mother, with Fira, insisted on returning to our home on the Moika. The war sanctified as it were my parents' separation, granting them the excuse they desired. It was the virtual end of our family as a unit, the end of a fiction if you like, and yet eminently respectable. Weren't there reasons enough for stationing Benensons in both cities?

'Fenya will come with me.'

Father uttered the matter-of-fact words as though he were ordering an item from a restaurant menu, and thus was my destiny entirely settled. Manya, her private logic an enigma to the rest of us, clung to me as a surrogate mother. At Bergen we boarded a vessel for Newcastle. Leaning over the deck father discarded the last of his dressings and dropped them into the sea, to mark his resumed role of financier, capitalist and international entrepreneur. If the face was shockingly altered, and the eyes half-closed, the determination was as strong as ever it had been. England being Russia's ally he nominated London a province of the Benenson empire.

London was also a crowded war-time capital, and Claridge's was not immediately available, so Herbert Guedalla arranged for us to stay provisionally at the Berkeley, overlooking Devonshire House. According to Manya, whose memory of those times carried the meticulous details imprinted on a child's mind, we started life there with coffee brewed by Rikarna on her portable spirit-stove.

Devonshire House, since demolished, was given over as a headquarters for the Red Cross, but my recollection of the world around Mayfair was not of a place burdened by a painful war. Not that I would dare to essay a faithful picture of what England termed 'the home front'. We were soon restored to Claridge's, our rightful estate, threading our way through the lobby at the very moment the actress Marie Lohr was conducting a dolls' auction in aid of Belgian refugees. It soon became obvious that distractions existed in abundance for the favoured, or perhaps I was witnessing a *danse macabre*, the young men whirling into amusement with the thought that each day might be their last. Freddie Cripps's Petersburg *amie*, Teddie Gerard, was the toast of the town, packing them in at a Palace Theatre revue where, daringly attired in a dress cut low at the back, she shared top billing with Gertie Millar.

To my intense relief father at once harnessed himself to that mysterious place called the City. London seemed relaxed: the words 'business as usual' hung from shop windows, with civilian suits more frequently to be seen than khaki in the streets. Unlike Germany, this country conducted her war with just a volunteer army, and only the occasional Zeppelin visit brought us a touch of blood and a hint of fire. By all published accounts Britain, not her enemy, was in sight of victory. They gave it as fact that she had only just been cheated of it: her troops had covered themselves in glory at the Dardanelles and, but for some understandable failure of the army commanders to get together with the naval commanders, she would have knocked Turkey out of the war to bring Russia the support she needed for a final drive in the East.

Some of my old London friends were away at the front, some were already dead. Philip Guedalla had at last found a use for his legal training with a job at the War Office. He was engaged to Nellie Reitlinger, who was something they called a VAD and worked in a hospital. Her brother, my old beau Henry, commanded an artillery battery in France. Being Russian, I found, was something of a help: our armies were taking the strain away from the Western Front and I received full credit for this. But I went rather mechanically about my affairs, such as they were, and missed Fira more than I admitted to myself.

Patterning my attire on pictures of the gentry in the *Tatler*, I took to riding several times a week in Rotten Row and on Wimbledon Common. Chaperones became a thing of the past during the war. Father occasionally joined me, and I found that despite my bulk I could sit side-saddle with the adequate graces. A close eye had to be kept on my young sister, for her expeditions with Rikarna in town invariably seemed to terminate in a visit to a church. This will not do, I told myself, and found a little school where Manya could while away her mornings. Then I marched her off to the children's department of Swears and Wells in Regent Street and allowed her to choose whatever

69

clothes she wanted, eschewing the kind of elaborate performance, with ecstasy alternating with despair, that mother indulged in on similar expeditions.

One day the hall porter of the hotel came to inform me that my
motor-car awaited outside. My motor-car? I felt embarrassed,
and went to investigate. There indeed was a motor-car. A
uniformed chauffeur, looking far too tall for this small auto-
mobile, stood beside it. He introduced himself.

'Miss Benenson, I am Mr Guedalla's chauffeur. Your father
has instructed me to teach you to drive.'

I was angry. Whoever heard of a girl just twenty years of age
driving a car! Had taxis been abolished in London? Father was
evidently making plans for me behind my back. I dismissed the
man, by the simple act of turning tail and returning to the hotel.

Father listened in patience to my tale of humiliation when he
returned that evening. 'But the times are now different,' he
explained, 'you must have seen how so many women in London
are doing men's work.' (In fact, I hadn't noticed this at all.) 'I
want you to learn to drive, and to use a typewriter. You will find
these things useful.'

'Do you mean I have to *work*?' I almost shrieked.

'I haven't asked you to work, only that we have to be prepared.'

Next morning the car stood outside Claridge's again. Meekly I
greeted the chauffeur.

'This car is called a Scripps-Booth,' he announced, as though
its name might strike me as information worth knowing. 'If you
will kindly get in, Miss Benenson, I'll show you how to make it
go.'

I made myself comfortable in the passenger seat, but he
expected me to take the wheel. He showed me a few hand
movements, a few foot movements, a few neck movements. He
seemed satisfied. He then got in beside me. 'Right, off we go,' he
said coaxingly.

Within an hour I had crashed the gears round Brook Street,
Davies Street, and into Piccadilly. One-ways didn't exist, nor
traffic lights, but motor and horse traffic cluttered the thorough-
fares, almost as today. I was not very absorbed with driving on
the left, the right, or in the middle of the road.

'It's a beautiful new car, you won't want to work it too hard to
begin with,' the chauffeur advised. I had no intention of doing
so, but was far too concerned lest he saw an unwarranted extent

70

of my ankles to be gentle with the engine. At Hyde Park Corner I had what was normally a jungle of wheels entirely to myself, for the policeman on point duty stopped everyone else dead at the sight of me. I might have been a nanny struggling with her pram across a busy road.

It was the only lesson I had in over sixty years of driving. Back in Brook Street the chauffeur touched his cap and left me in sole command. I grew to love my Scripps-Booth, a little red devil of a machine that made me queen of the road. After a few days I took it along Oxford Street, to change my library book at Mudie's. Reaching the crossing with Bond Street my reflexes somehow refused to co-ordinate, and a huge jam of traffic grew around me. A bobby called, 'Reverse, miss, reverse!' I failed to understand him, got the thing moving and ploughed relentlessly forward, causing everything and everybody to flee in all directions. Only later did I discover that a car could be made to go backwards as well as forward: the chaffeur had omitted to instruct me in the reverse gear. As for father's injunction about the typewriter, I held my ground. I gave the toy to Manya, refusing all association with the beastly instrument.

Father was caught up in much else beside his business. The arrival in London of a Russian Jew with connections taking him into the drawing-rooms as well as the banking halls of leading citizens – some with titles, an adornment to draw a gasp of obsequiousness in First World War England – brought a trail of other Jews to his door. It is a characteristic of our tribe that however much you wish to forget your origins, no other Jew will allow it.

Of course, father had no wish to forget he was a Jew. He was known as a man of conscience for his part in the defence of Mendel Beilis in the notorious ritual murder trial. He was on terms with friendship with Nahum Sokolow, who as Zionist representative was now also in London to press upon British politicians, as well as anyone else who would listen, the cause of re-establishing the national Jewish home in Palestine. Sokolow was joined in this endeavour with the chemist Chaim Weizmann, who had made his home in England a decade earlier and now served the government on a project related to the munitions programme. Also of Russian birth, he had a flair for capturing men and women of influence for the ideal.

The story of how Britain came to make the cause of Zionism her own in the First World War, which had much to do with her

71

own aspirations for a foothold in Palestine, has been described more effectively than I can hope to do. In any case, I was privy to few of the important discussions. And I was young, female, and of little consequence except as a link with Grigori Benenson. So I don't propose to enter into detail here. I had been converted the moment I discovered in St Petersburg that as a Jewess I was forbidden to sleep anywhere except under the parental roof. Zionism meant natural justice to me; I espoused it as one supports kindness to animals and goodwill to all men.

Father was not a passionate Zionist. He lacked the single-mindedness, not to mention the vanity, that leads a man to the top of a political movement. But he would not avoid his responsibilities when it came to bringing succour to his people, the great majority of whom were impoverished, vulnerable, and the victims of anti-Semitic governments throughout Eastern Europe.

He enjoyed using me as his chauffeuse. And this was why, early in 1916, I brought my little Scripps-Booth to the front door of a house in Porchester Terrace, Bayswater. It was the home of Herbert Samuel, the Home Secretary and first professing Jew to sit in a British Cabinet. Samuel was in his mid-forties at the time, young enough for England's Jews to anticipate another Disraeli in the making, and withal one who, unlike his great predecessor, had remained loyal to his ancestral faith.

Father was calling on Samuel as unofficial representative of the Russian-Jewish community in this country. This comprised mainly recent immigrants heavily concentrated in the East End slums, and people were asking why more of these aliens were not in some army, British or Russian, and fighting the common foe. Britain had at last, with her appalling losses of the previous years, introduced conscription; but it applied to her own citizens alone.

I was not present at the interview. Instead, I waited with Mrs Samuel in a distinctly airless parlour. With great ceremony she poured me some tea, and with gentle persistence interrogated me about my past life, present activities and future prospects. I was careful to be deferential to the lady; a lorgnette suspended from a silver chain rested on her bosom.

'How well you speak English, my dear,' she told me. 'My goodness, you *have* had some experiences for a young gel. To have been in Germany at the start of the war! Did you find them brutal? Those poor Belgians! The Germs will have to be punished when all this is over. What a clever gel you are to be able to drive a motor-car.'

72

I had not found it brutal over there, but kept my silence on the subject. It hadn't escaped me that the 'Germs' were regarded in this country as savage Huns. In fact what the British and their enemy had in common at this time was an addiction to tales of atrocity. Anyone disputing this in London was stamped a traitor and a spy.

Beatrice Samuel spoke about her family, the Franklins, which she described as though recounting the dynasty of the Plantagenets. She had married her cousin, and their forefathers had settled in England over a hundred years before. Her eldest son Edwin was a senior at Westminster School, marking time in his top hat and striped trousers – she showed me a picture – until he reached the age to go into the army.

'You know, even the gels in England have to do their bit.'

Speak English well I might, but she employed a phrase that was incomprehensible to me. Nevertheless I recognized in the statement a subtle reproof: I was an idle, frivolous thing, having a good time at the expense of all the other women who, standing behind their menfolk, were in the struggle to make the world safe for democracy, the British Empire, the Jews and everyone else.

'Perhaps you would like to meet some of my nieces. One of them is a VAD, you know. Did you say' – here the ponderous implication of degenerate luxury – 'that you're staying at Claridge's?'

I knew of that British war-time institution, the recruiting-sergeant. Beatrice Samuel was evidently of the breed. But I was not going to give her the satisfaction of ensnaring me. The next day I got in touch with Nellie Reitlinger and soon I was escorted to Devonshire House where, without ceremony, I was inducted a VAD and ordered to accompany Nellie to Charing Cross Hospital and report to the matron for duty. A banner across the frontage of the hospital proclaimed the admonition 'Quiet for the Wounded'.

The Voluntary Aid Detachment – and I think I am offending no cherished illusion in saying so – was a cosy niche for women who refrained from 'doing their bit' in the factories, on the buses, on the farms, all of which were increasingly absorbing the less well-placed. It attracted those who customarily opened charity bazaars, rode to hounds, and revealed by their dress, accent and politics that the egalitarian society was as far away as in the days of Henry the Eighth.

True, I was directed by a martinet of a ward-sister to polish brasses, roll bandages and wander up and down the ward finding bottles to empty. True also, the aristocracy of Britain demonstrated, by the copious flow of its young blood, that it was in the battle heart and soul. Many VADs were operating close to the front in France. And, after all, women had never before in this country occupied any role that was not decorative or domestically utilitarian. But the VAD organization was, nevertheless, a preserve. I had never, throughout my life, been either decorative or domesticated, and hence should have stood at the bottom of the ladder. I fitted in because my father's money was a tolerable substitute for that purer metal, class: it promoted me to the section of society recognized as 'society'. We were driven hard, but not hounded like ordinary nurses. We slept in our own home as before, occasionally played truant, and found ourselves in the company of officers and gentlemen rather than the uncouth baser ranks.

Even then I did not take easily to hospital drudgery of the earthier kind. Possessing my own motor-car I soon moved over to more congenial duties. The hospital trains arrived with tragic frequency at the station on the opposite side of the Strand. I loaded up every morning with these 'Blighty' cases, taking them to their homes, or to convalescence, or to other hospitals in the Home Counties. One hardened quickly to the sight of mutilated limbs, and I had ways of introducing a little colour into my work. Many a good-looking lad was gratified to find his journey homeward beginning with a slap-up lunch at Claridge's.

All that year the French held on to Verdun by the skin of their poor soldiers' teeth; their heroism would, we were advised, cost the Germans all their remaining strength. Britain saw victory in her grasp yet again, at the Battle of Jutland, apparently to have it cruelly snatched away through some misreading of signals the admirals were sending each other. The Somme should have turned the tide after that, but the weather had the effrontery to favour the enemy. The Russians, it was insisted, were at last getting their steamroller going towards Berlin. The German people, obligingly dying of starvation, would have to surrender at any moment. According to the experts, it was good news all round, and the fact that the Allies made no headway was nobody's fault in particular.

I suppose this was what was known as morale. I was too new to the country to understand that Britain always fought her wars

74

like an amateur. There I was at Charing Cross Station to encounter men, some blinded, some minus a limb, who only days
before had been in the trenches up to their knees in filth, and yet
the war was really so far away. The soldiers spoke hardly at all of
the battles, nor of the futility to which they were condemned.
Indeed, their tongues would loosen on no subject. I was beginning to see the war as a clash of national conceits and found I
could not take sides, as if I were a neutral spectator at some
horrific football match. Guiltily, I ascribed this to the shallow-
ness of my emotions, or that I had no person dear enough for me
to test them upon. I observed many scenes at the hospital that
should have rent my heart. When this didn't happen I blamed it
on my old sense of isolation, of not really belonging anywhere,
which I called my detachment. I recognized with a tremble that I
felt no genuine pity for anyone, and no self-pity.

Beatrice Samuel was as good as her word, and I found myself
enmeshed with a great clan of female Franklins, each highly
intelligent, some totally disorganized, none really beautiful.
Jeanette Franklin, about my own age, brought me to her mother
Laura, to whom I was a somewhat pathetic refugee who had
strayed by mistake from the East End, where cohorts of Franklins did social work among the poor. Laura was the darling of the
bunch. After one Zeppelin raid over London – it caused considerable loss of life, though nothing of course to compare with
the Blitz in the Second World War – she insisted that I bring
Manya to her country house in Kent to eat strawberries and
enjoy some peace. We arrived together with Rikarna, and her
canary.

'We are strictly kosher here,' Laura stated by way of greeting,
'and there's no smoking on the Sabbath.' She eyed the canary as
though it might be the first to lapse.

Laura had cats, so it was decided to lodge the bird in the one
room of the house where no uninvited creature, animal or
human, was permitted to enter: Mr Franklin's study. Jeanette
told me of the significance of the gesture, indicating that I was
acceptable within their circle. Jeanette was a sculptress, and
dressed like one. Her hair was usually flecked with white, from
the materials of her trade, and from time to time she would
absently pick pieces off and eat them. She had a sister Ruth, a
cousin named Dulcie, and all hinted that a trail of young men
stood in a queue to marry them.

I suppose they felt sorry for me. Despite my distinction as the daughter of a man credited with untold millions, it was inconceivable to them that any man of their acquaintance would wed a foreigner. I would have to wait till the war ended. I could then return to Russia and find someone of my own inferior kind.

(By all the ironies, the husband Ruth Franklin eventually settled with, several years later, was first to be engaged to my sister Fira, and rejected by her. He was Fred Kisch, in 1916 a colonel with the Royal Engineers serving in France. Fred belonged to the same aristocratic Jewish set as the Franklins, and was subsequently picked by Chaim Weizmann to work for him in Palestine, on the grounds that to deal effectively with the British the Jews needed a pukka sahib. Fred Kisch was certainly that, having been born in India.)

Weizmann picked me too, in a way. In 1916 he was a scientist with a brilliant reputation, though still grieving that Manchester University had turned him down for a professorship. Here in London he was charged by Lloyd George, then Minister of Munitions, with producing the acetone essential to keep the guns firing. Weizmann supervised its manufacture from maize by a process he had discovered. He rushed from his laboratory to chemical factories all over England, taking in meetings with Whitehall civil servants on the way, and usually gave the impression of being on the point of collapse.

To have all this, and engulf himself besides in the politics of Zionism might have felled a lesser man. Weizmann throve on it, though he occasionally expostulated that he was 'walking on eggs'.

So how did he regard the plump, horse-riding VAD Flora Benenson? Not too highly, I imagine. I was some twenty years Chaim's junior, and not to be taken seriously even as a woman. But I was the daughter of *that man*, and the Zionists were perennially in need of money. Also, my language, like Chaim's, was Russian, and this was qualification enough to draw me into his circle: I could not in his estimation be totally a non-person. He needed an easy-going companion, driver and general help for his wife Vera during his frequent absences making speeches, attending meetings and scrutinizing the bacilli under his microscope, and I was the natural choice. I loved the Weizmanns, but those two were unhappy both when they were separated and when they were together. Though ten years married, they were so temperamental they each acted up in the other's company with conduct verging on emotional blackmail.

76

In consenting to become Mrs Chaim Weizmann Vera did not immediately understand that she was marrying not a man but a political organization. She was not overwhelmingly in love with the business of being Jewish, yet it was this that filled her house with people she didn't particularly like and rendered their partnership a subject of public interest. She frequently protested, but in truth I don't think she really objected. Her plans for Chaim knew no limits (neither did his for himself) and she laboured methodically and successfully to build her home into a centre of discreet but generous hospitality. He never pretended to be other than a ghetto Jew from the Pale of Settlement, she never pretended to be anything but a French-speaking Russian aristocrat. The poses worked, and they entertained the great, the not-so-great, those aspiring to be great, until an invitation from Vera Weizmann would become an honour and almost a royal command.

When I first knew them this was not yet the case. They had only just set up house in Addison Road with their first son Benjy, a nine-year-old handful of a child of whom Chaim expected great things. Vera was pregnant with her second, due late in what was proving for them a difficult and strenuous year. I would often collect her, Benjy and his nurse and run them down to Brighton so as to rest the nerves of everyone concerned. Nothing disturbed me, I had the nerves and physique of a mountaineer.

Weizmann had gathered a group of young men around him, some with Lancashire accents, who, in the promotion of his Zionist affairs, performed his every bidding. They had been his disciples while Manchester was his base of operations, and were now his counsellors, benefactors, secretaries and messengers. They adored Chaim's acid humour, his manipulation of the Yiddish language, his devastating judgments of Sokolow as a leader. The one I took to most, and to whom the others deferred most, was an unassuming man whom I first encountered in the uniform of a private soldier. He introduced himself as Simon Marks.

'What do you do when you're not working for Chaim?' I asked him.

'What do I do? Haven't you heard of Marks and Spencer?'

'No, what is Marks and Spencer?'

'Shops, dear girl. Shops. Do you mean to say you've never been inside one? In that case I'll ask my wife Miriam, she's the sister of that man over there' – pointing to Israel Sieff – 'to take you. We've a branch in Soho. Buy something, the price won't break you.'

He was not yet thirty in 1916. He had inherited a major share of the business, famous in the North Country as a chain of 'Penny Bazaars', when he was nineteen. Now he was embarked upon an offensive to spread his wings in London.

Simon Marks had a David and Jonathan relationship with Israel Sieff that is now part of Britain's commercial history. They had been together at Manchester Grammar School, married each other's sister, and would one day jointly command the family concern. They were so interconnected that at first I found it difficult to sort out their wives. I learnt to distinguish who belonged to whom by observing which of the two women could dare to be unkind to Simon; that would be Israel Sieff's wife Becky. This little rule worked for everyone else besides me.

Simon had three more sisters. The next in line, another Miriam, had married Harry Sacher, the only truly erudite member of the family. Harry was an East End boy who had made good – or rather, he would have made good had not marriage into a wealthy clan deprived him of all ambition. After Oxford, where he read law, he entered journalism and became a leader-writer on the *Manchester Guardian*. Harry was a cynical 'Litvak' (that is, a descendant of Jews from Lithuania, where cynicism was an incurable disease). He it was, I believe, who understood Chaim Weizmann best of all, recognizing his weaknesses where Marks and Sieff saw nothing in their mentor except virtue, wisdom and statesmanship. His wife Miriam struck me as the most brilliant of the girls, a truly exceptional woman, and quite without airs. Her face was a striking composition of character, revealing the artist in her, though when painted by Augustus John she declared, flattered and delighted, that he made her look like a prostitute. Anyone with a deserving cause could get money from Miriam Sacher.

The two youngest, Matilda and Elaine, I did not know very well till much later, but I cannot forget how the Marks sisterhood constituted a phalanx, thinking and acting in unison. Sing the praises of one and they were all grateful; criticize one and you made four enemies. The unwavering loyalty their menfolk gave to Chaim was not extended by this quartet to his wife Vera. They found her sophisticated foreign ways and accent uppity. She was a qualified physician, a rather special distinction for women at that time; they, like myself, had no formal education, and this made them feel uncomfortable, which was a rare experience for the sisters of Simon Marks. They simultaneously loved and feared their brother, who was given to uncontrollable explosions of temper. He told me he would in no circumstances allow any of his sisters into Marks and Spencer, except as customers: they would overwhelm him, and he was sure Becky would want to be the boss.

Close though Weizmann could be to people of this group, who were first-generation Britishers, he rather scorned the old-established Anglo-Jewish gentry as being 'Members of the Order of Trembling Israelites', meaning they hadn't the spunk to face the realities of the Jewish minority position and cringed to remain on good terms with their neighbours of Anglo-Saxon origin. It was a calumny, I knew from my own brief knowledge of them. But it arose in part with the problem my father was concerned with: what to do about the reluctance of the aliens in the East End of London and other cities, most of them Russian Jews, to rally to the colours. While the cream of Britain's manhood lay dying on the Western Front these 'slackers and shirkers', as the Press described them, were being handed a collective white feather.

One of our friends, Vladimir Jabotinsky, himself a regular at Addison Road, had his own solution. He wished to form a Jewish Legion to help conquer Palestine. Then, he maintained, they would join up in their thousands. Vera and I always looked forward to Jabotinsky's visits, for one was certain of good entertainment. He would transform an interview he had achieved with some politician into high drama, or he would sing for us in Italian, or tell a hair-raising tale of his journalistic derring-do in Odessa, his home town. Volodya, as we called him, was thick-set and ugly, but he had enormous charm, and we went along with his theatrical protestations of eternal love for the two of us, which, he said, left him in a constant state of painful dilemma. The truth was, no woman could be trusted alone in his company.

Jabotinsky was intensely serious in his plan for a Legion, and this disconcerted the established leaders of the Jewish community (he was, to them, 'Jug o' Whisky') because they dreaded the thought of suffering the indignity of segregation for military service. And Herbert Samuel, facing a barrage of criticism in the House of Commons, was in a cleft stick. As these Russians abstained from joining the British Forces a clamour rose that they should be deported to their old homeland and fight for Russia. Father had to make the Home Secretary understand that the Jews had little cause to be Russian patriots, most of them were treated abominably there. He pleaded for more time, to persuade them to join up in England. Jabotinsky elected to take his soap-box to Whitechapel and exhort them.

Volodya had a reputation for speech-making to put Demosthenes in the shade. He begged Vera and me to go down to the East End to hear him. So one Sunday morning we drove to Petticoat Lane hoping for a *tour de force*, hand-claps, a procession of eager young men abandoning their second-hand clothes stalls to queue up for the king's shilling. We stood at the edge of a restless crowd as Volodya mounted his rostrum to begin his oration in the flowery Yiddish for which he was reckoned to be famous.

I don't suppose a complete sentence left his lips. Those tailors and cobblers greeted him with a cataract of disapproval. 'Warmonger!' they bawled. 'Go home! Capitalist lackey!' He gripped his platform tight, scarlet with anger.

'If we want Palestine we have to fight for –' But at that moment the platform collapsed. A policeman had to intervene to prevent poor Jabotinsky from being dragged to the ground.

Later he explained that such a scene was not at all typical of his audiences. Most of them listened to him spell-bound, but a band of anarchists made a practice of following him around to break up his meetings.

'If Chaim would only come down and speak in my support we could swing them,' he declared. But Weizmann had troubles enough with his own supporters over the Legion idea (Harry Sacher for one was against the scheme) and had no wish to add to his enemies. Jabotinsky saw that there was only one way to obtain his Legion: by personal example. He took a group of volunteers to Winchester and they all enrolled. It was now January 1917, and he continued to keep the pressure up, especially when he was promoted to sergeant. He reported his advancement in a long letter to Vera implying that he would probably be a general before the war ended.

Over at Charing Cross Hospital I found Nellie Reitlinger explaining to another girl that, with Lloyd George as Prime Minister instead of Asquith, the war would soon be won. The girls were sharing a tea-break.

'Flora, you must meet Gladys Solomon,' Nellie said. 'She works in the operating theatre.' Then, in a slightly lower key, 'She's Jewish too.'

I had seen Gladys Solomon before, several times. I was even mistaken for her once, for we were fairly similar in appearance. Gladys was one of those effervescent creatures who find the most minute scraps of information to be of absorbing interest. This was just a casual introduction as far as I was concerned, but henceforth Gladys greeted me at every encounter as though we had been bosom friends for years. One afternoon she collected me and hopped into my Scripps-Booth with such determination I had no avenue of escape. 'You're coming to tea,' she ordered. 'I want you to meet Mummy.'

Their home was a mansion in Hyde Park Gate, directly facing the park. It was furnished in exquisite taste in Empire style, and Mrs Solomon received me with such a relaxed smile I took to her at once, and felt a pang of guilt at having been so off-hand in the past with her daughter. She led me into the garden, which was enormous.

'When my husband Henry bought this place,' Frances Solomon told me, 'it was practically the edge of London, almost a suburb. He's asleep now.'

'Not ill, I hope?'

'No, he enjoys his bed.'

At tea I gazed around the curiosities in their sitting-room. Portraits of various members of the family covered the walls. 'You've heard of Solomon J. Solomon, of course, the artist. He did most of these portraits. You've not heard of him? Well, I forgive you, being foreign.' The *objets d'art* indicated connections worldwide – Indian temples, African idols, dwarf-size totems from the American West. Then my eyes fixed upon a photograph.

'My darling brother, Colonel Harold Solomon,' Gladys said. 'He's a regular, been in the army I don't know how long. He's due home on leave next week. I'd love you to meet him, Flora.'

So I received a phone call at Claridge's. A voice said: 'Colonel Solomon heah. I've got tickets for *Chu Chin Chow*. Care to come?' My heart took a bound. What a splendid way the English had of doing things! We had not even been introduced, and here he was inviting me to the theatre.

I don't know what Harold saw in me, but I found a vision. He wore red tabs on his uniform, spoke in quick, brief sentences, and must easily have been the most handsome officer in the entire British Army. I knew at once I wasn't good enough for him.

We met several times that week, for dinner at the Café Royal, to ride in the park and, amazingly I thought, I joined him at his tailor's being measured up for a new uniform. He asked me not a thing about Russia, my family or, as men would say, where had I been all his life. We never kissed once, but I allowed myself to dream that I too was now a 'soldier's sweetheart'.

Vera Weizmann gave me one of those knowing looks of hers. 'He'd be lucky to get you, Flora. Those assimilated Anglo-Jews regard us as savages. I'm not sure any of them deserves a beautiful Russian heiress.' That observation made me cross.

Vera had had her second child, a son Michael, the previous November. Chaim turned the circumcision ceremony into a state Zionist occasion, with the distinguished Rabbi Gaster given the role of honour (apart from the child, that is) of holding the poor little thing's legs apart while the Covenant of Abraham was enacted. The catch of the day, for all to wonder at, was the presence of James de Rothschild, accompanied by his beautiful young wife Dolly. Chaim, with his instinct for enlisting the right people, had found in Dorothy de Rothschild a stalwart recruit to Zionism. James was the son of the mighty Parisian philanthropist Baron Edmond de Rothschild, and his presence at Michael's *Brith* marked the enlistment of a powerful figure to the side of Jewish nationhood. This baby's foreskin was a step to the Balfour Declaration, if only the politicians could know it.

I should have been weeping for Russia, that endless greyness of desert and forest and ice of my roots, where starving peasants and exhausted armies ached for release from the Tsar's war. Even princes of the blood royal, horrified and humiliated at the twist of destiny, had revolted, striking at the Imperial Family through its evil genius Rasputin.

'We cannot continue as before,' father remarked to me. 'The Empire is diseased. It's time the Russians arrived in the twentieth century.' Was he speaking with foreknowledge? I have often wondered.

The Duma defied the Tsar and assumed power at the end of February. Prince Lvov became head of the Provisional Government, but the name on everyone's lips was Kerensky. His speeches sent waves of hope across the world, not least to the millions of Russian Jews now living abroad for whom life had been unendurable in their homeland. Russia would now remain at arms to defeat the common enemy. She had a true cause at last, as Britain had, and France. It went by the name of democracy. At the Weizmann's in Addison Road we all cheered.

My thoughts travelled inevitably to the soldier with the red tabs. Harold returned to London for another brief leave. He was being posted to East Africa, a war front my feather-brain barely knew existed.

He took me to the Cavalry Club in Piccadilly. I had to be admitted through the side entrance, for women were not ranked as real people there. He gave me tea in the only room women were allowed into. There Harold proposed to me, in one of those clipped sentences which I supposed was the only way cavalry officers were permitted to speak.

Leaving the club an engaged woman, I noticed Dolman's painting of Captain Oates as he walked to his death in the Antarctic blizzard to grant Scott and the others a chance to live. Oh, the bravery, the grandeur, the glory of the British! And I was to be one of them.

4 Chain of Circumstance

Harold came to me a complete stranger. He left for Africa still a stranger. Such was khaki courtship in the First World War, infused I think for the soldiers more with resignation than romance. We discussed no immediate plans, it being assumed that we would await the end of the war before our marriage. I was pleased, for it meant mother and Fira could also be present at the ceremony. I wrote to mother that I had found not the Jewish prince she had hoped for, but a king. He spelt Solomon just like his biblical namesake. Perhaps there was a connection. Anything was possible in a country where the monarch was himself believed by some to be of the House of David, with the Robinsons and Smiths of Islington and Stockton-on-Tees descended from the Lost Ten Tribes.

Frances, Harold's mother, showed me off to her sisters. One of them looked me over as though I was an article in Harrod's end-of-season sale. 'Quite nice,' she said, turning her back to me, 'but aren't there plenty of English girls for him to marry?'

'Where do the Solomons come from?' I asked Gladys. She had an answer that defied invention: 'You know about St Helena, where the English kept Napoleon after the Battle of Waterloo?' Heavens, was I marrying into the Bonapartes!

The Solomons, Gladys explained, were sprinkled round the Colonies – South Africa, Australia and India. Some had stopped off on Napoleon's island, and ran the trade supplying ships of the East India Company. When Napoleon died St Helena lost its importance, so they returned to England. A great-grandfather or somebody had established himself in Exeter, and made a fortune by introducing the steel pen-nib to replace the old goose-quill. Then he came to London and entered the shipping business.

'Somewhere along the line,' said Gladys, 'we started Solomon and Company, Stockbrokers. That's where Daddy is today. At least, I think so.'

'Aren't you sure?'

'Well, it's like this' – and she stumbled into an account of her father's routine. 'He goes to his office when people usually come home, in the late afternoon. That's just after he's had his breakfast and read *The Times*. He likes to be in the City when all is quiet there, and he takes his dinner about midnight. He returns early in the morning with his evening paper.' Gladys gave an embarrassed laugh. 'He works to a clock ticking in reverse. In Throgmorton Street everyone knows him as the late Mr Solomon. Mummy has an awful time with the servants, because Daddy spends the day in bed, so the housework's never done. On Saturdays though, things are quite normal. We all go to synagogue.'

Synagogue, I discovered, was an important feature of life at the Solomons, for my future mother-in-law's antecedents were of the cloth, in its most exalted sense. She was an Adler, of the dynasty that produced two Chief Rabbis of the British Empire – Hanoverians they were, like the Royal Family, and Frances Solomon could mark off half-a-dozen relatives in the German Army.

I was now expected to join the family every Sabbath for worship at the synagogue in St Petersburgh Place. This I did by secreting my car some distance from Hyde Park Gate and arriving, as the faith decreed, as though I had come all the way from Brook Street on foot. We would then walk in solemn procession, rain or fine, across to the Bayswater side of the park. These trips transpired to be ambulatory seminars on the Solomon family. I had to know of its ramifications in Anglo-Jewish society, the charities it supported, the variants on the name adopted by its different branches. Solomon and Co., I learnt, was held in reverence at the Stock Exchange, and never mind the stories reaching my ears of Mr Solomon's unusual habits. Once, at the theatre, Frances told me, he had been mistaken for King Edward. I stole a glance at the short fat man, with his pointed little beard, and was not surprised.

At the synagogue the sexes divided, the women being segregated on their own to chatter away without unduly disturbing the service, and to rank their finery against the attire of the other ladies thus congregated: Franklin women, Samuel women, Montagus, Adlers, and lesser folk. On my first visit I was intrigued by the marble and polished pine of the interior, liberally spattered with lettering in gold. The architect must have been inspired not only by the glory of the Lord but by the Albert Memorial.

Much of what I was told of my husband-to-be required further explanation. His school had been Clifton, Polack's House. Polack's House? Yes, it was reserved for Jewish boys whose parents wished upon their sons the Spartan upbringing required for English gentlemen plus kosher food. After Sandhurst he joined a cavalry regiment, the 18th Hussars, and was one of the officers involved in the Curragh mutiny. The Curragh mutiny? That was just before the war, when Ireland was being promised Home Rule. Some officers stationed in Dublin proclaimed their refusal to lead their troops north should Ulster rebel against the policy. Harold, too young for the Boer War and afraid he would miss this one (which of course was due to end that first Christmas) subsequently transferred to the Service Corps so that he could get to France.

His mother proudly drew my attention to the red tabs on his uniform. They indicated that he was on the staff of the War Office, through his work with the British Military Mission to Serbia. This had been led by his friend Clive Garsia, a wonderful man and a brigadier, Frances told me. They had to bring up supplies to the Serbian General Pasich, whose army had fought so bravely against the Austrians. It was another glorious episode which unfortunately had not worked out as planned, with Harold saving what stores he could while the Pasich forces scrambled their way out of trouble. Now, complete with Military Cross and the Serbian Order of the White Eagle, he was on his way to Cape Town, where he too would surely be appointed a brigadier. We all prayed fervently in synagogue for his safe return, trusting there would be no gallant campaign in East Africa to join with the disasters of Serbia and the Dardanelles, Jutland and the Somme. I wondered whether I would still recognize Harold when the blessed day arrived.

Meanwhile, my father decided that his interests required his urgent presence in Petrograd. The liberal revolution was on a shaky course, and Kerensky's efforts to inject new determination into the prosecution of the war were not meeting with marked success. Too much of the Benenson fortune was anchored in Russia. Perhaps it could be dislodged. Early in the summer father departed, and I brought Manya and Rikarna to a flat in Kensington, practically next door to the Solomons. This England was to be my home, of that I was sure. I was finished with hotel life, which merely emphasized the family rootlessness.

Father had not succeeded in preventing the British deportation order against the Russian aliens who obstinately refused to don khaki in this country. And what a miserable, perplexed picture they made that September in 1917 when they duly mustered on platform 14 at Euston Station for the first stage of their journey back to their hated homeland. While Jabotinsky had been goading them to do the decent thing and join the British Army, other soap-box orators, anarchists and pacifists, had been encouraging them to hold out. Most of them were so green they lacked the ability to string a dozen words of English together, and under the press of propaganda and counter-propaganda they hopped from one decision to another. In company with others of the Weizmann circle I went to see the sad assembly off. They were only about a thousand altogether, for many must have been lying low, or were able, by some ingenuity, to postpone the day. Clutching sandwiches wrapped in newspaper and their cardboard suitcases, these men had the lost look of a crowd unable to move except where directed. But while some wept, others looked relieved, and joked among themselves. Wives had to remain behind, and I could see that many of them who had come with their children to bid their menfolk farewell were younger than me. Some of these women would never see their husbands again.

While I was preparing for my transfiguration into the colonel's lady, Sandhurst and all that, the Jewish people as a whole were rushing towards a watershed in their destiny, one to divide my personality afresh. The Solomons had no experience of anti-Semitism, knew little of Zionism, cared nothing for Palestine. England was their Promised Land, and the City of London their Jerusalem. But over in Addison Road my friend Chaim Weizmann, now the acknowledged leader of the movement, was celebrating a great victory. He had finally wrested from Prime Minister Lloyd George and his Foreign Secretary Arthur Balfour an undertaking to help restore the Jews to nationhood in Palestine.

The Balfour Declaration, Chaim insisted, was a promise of nationhood. Others turned the words upside down, analysed the clauses and sub-clauses into infinity, and read a quite different construction into the formula. Several decades and half-a-dozen Middle Eastern wars later, the argument still proceeds. But for the moment Balfour's was the finger of God as far as the Zionists were concerned, inscribing the fulfilment of biblical prophecy. So, whatever my sentiments in Hyde Park Gate, over in Addison Road I was for Zionism, one hundred per cent. We sang the Jewish anthem *Hatikvah*. It drowned out the strains of the *Internationale* reaching us from Petrograd.

Every morning I ran to the letter-box for word from Harold. I was rarely disappointed. He wrote regularly as he worked his way up the east coast of Africa to clear the Germans from their black empire. Harold was promoted Temporary Brigadier-General, as he had expected, with responsibility for collecting the spoils abandoned by the enemy in their long retreat over thousands of square miles of jungle and desert.

For a man addressing his fiancée ten years younger than himself Harold chose a rather curious style of correspondence. His letters rarely referred to our relationship, or his hopes for our future. I do not recall any declarations of eternal love in them. But they were splendidly informative on the economics, ethnic composition and physical characteristics of Kenya, Uganda, Mozambique, as well as other territories of the Dark Continent.

Now, geography was never my strong point. We told a story in Russia of the boy who excelled in many subjects but was totally uninterested in geography. When his tutor complained to the boy's mother of this, she replied: 'What does he need geography for? The coachman will take him there!' That just about summed up my own attitude. Harold's letters were so detailed my eyes frequently glazed over complete pages. I could not quite understand why he was recommending certain types of administration to me for this region, nor why I needed to know its potential for industrial development. He asked me to put the letters carefully away after reading them. Much later I realized their true purpose: they turned up in print, in the thick supplements periodically issued by *The Times* on the future of the colonial empire. Harold was mentioned in dispatches and made OBE on his return home, which was some months after the termination of hostilities.

For the moment I had far greater concerns than Britain's imperial prospects. I was becoming desperately worried by the absence of news from my family in Russia. The fragile constitutional system had broken down. Kerensky was on the run, Lenin sought peace at any price, and the country drifted into anarchy. In the Communist revolution it became obvious that all our Russian wealth would be expropriated. Did we still have a home? Had father been arrested? The thought haunted me that he might be dead. Weizmann wired Sir George Buchanan, through the Foreign Office, to contact Grigori Benenson about preventing the Germans from obtaining Russia's raw materials for their war effort. There was no reply.

Father, it transpired, was in hiding; I received the news from refugees reaching the West. Mother and Fira remained in Petrograd while he had gone to relatives, probably in Moscow, and they had tucked him away somewhere. Our home was occupied by the Red Army, though Mother and Fira were allowed quarters there.

At the London branch of the bank Herbert Guedalla tried to brush my anxieties aside. He was convinced the Bolsheviks would not dare touch Grigori Benenson. I exploded. 'Why not? They've touched the Tsar!'

'Your father is protected by his British connections, and in any case his assets are in large part in British ownership.' Then why had he gone into hiding? Herbert shrugged his shoulders. 'Wait a while longer, Flora. You'll see this crisis will pass.' I believed not a word.

Months went by, and still I was without news. Lenin made peace with the enemy while the war raged in France, and in consequence a deep hatred of everything Russian swept over a shocked Britain. No longer an honoured envoy of the gallant ally in the East, I was tainted by the Communist treachery.

Germany was throwing everything into a last desperate push to seize Paris, to a general belief in England that the Boche now commanded so much of Russia's resources he might well sustain the war for years ahead. With all this I wondered whether so true-blue an Englishman as Harold Solomon would keep his promise to a girl virtually belonging to an enemy nation, and possibly penniless into the bargain.

Leaden of heart, I plodded on with my VAD duties. Charing Cross Station reeked with the aroma of stale blood as trains loaded with the wounded steamed in night and day in that final carnage of the war. I was less talkative now and had no wish to proclaim my foreign origin. The Jews as a whole found themselves in a wretched spotlight. Even Winston Churchill spoke of the Communist movement as a Judeo-Bolshevik world conspiracy.

And yet the struggle in Russia was turning the Jews against

themselves. Some supported Kerensky, others Lenin. I had left a mother and sister at that sorrowful parting in Stockholm four years earlier. Perhaps I would never see them again. Then a letter arrived from Sweden and I knew my family was safe. For it was in Fira's handwriting.

I have never kept correspondence (apart from Harold's letters from Africa, which resembled dispatches from the front) so this letter too is lost. But I am unlikely ever to forget its contents. Though much was left unsaid, I detected from my sister's account of events that Fira, now nineteen, had crossed a bridge I had not yet reached. She was a woman in all senses of the word.

She wrote of father's disappearance from home with the first proclamation 'All Power to the Soviets!' He gathered a few valuables and made for Moscow. The Communists searched for him there, so he boarded the train again for Petrograd. In all the chaos the train schedules were maintained, and by keeping on the move people could often avoid arrest and interrogation. The departure of our servants made it simpler for father to conceal his movements. Fira and mother were allowed to keep two rooms, with another, held under guard, for storage space. Most of the treasures in the house just disappeared. Soldiers spread themselves everywhere but, said Fira, she extracted lots of favours from them and when mother saw how they reduced her boudoir to a mess, with her scent spilt across everything, she protested and an officer had it all cleaned up. Although food was short they never went hungry.

With jewellery constituting easily portable capital, she and mother kept as much as possible about their persons. The rest was in the storage-room. They were allowed to go there from time to time to retrieve things and to check that nothing was missing. Fira described how she would steal out a brooch or a string of pearls, sometimes in return for being specially friendly to the guards. They kept a case of jewels also for our cousin Lila who examined it one day and began making a scene that a diamond necklace was missing. Fira nudged Lila to shut up, and later extracted it from her skirt. (Lila survived for the rest of her life in comfort on the strength of the jewellery Fira filched on her behalf.) They had an arrangement to meet father from time to time, far from the house.

One day a Commissar came to speak to mother. But first he ordered the soldiers out of the room – he wanted a private conversation. He told her not to be afraid, and to trust him. Yet mother feared that father had been caught, and was probably in prison. The revolution was then almost a year old, the Imperial family were killed, but many royals had escaped to the West along with thousands of aristocrats and other people of influence, as well as Kerensky supporters.

The Commissar introduced himself as Comrade Goukovksy of the Department of Foreign Trade. He said he knew Mr Benenson, having met him before the war at Monte Carlo. Goukovsky had lost all his money at the tables. He was in despair and approached father, as a compatriot, for help. Father refused to give him money, knowing it would merely go the same way, but undertook to see that Goukovsky got home. He took the man across to the Hotel de Paris opposite the casino, and instructed the porter to buy a ticket and see Goukovsky on to the train. Goukovsky told mother he was now in a position to repay the debt. He would be leaving the following night for trade talks with the Swedes, and offered to take the family along on the pretext that father would be advising on international trade. They should meet at the docks, a ship bound for Stockholm was waiting. So here they were once again, and how were Manya and Rikarna, and would Fira be one of my bridesmaids?

Soon another message arrived. Yasha was dead, a victim of the Spanish 'flu just then sweeping across Europe. He left his wife Vera with a growing daughter. They too would live in England when the war ended.

As it happened, bringing the family to London encountered further difficulties. The British Embassy in Stockholm suspected that father, arriving with a Commissar for Trade, was himself a Communist official. They were reluctant to grant the necessary visas, and waiting for Foreign Office clearance consumed more tedious weeks.

I think I recall Fira's letter in such detail not so much for the relief it brought, but rather because it wrote *finis* to the confused phase in my life that I could almost call my extended, if not retarded, childhood. Also, it reached me towards the end of the war and was, after a fashion, my personal *laissez-passer* out of the collective gloom. Selfish this was I knew, only too well, for weren't there millions still oppressed by their losses and deprivations? So I guiltily hugged my good fortune, refusing to sorrow over Yasha, or that Russia's agony was multiplying, not diminishing, as civil war and starvation took their massive toll.

More than this, I determined to make the most of that last fling of girlhood, my wedding. Harold was due home in April 1919. Frances Solomon, with what I considered great understanding, said I was to go alone to meet the boat-train at Waterloo. I thanked her, but begged Gladys to accompany me. I was nervous at the thought of not recognizing my fiancé. I had never seen him out of uniform, and knew he would be travelling in mufti.

We stood silent at the barrier, Gladys and I, close together and expressionless, two among hundreds of women ranged as though in an identity parade. Gladys shouted 'Harold!' There he was, calm and tall, very bronzed. I advanced trembling. For a silly moment it occurred to me that I was being ignored. Perhaps it really was all over between us, as happened frequently with those whirlwind war-time romances. No, he saw me and smiled. Then he removed his hat. Our first exchange deserves immortality.

'How are you, my darling?' he asked.

'I am very well, thank you.'

That might have been the introduction to a fuller conversation. But suddenly Harold, staring over my shoulder, exclaimed, 'Good heavens, there's Garsia!' A uniformed stranger stepped forward. 'Clive, this is my fiancée, Flora Benenson. You remember to be nice to her.'

He was very nice to me. Clive Garsia, Harold's old Commanding Officer, was from New Zealand. Something had been forged in comradeship between these two during the Serbian war and its pathetic epilogue, and I observed that here was a friendship into which no woman, not even a wife, dared intrude. Harold seemed more pleased to see Clive at the station than either Gladys or myself! I almost felt in the way. But the mood dissolved into more pleasurable sensations with the continuation of the reunion at Hyde Park Gate. Henry Solomon, Harold's father, honoured the occasion by rising from his bed.

We were married at St Petersburgh Place the following month, an event that had my own family occupying an unsure place in a congregation of diverse Solomons, army brothers, and Harold's school-friends. His old Clifton housemaster the Reverend Joseph Polack officiated – school sentiment ran thick in the blood of this society. We left the synagogue trailed by eight bridesmaids under an archway of swords, drawn some of them by officers in Serbian uniform.

Henry Solomon, the Edwardian look-alike, greeted father with old-world courtesy, inviting him into his study for a private talk while the rest of us assembled in the garden for photographs. I expected they would be having a friendly chat over brandy and cigars on the joy brought to both families by our alliance. But there was much else besides.

'He gave me to understand that in England it's the custom to send a daughter into matrimony with a dowry,' father subsequently informed me. 'I thought that belonged to the ghetto. Well, this is the ghetto. We came to an arrangement.'

'Am I allowed to know what it is to be?'

'You will have a settlement in trust, the capital to go eventually to your future heir. The interest will bring you in a reasonable sum. In addition I am making you a personal allowance of £1,000 a month.'

'Is it enough?' I was still a child in money matters.

Father did not immediately reply. Then he said: 'You remember those men who were sent back to Russia in the Kerensky days? Most of them have not yet returned to their families here in England. Their wives receive an allowance of twelve shillings and sixpence per week, with half-a-crown for each child. Your income will be greater than two hundred of those East End families combined.' Evidently, despite the Russian Revolution and the passing of the Lena Goldfields to 'the people', something still remained in the Benenson coffers.

Father went on: 'And I don't suppose your husband is exactly a pauper.' Harold, throughout our marriage, never discussed money with me. No, he couldn't have been a pauper.

We left for Paris, and I now began learning about the man I married. He had the easiest of personalities, with a rather juvenile sense of humour that came, I suppose, from his eternally making the army his point of reference. Civilians in his eyes were somewhat ridiculous, largely incompetent, and verbose. We stayed at the Meurice, though I rarely saw him during the day. General Pasich, the grand old man of Serbian nationalism, commandeered Harold as adviser to the delegation working at the Peace Conference for the unification of Yugoslavia. Harold admired the craggy warrior profoundly, and would have wished for nothing more than to help his country build up its military force once the patchwork of Balkan races was knitted together. But some members of the delegation were by no means amenable to British influence, and Harold watched blandly as quarrels, exacerbated by religious differences, developed among them. I don't suppose his later withdrawal from the mission was even noticed.

With Harold's engrossment in the cause of the Yugoslavs, I involved myself with the Zionists. They too had sent a delegation to Paris, where a bewildering assortment of national groups came before the Allied leaders to plead for their rights; you could take your pick from Arabs, Koreans, Irish-Americans, Lithuanians and goodness knows what else. The one-time penurious journalist Sokolow was holding court at the Meurice. We met in the lobby, and he greeted me with that knightly pomposity that Weizmann so cuttingly caricatured: 'Ah, the talented daughter of the great Grigori Benenson!' He waltzed me over to a corner of the lounge where Jewish representatives were planning their approaches to Prime Ministers and Presidents, actual and potential, who were established in the city. Adopting an air of special intimacy with the great, Sokolow spoke of the Big Three, the Big Four, the Council of Ten.

Having grown up in a country where my people had few legal rights, I recognized the importance of the work. Harold however found the motley collection of Jewish notables hilarious. This great-grandson of a Chief Rabbi had absolutely no Jewish feeling in him. Or perhaps he had been trained to suppress his emotions. His attitude, almost cruel, puzzled me.

I don't know what I expected of him in our own relationship, I suppose transportation to some magic realm. But his love-making left me partly mystified, partly shocked, partly disappointed. I readily forgave him – indeed, what was there to forgive? On the other hand, he chose for our joint entertainment those brash sex parades in which Paris excelled. He deliberately introduced me to them and I watched his uninhibited enjoyment of the performances while I writhed in discomfort. Naturally, as women do, I blamed myself, and the upbringing which had left me so innocent and prudish, for the absence of electricity in our partnership.

Once, as I strolled in solitude with these discouraging thoughts along the rue de Rivoli, where the smart antique shops gave way to cluttered garment stores and market stalls, I was stopped by a young woman hauling a suitcase. 'Flora!' she called.

I could barely recognize the lined face and shabby clothes. And yet they belonged to my Petersburg friend the elegant Anna Becker. 'I knew you were to be married,' she said. 'It's as I told you years ago. I live here, not far from the Hôtel de Ville.'

Anna looked drawn, but I didn't know how to lie about her appearance, and said nothing. Her hair, streaked with grey, blew across her face. We hugged each other. She babbled six years of history away, in staccato sentences – lightly, lest I feel some guilt.

'Well, you remember I was always good with my hands. When I arrived in Paris I found work in a dress shop. Now I make underwear, and take it around in this suitcase. Feel the weight of it!'

She laughed. 'I sell to friends, and sometimes I open my case on the pavement here. It's beautiful underwear, Flora. Look, all sizes.'

Could I have done it, I asked myself? Could I have survived on my own, counted pennies, begged people to buy from me, dragged a suitcase from place to place? I would have sunk without trace, I knew, yet here was Anna, doing all this, and putting a brave face on it.

'It's beautiful, Annushka. Give me your address. I'll find you customers.'

'Here, I've got a card. Take two.'

The encounter weighing heavily on me, I travelled with Harold along the Loire and watched as he fished, silent for hours long. We took horses and trekked the foothills of the Auvergne, then lazed on the beach at Cannes. We allowed the days and weeks to pass without hurry. Harold had an extended leave and I could see that after four years of constant movement he relished any respite. Now I found a different Harold, confident in his knowledge of the terrain, anxious that no vision of the beauty of France escape me. He spoke of hills and valleys as though discussing a sculpture, emphasizing their harmonies and shadows. By fixing his eye on a mountain he could gauge its height. I was enormously impressed.

'Next stop, Rome,' said Harold. 'Now there's a city.' Indeed it was, for Providence took a hand in our destiny there, in the form of Herbert Samuel, erstwhile Home Secretary. I recognized him in a restaurant and proudly introduced my husband. The two made a perfect match.

Samuel had lost his parliamentary seat in the 'Khaki Election' at the end of 1918, and was moving closer to the Zionists, whose ideas he had long supported from the side-lines. We had met occasionally at the Weizmanns' in Addison Road. Graciously, he now suggested that we join forces for an inspection of the wonders of Rome.

Oh, the tedious, exhausting, Baedeker-guided days that followed! Together, they marched me round the city to ensure that I missed not a monument or ruin or picture. Herbert Samuel, in relaxation as in life and politics, went strictly by the book. He didn't merely scrutinize a painting, he measured it. And Harold was just as bad. They had to know whether a certain Caravaggio was larger or smaller than the one in the National Gallery, and whether the lighting was adequate. They counted the pillars enclosing St Peter's, just to check whether Baedeker had it right. After three days of this I left them to it, emerging only for a visit to the Opera, when Herbert called for us courteously bearing a box of chocolates to assuage the frail young bride. My instinct told me he got on famously with Harold in my absence.

Herbert asked about our plans. Harold sketched a picture of the next few years that included so many out-stations of the then extensive British Empire that I had a vision of myself trotting over the globe alongside the cavalryman's charger. As for Herbert, he was on his way to San Remo, where the final disposition of the Turkish Empire was to be hammered out between Britain and France. He was now coming from Palestine and was due to report there to Lloyd George and Balfour.

'There's every likelihood I shall be appointed to Jerusalem as High Commissioner. Of course, it's by no means official as yet. I shall be recruiting staff.

My ears pricked up. Why not my husband? Must we be condemned to army barracks till the end of time? Palestine was my dream! I looked beseechingly at Harold. He looked in another direction.

It took the rest of the day to convince him that all my grown life I had been close to Zionism. But the general idea of a Jewish homeland struck Harold as bizarre. What did Weizmann intend to do, ship all the Jews out there whether they wanted it or not? And what about the Arabs? Would they stand for it?

I brushed these observations aside, for I was intoxicated by the thought of Jerusalem. 'Herbert wants you to join him, that's obvious. Think how exciting it will be, Harold, among Jews working the soil, building the country from scratch. I've met lots of Zionists. They're not all dreamers, as you think. They want to turn Palestine into a modern state.'

Harold was won over in the end, albeit reluctantly. If Samuel could use him we would return home and he would arrange a War Office secondment. What blessed relief! We had been on the move, he and I, for nearly six months. I had had all the sight-seeing I could digest, and was more than ready to settle down. Thoughts of the Orient tingled my flesh. We would share a new life in the Holy Land, I would be a pioneer in tune with the spirit of a nation in embryo. Though try as I might, I could not visualize my husband in the process of shedding his English skin.

Before leaving on my honeymoon I had arranged for Manya to enter Malvern Girls School. She was then aged thirteen, and though it might have been better for her to develop in a more normal way – I was an expert in boarding schools – a family background simply didn't exist to receive her. Father and mother followed separate lives, revealing little inclination to build a home together in England. Then there was Fira. Between the two of them, she had no place, and I knew of her restlessness.

Father's business affairs underwent a radical change. His English and Russian Bank virtually ceased to function when the two countries broke off diplomatic relations. London was now too small to contain him. He chose to embark on new enterprises in New York. Fira decided to accompany him, while mother remained faithful to Europe, taking up residence alternately at the Hyde Park Hotel in London and the Plaza Athénée in Paris.

Did father's departure have anything to do with a certain lady with a bottle of concentrated vitriol? Mother lived in constant terror of a revival of the scandal. She trembled as she confessed to me, on my return to London, that she was forever glancing over her shoulder for Tamara Kolinskaya. The woman was alive, very much so, and spoiling for a battle. She had telephoned from abroad, uttering threats. As a result, lawyers' letters were exchanged, and Kolinskaya was awarded a settlement out of court, conditional on her never visiting England. Father stoutly denied paternity in regard to her son. Family skeletons have a way of leering through the greatest of wars and the bitterest of revolutions.

Grigori Benenson was no more than five weeks in America when the *Wall Street Journal* announced his acquisition of a skyscraper, No 165 Broadway, at a cost of ten million dollars, half of which he put down in cash. It was now to be known as the Benenson Building.

5 The Colonel's Lady

Jerusalem was a fairyland. Tilted against a promontory high above a desert of musk-coloured rock, the city named itself to the mystics as God's foot-stool on earth. It pulsated in its splendour with an Oriental rhythm whose dignity inspired awe. It stood defiantly unchanged against a tide of successive conquests. Jerusalem in 1920 was a fairyland also in the sense that it was not quite real.

It had a curious effect upon its inhabitants: on the one hand reverential and soporific, on the other nervy and quarrelsome. Here the past stared across a chasm to the future. Jerusalem on our arrival was already dividing time between the memory of centuries flowing from the Bible, and the aspirations of a political age bearing in its train national rivalries and the clamour of ambition. Chaim Weizmann came to Jerusalem in 1918 and was appalled. The scientist in him gazed upon the multitude of religious sects, sniffed the crumbling slums within its walls, noted the absence of sewerage and typewriters, then decided to transform this place by building a university. But soon the soporific took command, and seven years would elapse before the first lecture-hall was ready.

Herbert Samuel, now Sir Herbert, donned a splendid snow-white uniform with plumed head-gear and made of his leaky official residence, the Augusta Victoria Hospice on Mount Scopus, a Viceroy's mansion in miniature. Initially the Jews saw in him a new Prince of Israel, for the title of High Commissioner conveyed little to them. In the course of time, as he looked more the British pro-consul and less the Israelite anointed, their enthusiasm waned. I took Jerusalem joyously to my heart. I pretended to myself that here I could be a pioneer in my way, like the Zionists draining the Jezreel marshes in theirs. One of my earliest acts was rather odd pioneering, except in a figurative sense. It was to arrange the weekly delivery of a case of champagne from Fortnum and Mason in London.

98

Until Samuel took over, Palestine counted as occupied enemy territory, and was administered by Allenby, its conqueror, from Cairo. Below the surface discontent simmered, the Arabs fearing for their future while the Jews, then a small minority except in Jerusalem, saw the Balfour Declaration as their charter to fill the country with immigrants and start up all the engines of development. This is something of a simplification, for nothing said about Palestine in those days, or Israel afterwards, contained the absolute truth. A part of the native-born Jewish population was devoutly Orthodox and hence did not welcome Zionist ideas or progress. During four hundred years of Ottoman rule the Holy City had been a pietist backwater, with mosque, church and synagogue regulating the affairs of the three communities in a chaotic but nevertheless satisfactory way. They lived in fair harmony because they lived in each other's pocket.

Harold and I were promised a house of our own, but in the meantime we took up quarters in what went by the name of the Hotel Allenby just beyond the Jaffa Gate, which guarded one of the entrances to the walled town. The hotel boasted one bathroom, which you booked the night before you required it, rarely more than once a week. I obtained carpets and a comfortable settee, spread some books and flowers around the place and declared myself at home. During rainstorms the water poured through the ill-fitting windows.

Harold found our lodgings quite acceptable. Not so Miss Read. She was the maid I had taken with me on my honeymoon. Miss Read was a relic from a royal household and had been persuaded to join us in this new life, but she looked upon Jerusalem in disbelief. Her special talent lay in her crêpes Suzettes, and if she eternally protested at finding herself in a situation without damask napery she nevertheless proved as adept a pioneer as any in the handling of a primus stove. I promised her prompt repatriation to Norfolk at any time without notice, but she stayed several months.

Up on the hill, as we referred to the High Commissioner's residence, Beatrice Samuel transformed a portion of the premises into a replica of her environment in Porchester Terrace. She queened it over the officials' wives, insisting we call her Auntie Bea. At her side a real niece was in constant attendance, a regular Franklin, Helen, who had a Bedford College diploma in social studies and let no-one forget it. She was married to a saint, Norman Bentwich. An early disciple of Weizmann's, Bentwich had commanded a Camel Corps detachment in the Near Eastern campaign and now served the British Administration as Legal Officer, a title that subsequently blossomed into Attorney General. Everybody loved Norman; that is, everybody except the most extreme Zionists. Helen was something else; she might have been Britannia rising on her chariot from the azure main. When she entertained she organized a tolerable version of a Buckingham Palace garden party. She and I shared a certain fame in being the only two women in Palestine with our own motor-cars.

What of the Arabs? Their leaders, both Christian and Moslem, considered the country to be their inheritance from the Turkish Empire. While provisionally accepting the British presence they anticipated a future Arab regime with full independence. They refused to be placed on a par with the Zionists, whom they saw as interlopers. The Arabs left politics in the hands of their clergy, and as a result they made great strides economically, but politically they lost all along the line.

I felt sorry for Herbert Samuel. Having to appear all things to all men – Zionist to the Jews, protector of their rights to the Arabs, flag-waving governor to his superiors – he could barely put a foot right. He enrolled Englishmen, Arabs and Jews for his administration. Some of them were fiercely partisan. I often served drinks in my rooms to colleagues of Harold whose delightful, flattering drawing-room manner concealed a hatred for the Zionists that could erupt in crude anti-Semitism. On their side the Zionists detected betrayal round every corner. When we came to the country my friend the warrior-poet Jabotinsky was in gaol; he had organized an illegal Jewish self-defence force, precursor of the *Haganah*, in Jerusalem against an Arab attack upon the Orthodox Jews huddled in their mean dwellings within the walls. Samuel cleared him in a general amnesty on his arrival and Jabotinsky went into the history books as a national hero.

Pardonably, many outsiders failed to discover who really ran Palestine, whether it was the High Commissioner on the hill or the Zionist down town taking his orders from Weizmann in London. This difficulty did not trouble me inordinately, and Harold stood, as it were, on both sides of the fence, like Norman Bentwich and several other Jews on Samuel's staff. Because of his war experience Harold was appointed Controller of Stores, a post which soon qualified us for a handsome villa in the German

100

Colony, so named because it had previously been the Templars' residential area. The Bentwiches lived close by, as did almost everybody else recognized as anybody. We could see over the Hinnom Valley to the old city walls on one side, while below us on the other stood the fortress-like Monastery of the Cross. Opposite our house the railway station brought travellers direct from El Kantara via Lydda Junction, so we hardly thought of Egypt as a different country. The house had those high vaulted ceilings characteristic of Arab architecture, while the exterior was clad in mellow Jerusalem stone. At my young age I had to add my own particular extravagance: wallpaper, the first ever in the Holy City. I knew Helen Bentwich, on hearing the news, shook her head in despair.

What gave me cause for particular happiness was the transformation of my husband in this atmosphere. He had arrived in Palestine the unemotional, detached colonial servant. His work took him to every extremity of the country, for the troops were still here in strength. Already the first Jewish communal settlements, the *kibbutzim*, dotted the skyline. They were established on the drained marshland in the Vale of Jezreel, along the Jordan, and in the Plain of Sharon adjacent to the coast. During the day the settlements rang with the confident sounds of house construction, picks and shovels, the occasional tractor. In the evening their lights twinkled a welcome to every passing traveller. Roads were few, but Harold's Arab driver negotiated the tracks with great skill in his official Sunbeam, and I observed that suddenly my husband gloried in every sight of Zionist endeavour. He had not known such Jews before, tough labourers who attacked their tasks with a song, impatient to redeem the Promised Land in accordance with the doctrine taught them as pale-faced schoolboys in the ghettoes of Europe.

Harold laced his enthusiasm with his own brand of humour. 'Up in Galilee they're breeding Jewish cows,' he said. 'They don't say "moo", they say "nu?". And I've met a bull called Balfour. Looks like him too.'

Proudly he brought me the first pound of butter made on a new Jewish farmstead. And a basket of strawberries cultivated in an area where the native population had never seen the fruit. Just then I was able to break the news to him that I was pregnant, and this gave our relationship a touch of magic.

'We shall have a baby talking Hebrew as his ancestors did on these very Judean Hills,' I prophesied hopefully.

101

'Yes, but if he's a boy he's going to speak it in an Etonian accent,' was Harold's rejoinder. He himself had crammed in some Arabic lessons before leaving for Palestine.

Chaim and Vera Weizmann descended on Palestine from time to time, and I would fill the house with dignitaries of every race and colour to meet them. I had sublime faith (and the years proved this justified) that Chaim, if no-one else, could convert even the direst opponent to the justice of the Zionist cause. I liked to load up my Studebaker with visitors and locals so that we could all tour together, picnicking out in the wilds, against the beating of the desert wind and the long, mournful howl of the jackals. The nights were for poetry, and hopes for the re-born homeland, and for flirtation too, if Hadassah Samuel was with us.

She had married Edwin, the Samuels' eldest, a man so tall and erect we nicknamed him Nebi, from the lofty tower on the hill north of Jerusalem where the biblical Samuel was said to have judged ancient Israel. I loved Hadassah, who was two years my junior and an unbridled spirit with a taste for every adventure. Nebi Samuel, a minor government official at this time, had quite a task holding her in rein: she was very good-looking, and Jerusalem suffered no shortage of bachelors, and not only bachelors, who relieved their bouts of pioneering with the occasional romance. Hadassah's father described himself as the only Hebrew lexicographer in Palestine, quite disregarding another, more celebrated scholar in Jerusalem named Eliezer Ben-Yehuda, who was the true architect of the modern, spoken language.

Both these venerable gentlemen scolded me for not attempting to learn Hebrew, then being up-dated to cope with such ideas as 'aspirin' and 'internal combustion engine'. I was impenitent, it being a paradox of Zionism that most of the Jews long domiciled in Palestine preferred to converse in any language but Hebrew while we, the newcomers, were criticized for not learning it. Hadassah Samuel was a law unto herself in this regard too. She had perfect English and French, and I rarely heard her speak a word of Hebrew except to reprimand a servant, most of whom were Arabs anyway.

I had my favourite walk, skirting the valley – which did as the municipal rubbish dump – and taking a path near the walls in the direction of Ophel, the City of David. At Friday's twilight I could hear the prayers of the devout in chorus at the Jews' holiest shrine; from the Wailing Wall they reached my ears as the hum of a thousand over-excited bees. The Sabbath came suddenly to Jerusalem, so that one moment the winding streets were filled with a scurrying crowd, and the next they were deserted, given over to the stray cats brazenly emerging from their alleyways. One morning I passed by the Pool of Siloam to observe a sight that shattered my peace. An Arab milk vendor, a man I had frequently noticed plying his trade door-to-door, was bending at the pool and drawing the unsavoury liquid into his goatskin to dilute the milk. So this is what the poor drank in Jerusalem! And could this nasty concoction, by some devious route, also reach the child stirring within me? I could be guilty of poisoning him!

I rushed home and told Harold of my fears. Of course they were not justified, for we had our own sources of supply. He appeared unperturbed.

'If you are so shocked why not do something about it? Go and ask Antimacassar. She knows everybody.' Antimacassar was his name for Hadassah Samuel.

I spoke to Hadassah. She said: 'Flora, there's only one doctor I trust in this city, a woman, Helen Kagan. She's one of your Russians.'

Helen Kagan, still quite young, had been working for years as a paediatrician among the poor Arabs. 'We can have pure milk from tomorrow,' she explained, 'but who's going to pay for it?' I replied: 'My father.' That day I sent a cable to New York. Three thousand pounds came back almost by return. Now I could do something really useful.

Helen helped me find a little house inside the walls and we converted it into a milk depot and infant welfare centre. We had the place painted with a blue door, this being the Arabs' lucky colour, and put a trained nurse in charge. One room had half-a-dozen primus stoves, to pasteurize the milk. Then we went to a dairy farmer in the Jewish village of Motza, not far from Ain Kerem, birthplace of John the Baptist. We gave the farmer buckets and brushes so that he could bring us milk in clean containers. We also provided him with two donkeys to guarantee daily deliveries.

A large sign was made, 'A Drop of Milk', in Hebrew and Arabic. We bottled the milk ourselves, and Helen obtained scales to weigh the babies, and a carpenter to convert orange boxes into cots. (The native women usually bound their newly-born in tight rags and laid them on the earthen floor of their

103

homes.) Everything was free, though the mothers shied away at first. Once word got around, our centre was kept fully occupied, even arranging milk distribution for those who couldn't come in person. We had money enough to keep the place open for years, until welfare services improved generally. As for our depot, it was restored for family use and is now preserved as a museum of domestic life in Old Jerusalem. Nebi Samuel, a veritable encyclopaedia of knowledge about Palestine, described it in an article he wrote in 1977, a year before his death.

Lusty babies were being produced daily in the country, but Harold decided he wanted his child to be born wrapped unambiguously as it were in the Union Jack, and I returned home in April 1921 to prepare. Manya was in her last year at Malvern and mother at the Hyde Park Hotel, so I took a flat in Albert Hall Mansions, engaged some servants and awaited the day. Miss Read had retired by now, but I had a good friend, Zoya Rozovska, who agreed to come in as my companion. She was from Riga, the daughter of a synagogue cantor, and extremely plump. Her mouth was eternally full of food, but this in no way impaired her outstanding mezzo-soprano voice, which won her occasional concert engagements.

Zoya made one condition. She must have a piano. A Bechstein was duly heaved into place through a window. Then she told me why.

'I'm going to be so busy,' she informed me importantly. 'I'm booked for the Ballets Russes. C. B. Cochran is putting on a Stravinsky season for Diaghilev at the Prince's Theatre.' The news delighted me. I was obsessed by my forthcoming baby in a most primitive way. I believed that whatever I absorbed in experience would influence his personality. On my journey from Palestine I had spent a night in Marseilles and visited the aquarium. I took fright at the octopus there, and feared my child would be born with a hundred legs. (He certainly grew up with a hundred different ideas.) I now decided that in an atmosphere generated by Zoya Rozovska and the composer Stravinsky he could well turn out a musical genius.

Knowing my Russians as I did, I stocked up with ample supplies of vodka and caviare. Though London's hostesses competed fiercely to entertain the star performers, and this took Lopokova to the Bloomsbury set and into eventual marriage with Maynard Keynes, Zoya frequently brought the entire corps de ballet to my flat – there was space enough to eat, relax and often, as it happened, to quarrel. Of them all, Diaghilev was the most extraordinary. Already running to flabbiness and jealously watching his boy-friends like a sex-starved hawk, he held sway in the tyrannical fashion that had caused strife within the company when it burst upon the Parisian scene before the war.

Diaghilev was a gourmet with ill-fitting false teeth, an unfortunate combination. His favourite dish was lobster Americaine, and though he tucked a napkin under his chin French style he succeeded in spluttering his food in every direction. As a result he cut a sorry figure, though not half so much as Stravinsky, who was shrunken, morose, and with a catalogue of grievances against mankind in general. Above all creatures he abhorred music critics, no doubt with justification. And having spent the war years as a refugee, virtually poverty-stricken, in Switzerland, he was obsessed with a fear that world recognition had passed him by. Interestingly, he told me of his theory that all musical notation had its origin in the ancient Hebrew alphabet.

While Zoya bustled round the company as a whole, a pacifying mama with honeyed words for each of her difficult children, Stravinsky's head was bent low over the piano. He could not forget the famous débâcle of the first night of *The Rite of Spring* eight years earlier, when Diaghilev foisted the already unbalanced Nijinsky upon him as choreographer. According to the composer, Nijinsky was exclusively responsible for the disaster. More likely, the revolutionary nature of the score, for those days, could be blamed for the ballet's astonishing reception, with the cream of *tout Paris* stamping its feet or marching out in disgust.

I asked Zoya how it was that two men of such brilliance as Diaghilev and Stravinsky could so abominate each other and yet still collaborate. She would not hear a word of criticism against Diaghilev.

'Don't you know, Stravinsky is so greedy,' she said. 'He's always complaining about money. Diaghilev has to go cap in hand to his patrons to finance the ballets, and Stravinsky expects all the money to go to him. The rest of us don't complain.'

The idea of Zoya Rozovska coupling herself in art with the great composer struck me as somewhat *de trop*, an example of how public performers could stretch belief in themselves. I had little knowledge of this until Diaghilev, while sharing a bottle with Fokine one afternoon, suddenly launched into a diatribe against Pavlova. She had tried to destroy him, he said. She was a

105

venomous, egotistical little demon. She should be barred from every stage across the world. Karsavina, on the other hand, was perfection itself. I collected up my naiveté and tip-toed quietly away.

The season opened late in May, and I was in my fully-rounded seventh month. Cochran, I recall, liked to give value for money. The programmes were long and varied, till I was grateful when the final curtain at last gave me release from my seat. Lopokova bewitched us as Firebird, with no two performances the same – the delirious audience refused to let her go. I would not miss a single evening. Sometimes the programme included Fokine's *Spanish Dances*, with a set by Picasso to dazzle the eyes. If Stravinsky came on stage all would be well afterwards. But he often sulked, declining to show himself, and then the sparks would fly between him and Diaghilev. Once, during an interlude, the conductor Ansermet gave three short pieces by the youthful prodigy Poulenc while a few members of the audience took it into their heads to organize a demonstration á la Parisienne. They jeered in unison, hissed, and burst into peals of laughter. It wasn't exactly the music to introduce to a London soaked in its post-war frivolity, and *The Times* critic described it as puerile rubbish, words he would one day wish he had eaten.

Usually, my Zoya had to content herself with singing from her customary position concealed behind the curtain; only in the ballet-opera *Pulcinella* did she come out front for a duet with Kaedonoff. Extravagantly made up, she wore circus costume that gave her a striking presence but did absolutely nothing for her figure. Poor Zoya! Her life ended, with her mother's, in a concentration camp. She married a stateless businessman who represented his company in Berlin. He was a gentile, and Zoya convinced herself they were safe. Mother and daughter were picked up by the Gestapo during the Second World War.

Harold returned to London in time for the birth, which duly took place at my home, now swept clean of all traces of balleto-mania, on 31 July 1921. Yes, it was a boy, Peter, and Harold gave a squeal of delight. Though this was Sunday morning he rushed out to enter Peter, as he had vowed, for Eton, the required sponsor being Humphrey Bowman, Director of Education in Palestine. We took a holiday at Le Touquet. Since I was accustomed to having anything I wanted I seduced the sous-chef, Bréchbehl, from our hotel and brought him back to Jerusalem with us.

Today I look back upon the establishment in my German Colony home with some incredulity. Bréchbehl was important enough to have his personal kitchen-boy, and found a Jewish student for the post. I rarely penetrated the kitchen but when I did I discovered this boy reading Nietzsche. My lady's maid was Norwegian, my parlourmaid Katia came from the Russian convent in Jerusalem, my butler Nicolai, a Cossack, had been left over from the war. Peter had the ever-so-British Nurse Oldroyd, and Harold his Arab driver. The household, a regular League of Nations, operated however without an official language. This was just as well, for had everyone the opportunity to express his politics in public we would have collapsed.

Palestine, old colonial hands used to say, was the land of three Sabbaths and four tomorrows. This certainly applied to Jerusalem. Harold found it pointless to sit in his office on Fridays with so many Moslems, including his personal staff, at prayer. And he dared not be caught there on Saturdays lest he offend the Jews. Sunday was kept sacred by government employees whatever their religion. With leisure lying so heavily on the sahibs, Harold mercifully established a Sports Club and organized horse riding expeditions with his colleagues. Applying method to his recreation, he inaugurated a tournament in which fellow-enthusiasts competed for the Solomon Cup. Little wonder that in the twenties it seemed the British in Palestine, not the Jews, more exactly matched the description of the Chosen People.

One step down from the High Commissioner, Wyndham Deedes as Chief Secretary looked benevolently on all that the Zionists were creating and, in the biblical phrase relating to the cosmos as a whole, 'saw that it was good'. The expression is by no means inappropriate, for Deedes, a former staff officer in intelligence, came from a farming background of fundamentalist Christianity. His devotion to the Jews' cause did not impair his absolute impartiality between them and the Arabs. Probably the adjective that comes swiftest to mind in describing Wyndham Deedes is 'ascetic'. He spoke fluent Turkish, having, in a varied life, served in the Ottoman gendarmerie. I often wondered why he did not seem completely content in the Land of the Bible, until he confessed to me that he yearned for a more simple existence. He felt he would fulfil himself in social work among the poor in the East End of London. This is how I found him, some years later in Bethnal Green, and we resumed a friendship that endured until his death in 1956.

107

Wyndham Deedes recognized better than most the sensitivities of the Arabs, and counselled caution upon the Jews. They on their side insisted on doing everything in a hurry. For many Zionists the Sabbath hardly existed. They came to Palestine armed with their blue-prints, realizing that the true competition in this country was not between the horsemen rigged out for all the world as though hunting with the Quorn, but between themselves and the Arabs for ultimate possession of the territory.

Wyndham was very much a mother's boy. Mrs Deedes ('Didi') spent a good deal of time with her son in Jerusalem. She had a wry sense of humour. Once, as I set out to accompany Harold and others on a visit to the Emir Abdulla in Transjordan, she gave me an excellent piece of advice. 'Carry a sponge-bag,' she warned me. 'You'll need it.'

I did as Didi advised. Abdulla entertained his guests in his huge tent outside Amman. When the food came in, the usual roast mutton on a mountain of rice, the Emir passed a sheep's eye to me, a special courtesy to a lady. I slipped it into my sponge-bag. Then he presented me with another morsel whose provenance I suspected. That too went into the bag. Then something more, disposed of likewise. The sponge-bag was now full. I clutched it dearly to my bosom as we said our farewells, which was all the talking Harold and I did on that occasion, for Abdulla held the fort and through his interpreter spoke of his determination one day to take all of Arabia under his rule. I was terrified lest he discover my ploy, and regard it as an affront to his desert hospitality.

As for that sponge-bag, it accompanied me all the way to Petra, our next port of call, where I felt it could be safely discarded. Any sooner, and I feared it would have been discovered by one of the Emir's tribesmen and brought back to Amman, while I would have been guilty of starting a diplomatic incident!

As Chief Secretary, Wyndham had an opposite number of sorts in Dr David Eder, Weizmann's representative in Jerusalem. Eder struck me as an enigma. He was burly, with a gruff manner that easily lapsed into rudeness. Yet I was pleased to find, when he was together with Deedes in my home, how well the two got along. Deedes described Eder to me as more an Englishman than himself. Socialist, psychiatrist and world traveller (he had been up the Amazon), Eder came close to the *kibbutznik* in both ideology and temperament. He left his London practice for five years to work for Palestine, much to the resentment of his friend and patient D. H. Lawrence, who threatened to come out and join him in Jerusalem if Eder insisted on staying away.

In pressing Eder to return to London Lawrence found an ally in the doctor's wife Edith. She was an aunt of Ivy Low, who married the future Soviet Foreign Minister Maxim Litvinov. I think the mystic atmosphere in Jerusalem was proving too oppressive for Edith Eder – understandably so, for she had suffered misery when her previous husband, the Labour Party politician Haden-Guest, plunged into Annie Besant's spooky world of Theosophy. Mrs Eder was a kindred spirit of Helen Bentwich, which meant that she and I did not exactly hit it off; she was a feminist, I was merely feminine.

I was relieved, therefore, when David Eder decided at last to return home, about the same time as Wyndham Deedes. Eder had not followed the latter's advice to be more circumspect regarding Jewish intentions. On the contrary, he constantly pressed the government to relax its immigration policy. The Arabs took fright, and this caused serious rioting in Jaffa while I was away having my baby. From that moment Herbert Samuel, to Zionist consternation, held the number of newcomers down. Jabotinsky, our stormy petrel, blamed Weizmann for being too soft with Britain and began agitating for his old friend's removal from the leadership.

Measures to frustrate the Jews' ambition to become the majority in the country were regarded by them as a betrayal of the Balfour Declaration. A group of engineers, technicians and entrepreneurs were pressing like coiled springs, yearning to release their energies in the industrialization of the country. They maintained that with economic development Palestine would absorb immigrants on a scale hitherto considered impossible. In the event this proved to be the case, though no official British expert would admit it. I found that the British were just as devoted to Palestine as the Jews, though they regarded any change as defacement of the sacred soil.

A perfect example was Ronald Storrs, Governor of Jerusalem. The classic 'Arabia hand', he shamed many Jews with his knowledge of Hebrew, he could speak Arabic, translate Homer while standing on one leg, and was passionate about Jerusalem. Storrs opposed any new building construction in the city except in native Judean stone, as though Jerusalem were a museum and he its curator. I was very fond of him, and respected his point of view, though he clashed with the Zionists time and time again. Similarly, St John Philby, who sometimes dined with us together with his attractive wife Dora and stammering young son Kim, was devoted to the silent, rolling desert. Samuel sent Philby to Amman to keep the flag flying in Transjordan, and polite though he was to my Jewish friends, I could see how much he resented their intensity.

They had a champion of course in Harold. My husband was given the 'portfolio' of Trade and Industry when Ralph Harari (a Jewish favourite of Storrs because of his fluency in Arabic) found the position somewhat anomalous for him and took the train back home to Cairo. Ralph was an aesthete, a member of the wealthy clan of which his father, Sir Victor Harari Pasha, was head. Little wonder that Ralph preferred to admire Palestine from a distance, for he had been born in a palace and raised like a prince. Sir Victor, in the Egyptian royal service, held the reins of his country's financial structure, but economics could not then evoke any interest for his son. So with Ralph Harari happily back in Cairo with his collections of pictures and antiquities (they became world famous), Harold inherited, among much else, two industrial pioneers determined on turning Palestine into the Oriental Switzerland. They were Peter Rutenberg and Misha Novomeysky; one look at them and I recognized here a type of Russian I had so frequently seen in my father's company in St Petersburg.

When Rutenberg, then aged forty, came to Palestine soon after the war he echoed the words once pronounced by Lenin: 'What this country needs is electricity.' He had worked before 1914 on an electrical scheme in the Italian Campagna, where he was befriended by the young Socialist agitator Mussolini. Now he canvassed all and sundry for a concession to construct hydro-electric works on the Jordan below the Sea of Galilee, and on the coast. Harold was captured by the vision of the project. He brought Peter Rutenberg to a lunch-party I gave for Rosita Forbes, the explorer. Peter began loudly to expatiate on the benefits electricity would confer on Palestine. He went on and on, reducing my other guests, the Bentwiches and Eder's replacement Fred Kisch, to extended, pained silence. Not so Rosita Forbes, with her vested interest in keeping the mysterious East mysterious.

'You're in the wrong continent,' she said. 'The needs of the people here are much too simple. Your scheme will cost the earth, and will never be made to pay.'

Rutenberg turned on her. 'What do you know of economics!' he retorted. 'I'm not discussing romance, that's your province. I'm talking business.'

'Well,' she replied, 'I haven't made a bad business out of my romantic hobby of Arabian travel.'

When this discussion took place Rutenberg already had victory within his grasp, for Harold had persuaded the Administration of the scheme's feasibility, while Weizmann gathered the necessary finance together in the City of London. But most important had been the intervention of Winston Churchill. As Colonial Secretary, Churchill had arrived in the Middle East in 1921 to settle, he hoped, all outstanding differences between Jew and Arab and, perhaps more significantly for him, between Britain and her local Great Power rival France. Churchill separated Transjordan from western Palestine and made Abdulla, unemployed son of the old Shereef of Mecca, its ruling Emir, with his brother Faisal King of Iraq. That left the path clear for the French to engage in their own policies for Syria and Lebanon.

Churchill enthused over the electrification project, and shepherded the proposal for a concession through despite powerful anti-Zionist sentiment in London. I vividly recall how Rutenberg took the news, pronouncing a Hebrew blessing over the name of Churchill. He had hawked his scheme around desperately, a man possessed. A weight was now lifted from him. At vertiginous speed he brought light and power to every corner of the country. And wherever he planted his pylons he also planted lawns and flower-beds.

Rutenberg now had a future as well as a past. He had been active in Social Revolutionary politics in Russia even earlier than Kerensky, in whose short-lived government he had served, with jurisdiction over the capital. He subsequently affirmed that, given a free hand, he could have fired the few shots from his office window in the Winter Palace that would have sufficed to bring the Bolsheviks to heel. Once, while strolling with him through the covered markets of the Arab *suk* he confided a secret to me. He confessed it had haunted him all his life. This related to that Bloody Sunday in St Petersburg in 1905 when, as I have already described, a demonstration of workers, led by Father Gapon, approached the Winter Palace and was savagely mown

111

down by the Tsarist gendarmerie. Peter Rutenberg was among the Social Revolutionaries in that demonstration. The SRs later held a meeting where they decided that Gapon was a double agent and would have to be executed.

An Oriental bazaar can hardly be termed a deserted place, yet Peter barely dropped his voice. 'We drew lots as to who should do it. To my horror it fell to me. I traced Gapon to Finland and found him in a country shack. He greeted me as a friend. Then I shot him. And do you know, Flora, I'm not sure to this day whether his execution was justified, whether he was in fact an *agent provocateur.'*

I was a little alarmed at being entrusted with this confidence. But Harold, after our guests departed one evening, said casually, 'Did you know that fellow Rutenberg did away with Gapon?' And another day Novomeysky, who would win the minerals from the Dead Sea, gave me his account, though with slight variations. Later, Bruce Lockhart, British representative in Petrograd in 1917, put it in a book as though he was the first to know. Poor Rutenberg, who lived for many years like a conspirator, was incapable of keeping the deed to himself, albeit he never told the story the same way twice. How Gapon died must surely be among the worst-kept secrets in history.

Rutenberg was a bachelor (though another of his 'secrets' was the wife he left behind in Russia) and he regarded feminine solace as one of his prerogatives. This applied also to Misha Novomeysky, then also unmarried and the other's closest friend in Jerusalem. Both of them passed extended periods deep in the country living rough while planning their respective schemes, and when they returned they came to me, as their compatriot offering hospitality de luxe. It wasn't always easy to fend their attentions off, though they protested friendship and loyalty also to Harold. I had no difficulty in recognizing the danger signals: they lapsed into Russian like plotters, or begged me to come and see their frontier enterprises (the proverbial etchings), Rutenberg's high up north on the Jordan, Novomeysky's on the shores of the Dead Sea. This didn't trouble me, it was just one more hazard of the high life in a rudimentary region with more conventional amusements hard to find. My husband had the monopoly of my attentions and did not, I feel sure, consider a Russian-Jewish engineer prone to anything so frivolous as an affair.

Nevertheless, when I accepted their invitations to inspect

112

their good works, my little son Peter and his nurse usually accompanied me, as a shield of additional armour. 'Novo' was a chemist and mining engineer, born and raised in the Siberian *taiga*. Indeed, his family had controlled mines in the Lena Goldfields. Others before him had spoken of reclaiming the riches of the Dead Sea but he, from his earliest survey of the area in Turkish times, knew this was to be his life's work.

The Dead Sea is no great distance from Jerusalem – one caught the reflection of the long sheet of metallic water clearly from the Mount of Olives – but so sudden is the leap in temperature from the highland city to the lowest point on the earth's surface that in my day few would chance the journey by motor-car except in Palestine's winter, and without first having the engine thoroughly checked. One road alone led to Jericho. It was crossed by leisurely camel-trains and flanked with Bedouin encampments patterned black against the folds of ochrous rock. Bethany was soon reached, and then the Good Samaritan Inn to beckon the weary traveller. Jericho advertised itself in the twenties by its long aquaduct carrying the waters from Elisha's Fountain. The town was exclusively Arab, and a barely discernible track led one down to the lake-side and to Novomeysky, usually ankle-deep in water and with a large grey homburg protecting his head. Mercifully, he was oblivious at this time to the manifold problems still to be surmounted before he could at last create an industry out of his dream. The Palestine Potash Company was not allowed to undertake major operations until 1929.

Novo had built a timbered house for himself and his laboratory equipment. His great contribution was in harnessing the sun for his evaporation pans. Solar energy is now commonplace, but you were considered a crank in those days if you hoped for its industrial exploitation in the Orient.

Novo had a reason for bringing me down to the Dead Sea that was far removed from any notions of gallantry. Quite the reverse. 'You know,' he told me, 'Rutenberg and I see a lot more of the Arabs than most Zionists. We work closely with them, we wish to remain their friends, and given time we shall succeed. But we don't delude ourselves. The British Army is now being run down here, because it's required for the troubles in Egypt. When the riots broke out in Jaffa the British were there to defend us. Next time we may be on our own. At any rate, we have to be prepared. Now, look over there.'

He pointed to some hutments in the distance. 'Our boys do their training there. Rutenberg and I are working for the *Haganah*. Flora, we want you to help us.'

'I suppose you mean money.'

'Yes. When the first new immigrants reached Palestine from Russia you went to Egypt, and with the help of your young friend Harari, you got funds for them. We need you for this purpose too.'

It therefore transpired that I had a visit from a most remarkable woman, Manya Shochat. She was already a veteran pioneer, having arrived early in the century following participation in the revolutionary movement in Russia. She lifted the veil for me on another side of Zionism, the left-wing political movement. She was in charge of procuring weapons for the collective settlements.

'Chaim Weizmann is not our leader,' she declared. 'This country will never be built up by his speech-making abroad, but by the workers here on the land. The man who is going to bring us victory is David Ben-Gurion.' The name was new to me and I knew nothing of his ideas.

I gave Manya Shochet money, then and later. I decided not to tell Harold of her visit, thinking the British were entirely ignorant of the *Haganah*. In fact they were fully informed on the organization, though for the moment turning a blind eye.

Eder's successor Fred Kisch had arrived in 1923. We were already old friends. With his regular army background he was rather similar to Harold, and I was sure the ideal man to deal with the British administrators in Palestine from the Zionist point of view. (At least, he would never bluster along like the 'foreign' Jewish leaders, one of whom, Ussishkin, added Eno's Fruit Salts to Churchill's whisky because he was informed the English always imbibed the drink with soda.)

On one visit to London from New York I had introduced my sister Fira to Kisch. To my delight a relationship ripened and they became engaged. Fira then dithered, and finally announced that she would not dream of living in Palestine. She returned Fred's ring, upon which she had always looked askance, for it was a humble piece of jewellery to a woman accustomed to diamonds of more substantial appearance. This left the path clear, as I have told, for Ruth Franklin some years later.

Fred saw that I could be of value to him. I made a point of

114

bringing Arabs and Jews together in my home, where they had ample opportunity also of coming into contact with the British in an atmosphere rather more relaxed than at the Samuels' receptions on the hill. An Arab I very much admired was the scholar George Antonius, a Christian occupying the post of deputy to Humphrey Bowman in the Education Department – he was worth ten Bowmans, but Arabs rarely got the plum jobs. Another was the Mayor of Jerusalem, Ragheb Bey Nashashibi, whose Turkish wife constantly plied me with her home-baked cookies, made with goat's milk that turned my stomach. Nashashibi enjoyed three-cornered discussions with the rabbis and Anglican clergymen I entertained, but like all moderates of whatever denomination, he had little influence on his own people. I remember in particular another occasion with Rosita Forbes. This time the intrepid traveller (she never moved far unless accompanied by a servant exclusively charged with guarding her immense vanity case) declaimed at length on the virtues of the Arab land-owning class, the Effendis. To the Mayor's embarrassment she spoke of the Effendis' touching concern for the peasants, when he knew the Effendis were largely responsible for their dire poverty.

Still, everybody was talking, and people from abroad present at my parties were sure this augured blessed harmony between the different races in the future. How wrong they were! And how wrong I was! One outsider to arrive at this conclusion was Ethel Snowden; her husband Philip was Number Two to Ramsay MacDonald in the Labour Party.

Mrs Snowden had toured the new Soviet paradise and I read her book describing life there. Evidently she saw nothing to criticize in Russia, neither the rigid conformism imposed upon the population, nor the barbarism resulting when a doctrine of theoretical equality is applied by an all-powerful few. Now that she was assessing the situation in Palestine I decided to show her the new communal settlements, where socialism was voluntary, and how the Jews were making the land bloom again. On the first morning of her month-long visit I marched her off to watch 'A Drop of Milk' in operation. It was now a flourishing concern.

A former schoolteacher and devout Christian, Ethel Snowden was naturally keen to visit the shrines of Old Jerusalem, and Bethlehem. She could quote almost the entire Bible by heart. We also drove to Mount Tabor, scene of the Transfiguration, and

115

into Nazareth, which was like a colourful carpet pleated into haphazard shape by its surrounding hills. She wandered dreamily through the meandering streets, I thought unconscious of everything except the presence of her Saviour, when suddenly she spoke: 'What lovely slippers in that shop. I wonder if they'll have my size?' We came to the Jordan at Degania, the very first *kibbutz*, and there waiting for us was Joseph Baratz, one of its original settlers.

Ethel and I shared a room in a tiny hut. Sanitary arrangements were somewhat primitive, the shower and toilet being located a good ten minutes' walk from where we slept. Degania has now grown into a township, though when we arrived just a handful of families struggled to make a go of the farmstead. They had the rudiments of a dairy herd, a banana plantation and chickens by the hundred. In those days you were subjected to ordeal by flies; escaping them involved constant movement. I tried to brush a fly from Ethel's face, only to discover it was a mole!

Baratz was no reclusive country yokel. He loved showing visitors around and could regale them through the night with his tales of the *real* pioneering days, under the Turks. He spoke of his childhood in Kishinev during the time of its pogrom in 1903, and how the district in which he lived was sacked by the Black Hundreds. That had decided him to go to Palestine.

'One day, when I've the time, I'll write a book about all this,' he said. And he did. Or rather, he dictated his story in Russian to my sister Manya, and I gave it its title, *A Village by the Jordan*. It was one of the first books Manya published when, in the late forties, she started the Harvill Press. A child born in Degania won fame as Moshe Dayan, Israel's victorious general and later its Foreign Minister.

Out of this trip an intimacy developed between Ethel Snowden and myself that deepened over the years and led me into new paths. I was profoundly moved by her idealism. To amend a phrase belonging in another context, socialism represented to her 'Christianity by other means'.

Needless to say, Harold too became friendly with Ethel. His personality, always urbane, expanded under the Palestine sun. I felt we were truly made for each other. He adored little Peter, who had a playmate now in Hadassah Samuel's son David. The two English children (David was born in his grandfather's official residence, actual British territory) in their two English prams pushed by two English nannies were quite a feature of our little outpost of Empire. I observed that my son inherited one trait at least from the Solomons: the family clumsiness. In reading Beatrix Potter's stories to him I found his double in Flopsy Rabbit. The name attached to him, he rather liked it, and Flopsy was his sobriquet for years afterwards. The world seemed a contented, optimistic place when surveyed from our privileged vantage-point in Jerusalem.

In the Christmas of 1923 Harold arranged, as usual, a make-shift point-to-point for the horse-riding fraternity. Harold's mount, a six-year-old bay, threw him, and as he fell its hoof kicked against his spine. Picking himself up, he ruefully re-turned home by motor-car, because of the pain. He was not the man to fuss over himself, and was back at work almost im-mediately. However, after a fortnight or so, he confessed to a suspicion that he had ridden a horse for the last time in his life.

Soon, every movement of his body proved laborious. In the spring of 1924 he stood leaning on my shoulder as together we took in a vista of the city made golden in the crystal twilight. The scene had inspired poets and prophets for millennia.

'It's no good, Flora,' he said, 'there's nothing for it. I'll have to resign. Perhaps someone in Europe can patch me up.' But no-one could. Harold became paralysed from the waist down. He never walked again.

6 In Search of a Purpose

Money enables its possessors to elude many laws, but the law of averages isn't one of them. The home that Harold and I made on our return to London in 1924 lacked for nothing in human and technical aids. Our house in Hornton Street, Kensington, sheltered a nanny for Peter, a nurse for Harold, two chauffeurs, and other staff abundant enough to service a small hotel. A lift was installed for my invalid husband, while in the garage, beside my Baby Austin, there waited a large Buick adapted to receive a man, his wheel-chair, and whatever and whomsoever else his requirements or whims demanded.

Life could be described as normal. However, on the other side of the balance our existences entered separate compartments. We were never again to stroll together, sleep together, or engage in any endeavour of mutual enrichment. A married couple we might be, but one partner was a widower rather than a husband, the other a widow more than a wife.

One of our unspoken rules – we had several – was never to tell each other we had been cheated. Harold, by application and inventiveness, constructed a world that he could inhabit satisfactorily. He determined to educate and amuse himself, through companionship, travel and study. He intended to be a father to his son. I observed that he needed me less and less, and concluded that this was the same as not wanting me. I found myself gradually retreating out of his life.

Without entering his rooms on the first floor, I could recognize his mood at any given moment by the sounds. Absolute quiet told me he was morose, and seeking consolation in a book, or his stamp collection. If he was banging out a tune on his piano – usually accompanying himself to such favourites then current as 'And her mother came too' – I knew all was well and his day would end with friends at the theatre, or perhaps the Embassy Club. His loud laughter signalled a romp on the floor at some boy's game with Peter. For a further relaxation he liked to call

2LO on his wireless. Whatever my occupation in that house, my ear never rested. Clive Garsia, Harold's war-time comrade, came so frequently he suggested one day that he move in with us. A bachelor, Clive played the stock-markets and perpetually re-fought the Near Eastern campaign against the Turks, in which he believed Allenby had grievously blundered. He was also sweating over a novel; it came out in 1927 and indicated a literary style faithfully derived from *Boy's Own Paper*.

He fitted smoothly into our household and proved an affectionate foster-uncle to Peter. Clive and Harold would pour over large maps of Yugoslavia reconstructing their Serbian war, and sometimes they would take off in the Buick on an expedition for a closer inspection of the Pasich terrain. After Peter reached seven or eight he would go along too, together with Harold's nurse. She disliked me, spied on me, and was obviously in love with Harold. *Lady Chatterley's Lover* was not yet written; when in 1929 I obtained my illicit copy it struck a chord.

Their journeys across the Continent involved the preparation of a detailed itinerary, compiled in army jargon: hotels became billets, meals were rations, one of the chauffeurs was posted as duty-driver for the expedition. It was no holiday for him, or the nurse. They had to lift Harold with his wheel-chair and other appurtenances up and down the winding stairways of old-fashioned Balkan hotels and in and out of monasteries he wished to inspect. They lowered him into the lakes for a swim, his only physical exercise. Split-second scheduling was *de rigueur*. Each day's stage had to be worked out for speed of travel and time of arrival, based on the twenty-four-hour clock system. If, for example, they were journeying from Zagreb to reach the Palace of Diocletian in Split at 1400 hours, the chauffeur adjusted his tempo to do exactly that: a minute too early or too late and he was 'on a charge'. It would be Clive's function to make a preliminary reconnaissance of the sights, to assess facilities for a halt and their interest for a visit. I knew all this from their daily postcards – 'despatches from the front'.

England itself being only sparsely served for hotels in those years, we would between times take a house in the country for the summer. Our usual choice was the Kent coast at Saltwood, near Hythe, where Wyndham Deedes had his family castle, and near our friends Victor and Ruth Gollancz, holidaying at Dymchurch with their five girls. Ruth was related to my mother-in-law, and Harold, ever the organizer, planned daily games and competitions for the children. We wondered whether our son Peter would one day marry a Gollancz daughter. He never did.

The twenties peel year by year from my memory with recollections of the Lyons tea shops to which I would take my son, returning from his daily kindergarten school, for a bun and milk, and Coco Chanel's fashion revolution out of Paris, and of course the novels of Michael Arlen. He made the little green hat the worn thing, so sure enough one day Clive Garsia brought a chit of a girl to our house at Dymchurch and there it was, covering her shingled hair. What happened between her and Harold I do not know, but on one of those Dalmatian expeditions she went along too, together with a companion for Clive – I was a little piqued, Clive had already declared his love for me, absolutely unreciprocated – though I felt my husband if anyone was entitled to such friendships. The head in the green hat belonged to a vivacious young person named Joan Carr, who subsequently married the newspaper executive Lord Drogheda. Another girl in their travelling group, Ginette Spanier, wrote a lively book on those salad days; later she became *directrice* of Pierre Balmain's couture house.

Happy I wasn't; contented neither. I was busy, ever on the look-out for some diversion that could lull me, and convince Harold, into the belief that we were living as ordinarily as the very rich lived. But part of myself was left in Jerusalem, along with my closest friends, my deepest yearnings, and my Jewish heart. Harold neither encouraged nor deterred me in my pursuits. It seemed he was incapable of taking any woman seriously. Some of us had at last been given the vote, in 1918 (I qualified too on reaching the age of thirty, when females were deemed to be grown up), but as far as I could plumb my husband's mind we ranked as a species with thoroughbred horses, or perhaps we were expected to resemble Arlen's wanton heroine Iris Storm.

One day was made memorable for me by a letter from Ethel Snowden. This was still in 1924, and she invited me to No 11 Downing Street, where her husband Philip, his grave face drained of all colour, was battling as the Labour Government's Chancellor of the Exchequer with the country's deplorable balance-sheet. I saw now that she and I had a bond in common: Philip was grievously crippled, from a bicycle accident in his youth, and needed the assistance of sticks in standing and walking. It brought Ethel and me very close.

Philip Snowden treated me to a smile that came so painfully

through his thin lips it would have frightened the devil himself. It was a smile nevertheless; many people claimed they had never seen any expression on his face except granite. I must have been everything he despised – idle, rich and foreign. And indecently energetic too, to one whose every movement sent a dagger-thrust into his flesh. Yet I awakened his curiosity. He asked me to join him later that week at breakfast, and I found myself opening up to him about my previous life to a degree never attained with my husband. He enjoyed my stories of St Petersburg and himself grew expansive, recalling his early years in a Yorkshire village, his father's work in the mills as a weaver, and the exhilaration he experienced in passing a civil service examination that promised the security of a regular wage. Philip Snowden had little interest in foreign travel and knew no language but his own. This I found inexplicable. Didn't he need to understand French, at least, for he was constantly in communication with foreign governments?

Again, that icy smile. 'Waiters and hotel porters need foreign languages, my dear, not politicians.'

Ethel, his junior by nearly twenty years, ran their official residence like a Salvation Army citadel. No alcohol was allowed during their tenure in Downing Street, while a luncheon-party lasted one hour, not a minute more nor less. She prepared meticulously for every occasion. She would send a card inviting you for one o'clock, and you would then reply. If this was an acceptance she would write again, as follows: 'Thank you for accepting my invitation. You will be seated beside Margaret Bondfield' – or whoever – 'on your left. She was last year's chairman of the TUC and will prove most informative on the working conditions of shop assistants. On your right will be Monsieur Jean Longuet, of the Socialist newspaper *Le Populaire*. He's a grandson of Karl Marx, speaks excellent English, and looks a little like Charlie Chaplin.' I wondered how she described me to them.

The inevitable happened. They made me a convert to Socialism. I continued to maintain eleven servants at Hornton Street and a style requisite to an income possibly as large as any young woman's in the country. I still enjoyed a night of dancing to the saxophone section of Carroll Gibbons' Orpheans at the Savoy, or a weekend at Le Touquet's gaming-tables, and cheerfully addressed footmen and parlourmaids in my employ by their surnames. I refused to join the Labour Party but indulged in heated arguments with Harold at meal-times on the exploitation of the working classes, with Ripley our butler standing by expressionless, a bottle of good wine at the ready.

The door was only slightly ajar. My revolutionary fervour took the form of attending Fabian lectures at Conway Hall in Red Lion Square, passionately supporting the coal-miners – 'not a penny off the pay, not a minute on the day' – in their protracted struggle against the proprietors (the spectre of the Lena Gold-fields still haunting me), and smoking in public. I kept my admiration for Ramsay MacDonald secret: Philip Snowden considered him tactless and secretive, while Ethel suspected the Prime Minister's sexual morality. When I found occasion to discuss politics with my sister Manya, now through London University with a history degree, she was completely unmoved. Her own intention, she confided in me, was to become a nun. How childish, I thought.

Manya was then living with mother at the Hyde Park Hotel, and showed the strain. She seemed to pick her clothes off a washing-line. By the way Manya attached herself to me since my return from Palestine I knew she was desperate to escape from the atmosphere of faded grandeur that hung about hotel life with mother. Her closest friend was our niece Mira, daughter of our late brother Yasha. They had discovered each other while students, and Mira likewise contemplated embracing the Catholic Church. Manya, now twenty, had obviously drawn the worst bargain of all three sisters in the family break-up; she was deeply introspective, she was a waif. I suggested we go away together, and chose Geneva, enrolling in a vacation-course there arranged by Alfred Zimmern at his School of International Studies. I gave absolute loyalty to the hope of eternal peace through the League of Nations, and in promoting his ideas of the inter-dependence of civilizations Zimmern had, to assist him in the course, the Polish musician-statesman in exile, Paderewski. Two additional young lecturers were French scholars of Egyptian extraction, Jean de Menasce and Georges Cattaui.

I asked them: 'Do you know my friend Ralph Harari?' They looked at each other and laughed. 'Know him?' said Jean de Menasce, 'We're all cousins. We're the tribe left over by Moses when he crossed the Red Sea; some in Cairo, some in Alexandria, with an overflow in Paris.'

Jean lectured on philosophy and comparative religion, while Georges' subject was literature. They moved effortlessly from

French to English, a Mutt and Jeff couple, Jean being tall and intellectual-looking, Georges short and unimpressive, and, like his idol Proust, forever wrapped up in a coat and scarf. Neither might be described as good fun. Nevertheless we found ourselves taking walks that stretched the evenings along the Geneva lake-side to midnight and later, and I observed how Manya drank in every word uttered by Jean. He was oblivious to this. She returned to the Hyde Park Hotel like a child being sent unwillingly to bed. Something had to be done about this sister of mine, of that I was sure, whereas nobody needed to worry about Fira, who drenched her letters from New York in the vivid prose of a café society confessor. Perhaps Manya could find herself, as I had, in Palestine?

I was aching to see the country again. In the spring of 1925 the inauguration of the Hebrew University was at last to take place, with Lord Balfour, now aged seventy-seven, to perform the opening ceremony. Jerusalem would be *en fête*. Chaim Weizmann therefore made arrangements for Manya and me to travel with him and all the other guests from Britain on the *Esperia*, and I recall the Mediterranean being so stormy that many passengers, including Balfour himself, were taken ill.

A somewhat bedraggled company, we docked seven hours late at Alexandria. But the local Jewish population were not to be cheated of a lavish welcoming banquet for so august a delegation. Jean de Menasce's father Baron Felix (the title was Austrian, the splendour of his establishment Oriental) ran the show, as he ran almost everything in Alexandria. He therefore arrogated to himself the honour of putting up Balfour, his niece, her husband, the Weizmanns, and anyone else deemed to hold precedence. This left Manya and me to be consigned to a secondary branch of the family. We nevertheless slept on pillows so profusely embroidered with the Menasce coat of arms our cheeks the next morning were embossed pink and white. When we looked at each other we thought we had developed a rash! After breakfast the family hairdresser, who lived on the premises, came to perform our coiffure.

A ponderous diet of speeches was in store, so I suggested to Manya that we skip them and travel on alone to Cairo that day. The marvels of the tomb of Tutankhamen had just been placed in the museum, where they were attracting visitors by the thousand. This would be our opportunity to see them. I telephoned Ralph Harari informing him we were on our way, no doubt a couple of beds could be found for us in some corner of his palace.

When we reached Cairo the museum was closed, this being one of its numerous rest days. It seemed we would be disappointed. I had overlooked the influence of the Hararis in Cairo, not less than that of the Menasces in Alexandria. Ralph sent a servant to the curator, who arrived personally and himself gave us an exposition of the treasures.

Ralph used to ask me at my home in Jerusalem: 'Flora, haven't you a sister for me to marry?' Well, *voilà*, a sister! He seemed to get on well with Manya. I was sure I had been right to dislodge her from her London rut.

The university ceremony in Jerusalem, stage-managed brilliantly by Fred Kisch, took place on an open site in a natural amphitheatre on Mount Scopus. An audience of ten thousand, an endless panorama of sky and wilderness, a spirit of high optimism for the future of the country, all lent a biblical majesty to the scene. It was above all Weizmann's triumph. He sat with Balfour, Allenby and Samuel, the three British personalities who could be said to have brought an ancient dream of a Jewish homeland within the grasp of reality. This was Samuel's swansong in Palestine, for his term as High Commissioner was now completed. He utilized the occasion with a poignant address that had the gathering almost in tears, concluding with the prayer, spoken in Hebrew: *Blessed art Thou, O Lord our God, King of the Universe, who hast kept us in life, and hast preserved us, and enabled us to reach this moment.*

One other incident warrants recollection, as a gauge to the veneration Balfour had won among the Jews. The old man, still handsome and erect, and delineated in space like a prophet, raised his arms aloft to emphasize an almost dying wish, for harmony among the races of mankind. Now, Palestine was in the midst of a drought which that year was spreading havoc among the crops, for it was already April and no rain was expected until the autumn. Jerusalem was suffering above all. That night the rains suddenly descended, in torrents. To the cynical and the sophisticated it was a meteorological freak. Not so to the average Jerusalemite; he was convinced Balfour the Englishman had brought the blessing.

I was hoping for a miracle of another sort, and was not disappointed either. On the termination of the day's programme, as we dispersed, Manya and I were greeted by those

124

three cousins, Ralph Harari, Jean de Menasce and Georges Cattaui. They had, on impulse, decided to come up from Egypt for the ceremony. At their suggestion we made a tour together to show Manya this entrancing land. Jean lead the group – the civilizations of the ancient Orient were his speciality. And as we lingered below the rocks by the Sea of Galilee it became clear to me that he captivated Manya. She was in love.

That summer Jean took a post-graduate course at Oxford, Georges Cattaui in periodic attendance. Jean and Manya were now seeing a great deal of each other, and I recall the four of us travelling to Garsington in the Cotswolds to visit Lady Ottoline Morrell, whom Georges referred to as Lady Utterly Immoral – I expect he got this from a book, not personal experience. One day a letter arrived for Manya. It was a proposal of marriage – though alas, from the wrong cousin; not from Jean but Ralph Harari. It surprised and disappointed her, for she considered she hardly knew Ralph. She wrote back refusing him.

Jean de Menasce, by now well aware of Manya's feelings, came to talk to me, bringing a confession: he was homosexual and would never marry. He could only love Manya as a sister. She should find happiness with Ralph.

Shortly afterwards Manya and Ralph were married in Paris, in a synagogue ceremony with a reception for four hundred at the Plaza Athénée. For a woman to whom clothes had absolutely no significance Manya prepared her trousseau with a frenzy that was akin to an exorcism. Only the top couture houses would do: Chanel's afternoon dresses, Patou's black chiffon, Lanvin's lingerie, with shoes and matching accessories from Kirby Beard to fill a pantechnicon. She had the expert advice of Fira, who was spending part of every year in Paris in the regular company of Alfred Savoir, playwright laureate to the *beau monde*.

My two sisters were poles apart (the pun is unintentional, but Fira was addicted to Poles, Savoir having been born a Posnansky). Fira and Paris served each other perfectly. She was at home wherever elegance, intellectualism, easy living and easy loving, reigned. It was that post-war Paris presided over by Misia Sert, the friend of Diaghilev and Cocteau, the Misia immortalized by Proust (now as Princess Yourbeletieff, now as Madame Verdurin) in his great opus, creator of the Chanel legend and model of every renowned painter beginning with Renoir and Bonnard. As all Paris knew, Misia was then at the terminal stage of her third and final marriage to the celebrated ornamentalist whose murals decorated opulent homes and famous edifices from the town hall in Barcelona to the Waldorf-Astoria in New York. I spent memorable hours with her when I came to the Meurice, where she and José-Maria Sert occupied a suite.

Fira, the Benenson girl closest to father's millions, had with all this transformed herself into the complete American, right down to her nose operation (she and Peggy Guggenheim held each other's hand to have the re-shaping job done together, though Fira's was unsuccessful and gave her breathing problems ever afterwards). She had all but shed her Russian accent, and was, from all reports, so at home in Mayor Jimmy Walker's New York that her apartment at the Plaza took on the ambience of the Twenty-One Club, ever with its quota of vaudeville comics, impoverished Polish counts, *New York Times* journalists and Irish politicians. Now she taught Manya, who never hailed a taxi, even in the rain, if there was a bus queue nearby to join, how to spend. Whatever happened to the wardrobe Manya acquired with Fira's assistance no-one knew, for she was content all her life in a cardigan and worsted skirt.

Jean de Menasce joined the Order of Dominicans and entered a monastery near Paris as Father Pierre. Manya, as was the custom in their Egyptian circle, accompanied her husband to his family abode in Cairo, helping him in the charitable works expected of every Harari scion and which Ralph espoused with all earnestness. She established her own milk depot, described there as 'La Goutte de Lait', for the poor, took an active part in running a Jewish orphanage and heroically positioned herself with the local ladies in their activities for Palestine. None of this allowed Manya to forget Jean. He was always the person spiritually closest to her, and she travelled frequently throughout her life to Paris to visit him.

Paris in the twenties, for Britishers with money, had less the air of a foreign city, the capital of incomprehensible France, than an extension of Mayfair, Chelsea, Bloomsbury. Restricted though I might be by my domestic responsibilities, and duties towards my invalid husband, I nevertheless slipped frequently down to Dover and boarded the boat-train for that other life. Mother spent long periods there and in the South of France, tenaciously keeping herself in this world through a painful illness so as to be present at Manya's wedding. Then she retreated to her villa in Nice, where she died.

Paris continued to beckon. Perhaps this reflected a restless urge to fill the vacuum in which I found myself. I took hungrily to the society of painters and actors, dropping at every opportunity into that wildest of night clubs the *Ox on the Roof*, where literary men-about-town like Maurice Sachs drank themselves silly, Serge Lifar retailed the latest ballet scandal, and the couples danced while you were left guessing as to which was the man and which the woman. Here one saw how Misia Sert, profligate though she might be yet still beautiful, could produce heart-ache or ecstasy in Stravinsky by taking his latest composition either with a dubious shake of her sensitive little head or a smile of approval, and how she could make the reputation of an unknown artist from a single *vernissage*. So lavish was Misia towards those she loved, she drove the teenage Roussy Mdivani into the arms of her husband José-Maria Sert, till she was herself replaced by the little princess to emerge the gooseberry of the arrangement. Years later I could not persuade any British publisher to take Misia's memoirs; yet they sold and sold in France because the book was required reading for writers, politicians, hoteliers and courtesans alike.

Paris was to London what champagne is to stout, and Stanley Baldwin to Herriot – could one imagine the English Tory writing a study of Lady Mary Wortley Montagu as did the French radical of Mme Recamier? Yet I remained faithful in my love for London. I rejoiced in being British but was angered too, for I was learning about its darker side: Margaret Bondfield's earlier shop-assistant existence as a live-in drudge on her feet seventy hours a week for a pittance; the fire of resentment breathed by 'Red Ellen' Wilkinson as she fought and fought to improve the laundry girls' lot. When 'Didi' Deedes told me of her son Wyndham's work among the poor in Bethnal Green I got into my Baby Austin and took the route to Old Ford Road, there to find him among the ping-pong tables and fret-work benches of the Oxford University Settlement House. He barely slept, and rarely ate, until Didi herself came up from Kent to take him in hand. The settlement was a church charity, but Wyndham lamented that few Oxford undergraduates, even those aspiring to holy orders, would spend any time there, and join him in calling on the old widows – usually wearing a late husband's cap held in place by a hat-pin – or help put out the chairs for a prayer-meeting.

Oxford House had ideas for the spiritual welfare of the beer-drinking, unemployed slum-dwellers of Bethnal Green that were miles above its financial station. Its upper-class organizers quarrelled with the local clergy – and this meant the Reverend Sarel of St Matthew's, a character who deserves a place in East London's history along with William Booth – because not enough religion got into the week's programme. Yet nothing was so effective as the Lord's Prayer for keeping customers at a distance. Wyndham, his soulful, liquid eyes fixed upon the rising damp on the kitchen wall, where tea and biscuits were dispensed for a penny, explained to me that Oxford House had once owned the only indoor swimming pool and concert hall in Bethnal Green. However, they had got so deeply into debt catering for a community obstinately staying away that they had succumbed to the inevitable, virtually going over to the devil, by converting the Excelsior Hall into the Excelsior Kinema (only mission-meetings on Sundays, though) and could still not balance the books. Could I help?

Wyndham Deedes was the worst fund-raiser I have ever encountered. His transparent honesty was an advertisement for failure, I thought, as I recalled some Jewish meetings I had attended where an orator could start the tears and the shillings flowing with tales of heroism and sacrifice in the Holy Land.

'Our next project,' Wyndham revealed, 'is our most ambitious, though whether it will succeed or not I cannot say. At any rate, we must try.' They were converting premises in the vicinity into a library and arts centre, where young and old could sit in warmth, read, learn sketching and be introduced to folk-dancing and drama. They would open the place – here a roguish spark lit up his eyes – to both sexes.

'Of course,' he went on, 'the Reverend Sarel was against it at first, but at length he too admitted it was worth the effort, to curb what goes on in the back streets here after dark.' And so it was that I found a use at last for the pearls with the diamond clip given to me by my father years before on leaving Fräulein Wolff's at Wiesbaden. They became a library in Bethnal Green.

Didi entertained for Wyndham, at tea-parties which she summed up in a phrase that sounded original coming from her: 'It's where East meets West.' I was thus familiar with all the problems associated with the Excelsior Kinema. It was almost, though not quite, the worst flea-pit in the East End. Aided by a trained projectionist, the cinema kept going by exhibiting films not of the latest vintage, and did tolerable business when Smart's Picture Palace, further down the Bethnal Green Road, boastfully announced 'standing room only'. Alas, 1928 brought Al Jolson and the talkies. The Oxford House management, demonstrating the professionalism that had proved disastrous in nearly every venture it espoused, pronounced the new invention a temporary, passing fad. It continued its silent offerings as before. Takings dwindled, Bethnal Green denizens almost ashamed to admit to spending an evening at the Excelsior. Wyndham and his committee responded thankfully to an offer of purchase and, to the relief of everyone concerned, resigned from the film business.

In those times the club settlements of London were sectarian, and Oxford House, though it did not refuse Jewish money, could only welcome as volunteers upright, church-going Christians. My own desire to be of some use among the under-privileged sent me to the other side of the borough, to Butler Street in Spitalfields. The local girls' club, dominated as was much else in the Jewish East End by a relative of Harold's, Nettie Adler, awakened my interest. The experience was to serve me well in later years. Added to their extreme poverty, the girls suffered a sense of alienation in being, for the most part, daughters of recent immigrants. They were largely employed in the dress-making and millinery trades, a few in the local cigarette-making factory – all sweated industries.

Despite the range of activities available at the Butler Street club to develop latent talents and expand artistic and economic horizons, only one subject truly interested the girls, and it wore trousers. They practised the foxtrot in the wash-rooms so as to meet boys at the local 'hops'; they attacked the mysteries of shorthand solely to qualify for a job as secretary to some office Adonis, and they would steal away in groups to parade up and down the Whitechapel Road in the hope of a romantic encounter on that famous trysting-ground. Their mothers slaved all hours for large families, to become old women by the time they were thirty; yet marriage embraced the entirety of the daughters' dreams.

Nettie Adler, who adjusted her hectic day to a succession of committee meetings, could never understand it. She, as a matter of fact, was wedded to the local borough council, and her inauguration into each new chairmanship practically took the form of a religious rite. But I found the girls little different in this respect from the contemporaries of my own sheltered youth. Morality among the working classes was certainly more puritanical: to be seen out with a married man marked a girl as the neighbourhood harlot.

Though already in their teens, many of my charges had never smelt the sea, never in fact been outside London. The bulk of the population in the centre of the world's greatest empire received not a single day's paid holiday a year, any time off work constituting unemployment. The house Harold and I took for the summer at Dymchurch was located in fairly extensive grounds, so it was no problem to arrange a camp for the girls. They came down in groups, sleeping in the bell-tents discharged from active service in various theatres of war and now available for hire. Harold of course organized their sports events. Dymchurch offered little diversion for the young except a rather stony beach. However, just a few miles away Folkestone, with promenade and pier, exerted its magnetic pull as a potential hunting-ground among the other sex. We had 'Lights Out!' at ten o'clock, but there could be absentees, and at such times my heart pounded for the Butler Street reputation. Then I would hastily get into the car and cruise along the sea-front in search of any of our girls who might be treading that primrose path.

Social historians are wont to describe the twenties as a period when the pursuit of pleasure took precedence over all else. They must have had my sister Fira in mind. Her difficulty was to manage within her copious dollar allowance, though she had no problem in assembling friends to help her get through it. Her stamina, sophistication and extravagance never failed to amaze me. She wore so much jewellery no-one believed for a moment it could be anything but imitation. On one occasion, to celebrate a revival of Savoir's *Bluebeard's Eighth Wife*, she took a party by special train to Monte Carlo for a weekend and, with a private hotel booked entire as their base, they watched Suzanne Lenglen and Helen Wills in a battle of the giants (Lenglen won 6–3, 8–6). That little exercise could not have left her much change out of a couple of thousand pounds. And this apart from the money she left with the management after an evening at the casino.

For expiation, if any was called for, she knew something was imperfect about her life. She had not yet found a man she truly loved, and her undoubted creative streak languished for want of satisfaction. Fira had the instinct, without the training, to be an artist. But in what?

America presented its own answer. Its rich women indulged their love of clothes to the degree of rendering New York the glamorous reality behind the shadows of the cinema screen. Such women could fight like tigers to be at the top of the league, and that meant fashion as decided by Paris, then in its heyday as dictator of style. So why not bring Paris to New York? Father gave Fira a Madison Avenue building in which to open her salon. She invited Vera Heller, Chaim Weizmann's niece, to be her business partner. Fate had dealt not too kindly with Vera Heller, and she was then hovering, like so many Russian refugees, between an aspiration to glory on Fifth Avenue and a shabby reality down by the East Side. New York could be the transatlantic Babylon or the transatlantic Warsaw ghetto, depending on your star. The Fira Benenson–Vera Heller partnership was sealed in the name Fira gave their salon, Verben. My sister, of course, paid all the bills.

What was lacking in this city of ballyhoo for an auspicious launching of the endeavour? No doubt about it, Misia Sert was lacking. She had discovered and befriended Coco Chanel, transforming the unknown milliner into a leading figure of international society. She had even been responsible in part for the famous perfume attached to Coco's name. Might she not achieve something similar for Verben?

Misia was at a most critical period in her life. Still of strikingly handsome appearance, she continued to surround herself in Paris with the intellectual aristocracy, and was in demand as always for her judgments on the latest play and the newest music. But she now had to face the shattering reality of Sert's final desertion to the much younger, more amusing Princess Mdivani. Further, the death of Diaghilev, the man dearer to her soul than any other, was an intense and agonizing bereavement. Misia was tampering with drugs, and she hid her sadness behind dark glasses worn both in and out of doors.

She came to New York, was acclaimed as an ambassadress of supreme taste, and made the Verben label necessary to those women in the New World for whom adornment in the right creation was as important as sleeping with the right man, if not more so. Misia moved regally across the Madison Avenue landscape, though of course she could not be at home anywhere except in Paris. With three husbands and several lovers behind her, she now numbered my father, in his late sixties, among her conquests. Bearing though he might the scars of love's battles from a previous existence, locked as he was in America's business-boom, his larger-than-life personality continued to attract women as always. Misia was, I rather think, his final romantic affair.

Much of this was still in the future, though with Fira away in Paris with Vera Heller for extended periods preparing the elaborate opening of their fashion salon, father asked me over to New York in 1927 to help him entertain his business colleagues. He and Fira each occupied a suite at the Plaza, but I borrowed Vera's less spacious single-room accommodation at the hotel for my stay. I was now introduced to father's dominion, achieved after seven years of activity in this city. He showed me his flagship, the Benenson Building on Broadway, at that time one of the tallest office blocks ever built.

The property looked on to Liberty Street, Cortlandt Street and Church Street. Father took me up to the thirty-second floor, and we went over to a window. From what I learnt he was the monarch of all he surveyed. He was president of the New York Dock Company, owning piers and warehouses extending over several miles of water-front southward from Brooklyn Bridge, to make his holding the most substantial docking system in the hemisphere. It embraced thirty-four piers, a score of factory buildings and railroad sidings, with lighterage regularly used by a dozen steamship companies.

A mass of other down-town properties were in his possession, and he spoke quietly and confidently of developing all this real estate into a still greater empire. One day, he promised, the building in which we now stood would be torn down and replaced by a skyscraper to dwarf the Woolworth Building, then a wonder of the world. (It happened, in the form of the World Trade Center, though that would be another war and another story away.)

And something more: the Soviet Government, lacking the expertise to operate the Lena Goldfields profitably, had swallowed its pride to the degree of inviting father's participation in a reformed management. It fell within Russia's much-vaunted New Economic Policy. But father was too astute to do this in person. With a commitment to compensation for his losses in the revolution, he re-arranged the financing of the mines, establishing a company in which he nominated my husband Harold as a director (this I had not known) and turned the Lena Goldfields into a money-making concern by remote control.

I was reduced to silence. What does one say to a father who claims that money doesn't interest him, yet is obviously one of

132

the world's richest men? What he said to me that day indicated that he understood I could cope with the mentality that resides in Wall Street only by dismissing it from my mind.

'I don't suppose either of us will ever see Russia again, Fenya.'

'Do you want to?'

'I often catch my thoughts returning to the Nevsky, with that view of the Winter Palace. And Redkino! How can I forget that?'

'Now you have Redkino and the Winter Palace combined in America.'

Perhaps we were sharing the same suspicion, that here too, in this fantastic country, a revolution might come. There was no dearth of Communists in New York.

We were in the month of March, and on Sunday, as we were taking lunch, father said: 'I've tickets for the Kerensky meeting this afternoon. Will you come?'

I protested. That man didn't interest me particularly. If I thought about Kerensky at all it was with contempt for having surrendered so meekly to the Bolsheviks. Surely no-one had been more completely swept away by the tide of history? Father pressed me further, and I agreed to accompany him. At least, we would hear an oration by a master of the Russian language.

The meeting was to take place at the Century Theatre on the west side of Central Park, and we decided to walk. As we approached Columbus Circle, a biting cold wind howling from the park, we saw that this was just as well: the only approach could be on foot. Making its way towards the theatre an enormous crowd was being marshalled by scores of anxious police. I had not seen so many Russians together since leaving my homeland, and the tension in the atmosphere told me that Kerensky's was still, on the tenth anniversary of his revolution, a name to be either venerated or reviled. The situation on nearing the doors of the theatre looked ugly, and I was for abandoning the expedition. We could have been a multitude organized for a scene directed by Cecil B. de Mille. Father would not turn back.

New York hardly formed part of America in 1927. In that city every European conflict imaginable came up for re-enactment among the rival flotsam that had been sloshed across the Atlantic from the Old World. And this was the day dedicated to re-living the Russian Revolution: White Russian monarchists, Communists, Kerensky's Social Revolutionaries, they all had arguments to ventilate at the top of their excited voices. Nothing

133

of the year 1917 was forgotten that Sunday afternoon on Central Park West. In vain did the police endeavour to regulate the stampede at the meeting-hall, for many people without tickets pressed through the doors.

With difficulty father and I reached our seats in the front row. Red Army songs reached us from the gallery, the Imperial national anthem defiantly from the Tsarists in the orchestra. Kerensky supporters packed the stage, together with American personalities brought along (in vain, as it happened) to dignify the proceedings. I thought of my draughty Conway Hall lectures, with their audiences of a score or so thinly spread across the rows of vacant seats. Here the smell of human flesh choked the atmosphere. Alexander Fyodorovich Kerensky stepped up to the dais amid a thundercrash of boos and cheers.

He stood silent for a moment, a tall and powerful-looking figure with crew-cut hair, waiting for the hubbub to die. From the rear of the stage a young woman stepped forward holding a large bouquet of red and white carnations. Ah, I told myself, how typically Russian! Where else would a political speaker be greeted as though he were an operatic diva?

The lady came close, extending the flowers in her left hand. He turned to acknowledge them. But in her right hand she held a glove, and with it she struck the former Prime Minister of Russia across the face, again and again. It must have concealed a heavy metal object, for blood poured from his cheek. We all gasped. Stewards rushed forward and carried the woman off the stage and into the arms of the police.

Kerensky seemed unmoved. He lifted his arm for silence, and began to speak as if no incident had occurred. A hush now descended upon the hall. I heard for the first time the voice legend still spoken of as the peal of Kremlin bells. Though shaken by what I had observed not ten feet away, I was transfixed. He told of his efforts to save Russia for democracy, of the treachery of Lenin, and how her Western allies had betrayed Russia in her hour of supreme need. The Russian people, he declared, the tragic, misled Russian people, were now held in a despotism as brutal as any the world had known. But one day it would end. He was ready to return the moment he was summoned. And all the time he held a handkerchief to staunch the blood flowing down his cheek.

That evening I accompanied father to a reception in the orator's honour. It was given by his influential friends the

Bookmans, wealthy Jews of German, not Russian, descent. Judy Bookman, related to the Morgenthaus, was a regular head-hunter, her doors open to any famous personality whose presence in New York would also attract the Democratic Party élite.

I remember entering a large drawing-room. Most of the gathering spoke English, and Kerensky stood there a little out of things. Almost unconsciously I approached him. He noticed me and smiled, or perhaps it was an expression of appeal. A sensation swept over me that may have been a combination of admiration and compassion: admiration for the way he had continued with his speech after the assault, compassion for a man who must travel always in the possibility of an attack still more serious, perhaps fatal.

A few pleasantries were exchanged, of little moment, but soon we were walking from the Bookmans' party, leading each other, and evidently unperceived. We hailed a taxi and Kerensky accompanied me to the Plaza. I had only the single room of Vera Heller, without a sitting-room. The house rule was firm, no woman might entertain a man in such accommodation alone. Nevertheless I took him upstairs. We talked desultorily about the day. No, he would not have his attacker charged. She was a White Russian, he had been informed, and she blamed Kerensky for the execution of her fiancé, a Tsarist officer, during the war.

Suddenly there was a banging on the door. Kerensky disappeared into the bathroom. I opened the door to the night-manager. 'You have brought a visitor to your room,' he said. 'You must know such things are not allowed.'

I pleaded with him to avoid a scandal. If the man was discovered to be Kerensky the papers would be full of it. The night-manager departed, reluctantly I thought. The ex-Prime Minister emerged from the bathroom. It was not the first time, he confessed with a smile, that he had had to elude his pursuers. Then we were in each other's arms.

I knew this signalled another complicated period for me. But I was experiencing an emotion I never realized could exist. The next morning I took Kerensky openly through the foyer of the hotel. Though a little confused, I was not displeased with the turn of events.

7 The Old Order Changeth

To the world at large, Alexander Kerensky most likely appeared less a human figure than one of Madame Tussaud's historical waxworks escaped from her museum. This spared me a host of explanations. Our relationship was emotionally intricate and geographically wearisome. I was attracted to the man with a passion which told me that hitherto my womanhood had been a hollow thing. Suddenly, I became aware of new aspects of my personality, so calming, so strengthening, I felt confident enough to risk everything, including my destiny. My love affair was not so much a restoration of my sexuality as its discovery.

Was Kerensky's love equal to my own? I can reply honestly to this question with the admission that I neither expected nor demanded it of him. And I did not punish myself with jealousy when, after magic days in New York, we separated; nor, between our hurried meetings afterwards, we went our different ways – for weeks, perhaps longer. We each took from the liaison what we needed. As to marriage, he knew I would never leave Harold and break up my home, so I paid the price of not knowing whether I was the only woman in his life: such an assumption would have been stupid on my part. He lived in Paris, his estranged wife and two teenage sons being domiciled in England.

Kerensky was a true romantic, and dressed meticulously. I was therefore appalled, on visiting him in his little flat, to find a scene of utter disorder. He did not consider this his home, it was where he slept, did his writing and awaited the summons back to Russia as though it might come in a telephone call that very evening. Nearby, in the rue Vineuse beside the Trocadero, he published the newspaper in which he kept his anti-Leninist, now anti-Stalinist, mission alive. A small group of torchbearers, pathetically small, survivors of his short-lived regime when he held the fate of an empire in his hands, comprised his entourage. I suppose revolutions have been created from less, but this

136

hardly struck me as the spearhead of a movement directed to the heart of the Soviet population. More, it seemed the shadow of the tail of a long-extinct comet.

Two of the faithful I already knew from my contacts with London's Russian colony. They came regularly to Paris to review the mistakes of 1917, and check the proofs of the leader's newspaper, sustaining his spirit when it flagged. One was the journalist David Soskice, married into the Madox Fords of the Pre-Raphaelite brotherhood and father of the Labour Party politician who would become Lord Stow Hill. The other, Jacob Gavronsky, still had money left over from being on his mother's side a Wissotsky, the princely tea-merchants of pre-war Moscow. A physician, Gavronsky was in 1917 the London representative of the Kerensky Government. These two saw me as a valued recruit to the cause, but to demonstrate my interest in the man, not the mission, I rented a maisonette in the rue des Belles Feuilles from the widow of the painter Félix Vallotton. This became my bedroom paradise.

Naive though he surely was as a statesman, and at forty-six still the Volga backwoodsman marooned in the sophistication of Western Europe, Kerensky nevertheless plumbed accurately the mysteries surrounding relationships of the heart. I was forthright with him on the hopelessness of his cause, reasoning that, whatever the crimes of Stalinism, the Soviet masses had at least made a beginning towards cultural and economic progress impossible under the old Tsarist feudalism. Anti-Semitism, for example, was proscribed in Communist law. This infuriated him, and he accused me of judging the situation from a narrow point of view – Soviet democracy was a cruel sham, returning Russia to a constitutional ice age. Our differences on this score could not be resolved. Discussion would terminate by a softening of his expression, the reach to my cheek of a sensitive hand – the hand bearing its scar from his time at the front greeting his troops and exhorting them to continue the war – and then politics would dissolve and give way to the more urgent impulses of our love. We only ventured out in the evening, and never to a theatre or a cinema. Kerensky constantly received threats to his life and had once been attacked in broad daylight, so I sensed danger everywhere. We ate at Chez Maurice, a tiny restaurant on the Left Bank, with Mme Maurice and her great black cat at the cash desk.

He confessed to an almost superstitious belief in omens and

coincidences. He related to me how, on his return to St Petersburg after his investigation of the Lena scandal, when he was being pressed to embark on a political career, he had once walked past the Winter Palace and caught a glimpse of the Tsar standing at a window. Kerensky became seized by the conviction that one day he would appear at that same window, in a position of power. This decided him to accept an offer of candidature for the Duma. He even visited a fortune-teller, who read in his hand the path his life would take.

I held enough of myself back for my pride not to suffer. Moreover, I am certain my husband did not suffer from my liaison with this other man, this Russian who spoke little English and arrived on occasion at Hornton Street to dine with us and depart into the London night with our other friends. But did Harold know? His nurse listened in to my phone calls and was not above retailing the intelligence she gathered. If Clive Garsia suspected anything he remained a model of discretion. I would never be sure about Harold; his disability joined us irrevocably together, but it also divided us.

What about my son? There I plead guilty to being less a mother than before. Yet this need not have been to Peter's disadvantage. Were he of the House of Windsor he could not have been the object of greater adulation. Uncles, aunts, a dedicated Solomon grandmother, a father who adoringly recorded his son's every development in albums of photographs; they swamped the lad with attention. Where they left off, the household apparatus took over. And if that sounds like an alibi for my parental deficiencies I make no excuses for it. His nanny was still wiping the eight-year-old boy's nose. I decided Peter was of the age to have a tutor rather than a nanny. My sister Manya's friend Margaret Gardiner, one of the Communist scientist J. D. Bernal's many 'wives', and guardian angel to a variety of intellectuals stricken with an inability to cope with the prosaic daily round, informed me she could recommend the very person: a young poet of promise. When, in the autumn of 1929, W. H. Auden arrived in Hornton Street no-one had heard of him except a minute coterie of Oxford admirers.

Meanwhile Harold and I had separately reached the conclusion that we were pointed towards a blank wall. Clearly, we had lost each other, with warnings of greater stultification to come. Kerensky, by his tenderness, assuaged the hunger of my feminine soul, but he was also a reminder that for the rest, my life was over-cloistered and superficial. As for Harold, I detected in his constant search for diversion a fear of being turned into a creature of self-pity. I knew I could do something about my condition, but what could he do about his? One day he gave me the answer.

'I'm going into politics, Flora, as a Conservative. I've been adopted for North Tottenham. It'll be a tussle, Tottenham's considered a safe Labour seat. Will you help?'

'Of course.'

Why had he chosen this way? I had no sympathy for the Tories, he knew that. My friendships and inclinations placed me on the Left, among people who regarded the government of Stanley Baldwin as the heartless tool of a cynical ruling class. My initial reaction, unspoken, was to seek an element of malice in Harold's decision, a gesture of resentment and defiance against the wife who could not be a wife by a man unable to be a husband. Then I felt ashamed. Weren't we of the ruling class, with our inherited wealth, privileges, servants, travel? Surely Harold was the logical one, I the sentimentalist! What had I sacrificed for the working class?

We were still in 1928, with no election in sight, so our visits to the constituency did not as yet evoke scenes of soap-box rowdiness complete with clowns heckling from the side-lines, and chanting demonstrators who made the British elections in the days before television jolly forms of street theatre. Tottenham was located on London's outer edge. It embraced tenement slums, neat terraces of bay-fronted houses and acres of gaunt council estates. Railway workers and dignified artisans intermingled with minor civil servants and a solid bourgeoisie in one-man businesses along the Seven Sisters Road, a name I loved. Valiantly, I joined the Primrose League (what would Ellen Wilkinson make of *that*) and introduced myself to the Tottenham Ladies Conservative Association, whose chairman had the kind of name that only English people could award themselves: Mrs Smellie. I was a lot for them to swallow – Jewish, Russian, speaking with a heavy accent, and quick to confess my preference for Labour. But my husband deserved to be their MP, I told them, because he was a truly fine man. I came away convinced they detested me, though a few weeks later, at a meeting in the parish hall to recruit members, they presented me with a lace table-cloth on which each of the ladies had embroidered her name. I have it still.

Returning with Harold from one of these forays I revealed that I too had decided to engage in some real work. I was going into publishing. Having previously experienced Harold's caustic sarcasm I awaited his reaction with trepidation. But he received the information quite civilly.

'Where on earth did you get that idea? Hoping to compete with Victor?' Gollancz had recently departed from the old-established firm of Ernest Benn to found his own publishing house.

'Victor knows about it. In fact he's recommended a girl to help me who was at his office enquiring after a job. I'm going to call it the Blackamore Press and produce collectors' items, like Cresset Press' – owned by our friend Dennis Cohen – 'and Nonesuch Press.'

'It'll cost you a pretty penny. But good luck just the same.'

The Blackamore Press was born out of my association with Russian émigrés in Paris. One of them, an expert in European literature named Pouterman (married to a dress-designer acquaintance from the Baku days who did some work for Fira), put up the scheme. We would issue foreign classics in English translation. They would be illustrated by leading artists, of whom John Nash and Marie Laurencin were two, and designed by Oliver Simon, the noted typographer. I brought the idea back to Dennis Cohen, who had served with Harold in the Palestine Administration, and he encouraged me to go ahead. Pouterman took complete charge as managing director, with Prince Sviato-polk-Mirsky his chief editor.

Pouterman, a frustrated intellectual, tended towards depressions and lived unhappily with his wife. He rented a couple of rooms in Great Russell Street which became our publishing address. Painfully conscientious, he would not make a decision without my agreement. This applied equally to contemplated titles, printers' estimates, deals with American houses, all of which I would earnestly endorse as we sat together over an egg-on-toast lunch at the ABC in Holborn. We began with a medieval Japanese work, *The Lady Who Loved Insects*, rendered into English by Arthur Waley and bound in full Chinese silk. Copies signed by the author sold at three guineas, and following an excellent review in *The Times Literary Supplement* it won a prize at some Continental book fair.

Thus our first title turned a profit. Mary Hanson, the girl sent to me by Victor Gollancz, was placed in a cubby-hole in Hornton

Street, near the cheque-writing department. Mary spoke French well and had the patience to cope with Pouterman. She occupied a status in my home roughly corresponding to Auden's in the social scale. We took to each other immediately and are friends to this day.

I cannot say I learnt a great deal about publishing, an occupation which always has, and doubtless always will, attract the wealthy amateur. I have never been one to court the society of celebrated authors, whose company can prove an ordeal. But I enjoyed having an outlet among the men and women who ran to catch buses, lived on a weekly budget and strove for perfection in their craft. In contrast to Pouterman, Dmitri Sviatopolk-Mirsky, son of the Liberal politician of Tsarist days, was a rip-roaring *bon viveur* eternally short of the funds to finance his drinking. We met for dinner in Paris while he was working on our handsome edition of Milton's *Brief History of Moscovia*, last seen in print in the seventeenth century.

Dmitri had given his family tradition an ironic twist by espousing Communism, and eventually returned to Russia as a Soviet citizen. But at our dinner an excess of wine washed this momentarily out of his system and he reverted to his origins. He startled me by rising shakily from his chair and inviting the entire restaurant to join him in a toast to the dynasty of Romanov! He grieved at the complacency with which the West bore its ignorance of Russian culture and felt a special responsibility for making Pushkin available to the English reader. So we issued a selection of Pushkin's letters, with the master's own drawings reproduced in collotype, as well as a de luxe edition of *The Queen of Spades* bound in goat vellum and priced at ten guineas. I don't recall whether this sold like hot cakes or whether hundreds remained tucked away unwanted under Pouterman's bed in Great Russell Street.

The uninspiring Baldwin Government, teetering to its long-overdue demise, announced a General Election for May 1929. Growing unemployment and rancorous argument over measures to curb the power of the trade unions, combined with the Tories' unenterprising foreign policy, gave the impression of a Britain sagging under the burden of its own platitudes. Polishing up his Election Address, many times drafted, Harold took on new life as his rooms on the first floor filled up with helpers and echoed with the din of battle: once more the military jargon, the snappy commands, the colonel encouraging his troops.

Tottenham blazed with excitement, everybody suddenly feeling wanted. At his first meeting, packed with supporters, opponents and the merely inquisitive, Harold said: 'Don't vote for me out of kindness. I was not wounded in the war, but in a horse-riding accident.' And he told them how the wise Stanley Baldwin alone would find work for the jobless, save the British Empire from the 'Bolshies' and bring peace to the entire world. I hid my face in my hands.

Harold's Labour rival, the existing member R. C. Morrison, had only just scraped through at the previous election but was now in a much stronger position. Morrison was a local man, and Harold kept the campaign close to home with the allegation that Morrison had been frustrating what was apparently the borough's dearest wish: to have a branch-line of the London underground system! It became a subject of intense controversy, with challenges of misrepresentation and counter-challenges hurled into the columns of the *Tottenham Weekly Herald*. At a demonstration in support of Harold one part of the crowd sang 'God Save the King', another went into 'The Red Flag', while a third, of indeterminate affiliation, bellowed 'Tipperary'. Then off they marched, the streets ringing with a ditty that could be adapted for either candidate:

> Vote, vote, vote for 'Arold So-lomon,
> Chuck old Morrison on the floor,
> With 'is high topper 'at and his belly full o' fat
> No, we won't vote for Morrison any more!

A Liberal was also standing, but few rated his chances good enough for a chorus.

Another thing: the Labour camp discovered Harold was a secret Communist! 'Yah, hypocrite!' they shouted after him as he toured the district, the hood of his Buick open to the sunshine while he proclaimed Tory virtues through a hand-megaphone. They had unearthed details of father's bank, still managing the finances of the Lena Goldfields on behalf of the Soviets, with Harold listed as a director. So into the *Weekly Herald* went an explanation, but how could Tottenham be expected to vote for the director of an international bank?

Mrs Smellie and her ladies were convinced it would. Tottenham, they emphasized to me, was famous not only for its football team but its sense of fair play. It voted with its heart, and

142

who could resist the colonel gallantly canvassing the streets in his wheel-chair? A thick wad of leaflets in my hand, I took my share of endless grey council houses and crumbling tenements. Tottenham, I found, loved cats, and sat its babies on their potties in the living-room. Canvassing can prove a disconcerting experience. One dear old soul confused me with the borough sanitary inspector and insisted upon showing me her kitchen sink, silted up with dark waters which refused to drain away. Guiltily, I beat a hasty retreat.

However, the result was a foregone conclusion. Morrison romped home with a huge majority. I wept for Harold but cheered for Ramsay MacDonald, the new Prime Minister. Once again Ethel Snowden, a glint of triumph in her eye, took over as the industrious mistress of No 11 Downing Street. We shared a thrill on learning of Margaret Bondfield's appointment as Minister of Labour, the first woman Cabinet minister in Britain's history. But MacDonald failed to secure an overall majority so, haunted by a growing economic crisis, he had to lead a government without real power. Socialism was still a long way from achievement in Britain, as was Tottenham's underground extension: not for fifty years did the tube materialize, in the Victoria Line.

Smiling stoically through his disappointment, Harold returned to his books and travel. He now interviewed the lanky youth sent to me by Margaret Gardiner as a likely tutor for Peter, and was somewhat surprised by what confronted him. Wystan Auden was off-hand, ill-kempt and a chain-smoker. He spoke with an upper-class accent so grotesque as to make for near-incomprehensibility. If this was the best Oxford could do then manifestly that ancient institution was ripe for reform. In taking on the tutor Harold showed his good faith, for apparently the twenty-two-year-old Auden had not until then been in employment, either as a tutor or anything else.

Margaret Gardiner had been less than frank with us in singing Auden's praises. It subsequently transpired that she was more concerned with the well-being of her poet than the educational progress of my son. I was to learn this from Manya, who now lived in London with Ralph because Lady Harari, a lady-in-waiting at the Egyptian Court, was offended by her daughter-in-law's propensity to venture hatless into the Cairo air. Margaret had become acquainted with Auden during an expedition to Berlin to save another of her protégés, the anthropologist John

Layard, from suicide. She did not of course divulge to Manya that Auden and Layard were lovers, and that Auden's Oxford fame rested not on his academic achievements – third class honours – but on his flagrant homosexual escapades. I don't say I would have objected, I knew little of homosexuality; but in retrospect I have no doubt Harold would have had some not very tolerant ideas on such non-conformity. This was 1929, remember, not a very good year for homosexuality in Britain, whatever the climate of France at the time.

Wystan took over nanny's room next to the day-nursery, now termed Peter's school-room. Their meals were sent up. It was not until Auden left us that Peter revealed what meal-times could be like with the poet.

'He threw the food over the floor,' Peter said.

'What do you mean, over the floor?'

'He thought the house was too tidy, everything so clean and in its place, that sometimes he spilled the plateful on to the floor. He said I've got to learn to eat some dirt, it did me good.'

'And did you?'

'Of course not. I spooned it back on to my plate, and ate it then.'

I learnt also of another occasion, while both Harold and I were away, when Peter caught the measles and Auden, whose father was a doctor, dabbed iodine on every one of the spots. It must have worked, for Peter was quite well when we saw him next, except that his entire body was dyed a funny shade of brown.

One evening Ripley the butler brought some news to me: 'I don't know whether you are aware of it, Madam, but Mr Auden has a companion sleeping with him in his room.' It was Christopher Isherwood making his discreet exits and entrances. I couldn't think of an appropriate comment and let the matter drop. Then Wystan stopped me on the stairs and asked if I knew where he could have some material typed. Well, I did know someone, Hilda Brighton of the Brighton Bureau in Regent Street. (Her father had shared Lillie Langtry with King Edward VII and was a director of Harrod's, though why Hilda felt the need to go into business on her own account I had no idea.)

I sent the manuscript over to her. Later she telephoned. 'This is the concoction of raving lunatics,' Hilda declared. 'Even the title doesn't make sense. Do you want me to continue with it?'

144

'I haven't read it,' I replied. 'But you'd better finish it. I'm told the author is a brilliant poet.'

'Two brilliant poets, you mean. It says here, "Auden and Isherwood".'

She was typing a play, *The Enemies of a Bishop, or Die When I Say When*, interspersed with poetry. The work never passed beyond the manuscript stage, though years later its authors re-wrote the piece as *The Dog Beneath the Skin*. Literature specialists may wish to know that the original belongs to Auden's canon of lewd writings. One of Hilda Brighton's typed copies has survived as a highly valued artefact in the manuscript collection of the New York Public Library.

Wystan was not shy by any means, especially in doing his friends a good turn. Learning of the Blackamore Press from Mary Hanson, he enquired whether I had any French translation work for Isherwood, 'a first-rate French scholar' who needed money. He must have had a hint from Mary that Pouterman was planning an English version of Baudelaire's *Intimate Journals*.

I arranged for Isherwood to be given the work. Further, Auden was indebted to T. S. Eliot, who was encouraging the young poet from his desk at Faber, so Eliot received a commission to write an introductory essay to the Baudelaire. Pouterman was none too pleased with Isherwood's translation, protesting it was full of inaccuracies.

Auden left us early the following year. Peter was due to enter Summer Fields, a preparatory school with a strong Eton connection, in 1930, and Wystan began looking for another post. He first went as coach to the son of Naomi Mitchison and then replaced Cecil Day-Lewis at a boys' school near Glasgow. Before leaving us he put Harold, somewhat gruesomely, into his poem 'Will you turn a deaf ear' (no interrogation mark). It appears in *The English Auden*, edited by Edward Mendelson:

> Will you wheel death anywhere
> In his invalid chair
> With no affectionate instant
> But his attendant?

Perhaps Auden was a seer. His mannerisms – he was too young for me to describe them as eccentricities – left Harold speechless, that is, until we were alone together when I would be roundly rebuked for introducing a man so slovenly into the household. Fortunately, Harold never appeared on the third floor; his lift reached directly to the roof-garden, so he was spared a sight of the tutor's room. Nothing, not clothes, nor books, was stored in cupboards or on shelves; what could not be accommodated on his table lay scattered over the floor. From his window Harold observed that Auden failed to carry an umbrella in the street. He expressed hostility towards this defection from the proper Englishman's style of walking out by stationing Wystan over Peter with an outsize brolly on our roof-garden as he took a photograph of our son in the fancy-dress of an Oriental potentate. Harold captioned his pictures in considerable detail, and labelled this one 'His Tartaric Majesty and his Royal Umbrella Holder', the poet looking decidedly aloof.

Peter could not have learnt a great deal from his tutor, for he spent most of his waking hours with Harold in the library. My husband held geography and history in reverence, and usually taught Peter himself. Domestic harmony was restored to Hornton Street with Auden's replacement by a governess.

In the summer of 1930 I was at the rue des Belles Feuilles with Kerensky. Not for the first time he was narrating to me how, while in control of Petrograd he had reached a relationship of friendliness with the ex-Tsar, then detained with his immediate family at the Alexandrovsky Palace at Tsarskoye Selo; and how with profound relief he had gone to Nicholas to inform him that soon a British warship would dock at Murmansk and take them to safety as guests of Nicholas's English cousin, King George V. Unexpectedly the invitation was withdrawn, in Kerensky's view due to the intervention of Lloyd George. Not daring to inform poor Nicholas of the sudden change of plan, Kerensky merely told him to prepare for a long journey.

'I assured Nicholas they would all be safe, that he could trust me. And Nicholas said, "I believe you".' Kerensky heartily despised Lloyd George, though it later transpired that the British Prime Minister was not really the guilty one; public opinion in England, especially of the left-wing, had voiced displeasure, and King George himself finally made the decision not to rescue his relative.

I knew better than to interrupt Kerensky when he brooded, as so often, on the Romanov tragedy. But at this point my maid called me to the telephone, 'It's your brother-in-law Arthur Solomon,' she announced.

Arthur said that Harold, who was touring his beloved Serbia, had been taken ill. He had caught an infection while bathing in the Danube. The place was Osijek.

I left immediately, Arthur arranging to bring Harold's mother and Peter. Fira was then in Paris and accompanied me. We found Harold with fever, in a squalid, sour-smelling room at the local hospital. He was being tended by his own nurse, 'Soph' as he called her, and she was mainly engaged in keeping the mosquitoes from his face. A special railway carriage had been reserved by the Yugoslav Government should we wish to bring Harold home. He was too weak for such a journey. We took him to Glion in Switzerland, where I knew of a well-equipped clinic near the villa of the writer Stephen Hudson, one of my Blacka-more authors (his story *Céleste* commemorates his long associa-tion with Proust).

Harold's condition worsened. On 30 July he spoke to me, with great difficulty, about Peter, whose ninth birthday fell the fol-lowing day. 'Give him a really happy birthday, Flora, with lots of presents. It'll be his last before boarding school. Now I'd like to write to Dr Williams at Summer Fields.' I brought him pen and paper, and he wrote to the prep-school headmaster. Harold had always wanted to enrol Peter himself.

I bent over my husband. I was moved to kiss him and found his lips so dry I pressed a sweet into his mouth. Soph called out sharply: 'Don't, you're poisoning him!' By this time he was more hers than mine.

Harold died that night. We all gathered around Peter the next morning with our presents, but of course he was not to be consoled. Ours was hardly a loss compared to his. He had been the big man, with arms outstretched and socks round his ankles, pushing Daddy's chair to the Round Pond in Kensington Gardens. He had been the fellow-explorer on those trips across the Continent. He had been the limbs the man on the first floor no longer possessed, and I believe he prayed daily for the miracle to make his father whole. What place could I occupy in all this?

We buried Harold at Vevey beside Lake Geneva. It is not our custom to wear mourning at a funeral, though one person present was attired in heavy black: Ethel Snowden. She had rushed over from London and only then, as she gripped my hand, did I break down and weep. More than half a century has passed and Peter, now a Roman Catholic, continues to visit his father's grave in the Jewish cemetery at Vevey.

The Hudsons (it was his pen-name, they were in reality Sidney and Violet Schiff) looked after Peter and me for a few days while I sought my bearings. I found their stories of the celebrated writers in their circle tedious in the extreme – Proust and his peccadilloes, James Joyce, David Garnett, they tripped off Sidney's tongue so frequently I could have been in a seminar of the Workers Educational Association. They were in fact being kind, conceiving their duty as steering my thoughts away from my bereavement. I thanked them with a great bouquet of roses, together with a rather splendid vase to put them in. As I left I noticed the vase on the grand piano empty, without the flowers. Violet explained: 'You know Proust suffered from asthma and could not remain in a room with flowers. We didn't have them when he used to visit us here and we don't have them now.'

No doubt loose ends have to be tied up to make a neat narrative, but it doesn't quite happen in real life. Odd corners at Hornton Street continued to be filled by Harold's possessions, and at times his presence seemed almost tangible. My thoughts dwelt on leaving the house. Clive Garsia helped my transition to widowhood and then tried to terminate it. When he first asked me to marry him I took it as a joke, but he repeated his proposal every year, on the first day of February. I owed Clive a great deal in the early days, especially for the care he took of Peter, and for his toleration of my caprices.

One of my loose ends had a strand tied to Palestine. The subject meant nothing to Kerensky. He lumped Zionism with what he regarded as the many half-baked ideas I cherished close to my somewhat ample bosom, like my left-wing politics, and welfare work in the East End, and my posturing at being a publisher. Kerensky was a man in blinkers to whom every move had to be a step towards the only goal – the liberation of Russia. But he was wrong about me.

I was absolutely serious in my Zionism. The years 1929–31 were a period of crisis in the Jewish enterprise, albeit over-shadowed in the world at large by the great depression initiated by the Wall Street Crash. I watched Chaim and Vera Weizmann being harried by the troubled situation in Palestine and knew how this was affecting their domestic life. Vera put on a courageous front in support of her husband, but at home in Addison Crescent she saw Chaim as hostage to a political organization which criticized his every move though it could not produce an alternative leader of equal standing.

Eternally on the road both to beg money and to win friends for Palestine in the capitals of the world, Chaim neglected the family he truly loved. Vera suspected what I knew for sure, that he had a roving eye and was not above making a fool of himself with women prone to an occasional affair.

The peace of Palestine was broken in 1929 by an Arab insurrection resulting in the death of nearly three hundred people, Jews, Christians and Moslems. It was followed by an inquiry commission in which the Arabs were given the benefit of the argument. To my chagrin as a Labour Party supporter the government of Ramsay MacDonald thought to introduce measures to stop immigration as though the national home was now achieved and that would be the end of it. Less than 200,000 Jews were then living in the country.

Weizmann fought these measures like a tiger, with the help of Harry Sacher and Simon Marks, his two principal advisers. Through his great negotiating ability he managed to get the veto on immigration annulled. However, he was compelled to pay the price of his moderation. He was forced out of the leadership of his organization for a time and plunged once again into his scientific work.

My preoccupations were then being directed elsewhere. Father had sailed through the débâcle on Wall Street with all flags flying. He was still expanding his holdings in 1931 when huge loans outstanding with the Manufacturers Trust Company were called in. The great Grigori Benenson, with the reputation down-town of being a wonder-worker, couldn't immediately pay. Manufacturers Trust filed a foreclosure suit on his City Terminal Company. Then the dam broke. The multi-millionaire was reduced to disposing of his seat on the New York Coffee and Sugar Exchange to clear the last of his debts. An American bank was sending my draft of £1,000 every month; it arrived so automatically I didn't see it as money, rather as nourishment drawn naturally from the elements. One day the postman brought not the draft but a letter from the bank. It contained the laconic statement that, my credit having been used up, payments would now cease. The words left a ringing in my ears.

Characteristically, my mother-in-law Frances Solomon assumed I would be thinking only of my son. 'You're not to worry, Flora,' she hastened to say. 'I shall pay Peter's school fees at Summer Fields.' I was not worrying about Peter. Truth to tell, I was too inexperienced with money to worry about anything.

149

But I did give thought to my own position. My butterfly-life had had its twenty-four hours. Now, I told myself, I was in the same situation as everybody else, and must try working for a living. The novelty of the idea produced in me a sort of exhilaration, the sense of challenge. Heroism is remote from my character, but so is panic. I wondered whether I was qualified for anything – anything! Searching my mind, I found very little to reassure me on that score.

Chance took me to a dinner-party shortly afterwards at which Simon Marks was my immediate neighbour. I was being treated to an account of his business affairs, and how they were flourishing. Simon spoke of the vast expansion contemplated for Marks and Spencer since it had become a public company a year or two earlier. As I recall, he was then the proud possessor of a chain numbering about 160 stores. Some were large, others over-stocked shop fronts facing on to provincial market squares.

'Our most powerful competitor is Woolworth's,' he said. 'They're American, but a household word over here. Now we are going to show what a British company can do. The days of the "Penny Bazaar" are finished.' Simon had the fire of battle in his eyes. Unemployment hovered in Britain at the two million mark and was growing daily, but Marks and Spencer were developing as though these were boom times.

All the years I had known Simon Marks his business had not aroused the slightest curiosity in me. My way of life rarely brought me into shops and stores of any kind. Now my life had changed, and for the first time I found myself listening. On his fingers he ticked off the towns where he intended to plant new branches. It was an impressive list, without question. But against his proud assertion of commercial success I heard echoes from the talk of some of my Labour Party friends. They saw High Street trading from a different perspective: not the dividends announced in the city columns of the Press, but the conditions of those who toiled to produce them. It was an ugly story. Since the pre-war Lena Goldfields scandal I had developed a conscience. Mostly, it lay dormant. Suddenly, my dinner companion awakened it.

Voices came through of the struggles in which the working-classes were engaged. I heard again the passionate North Country accents of Ellen Wilkinson speaking of girls slaving long hours in miserable, unhealthy factories; of how Margaret Bondfield had started life in a draper's shop at the age of fourteen, opening up for business at first light. Of course, much had changed, though not enough by any means. As Simon Marks proclaimed his achievements I could not resist an intervention. Staring straight ahead, I flung a comment at him.

'You know you have a shocking reputation in the country.'

He was taken aback. 'What do you mean?'

'Your labour conditions are notorious.'

'But how do you know, Flora?' Simon retorted. 'When was the last time you ventured into one of my stores?'

'I have it from Margaret Bondfield. Before becoming Minister of Labour she was an officer of the Shopworkers' Union. She has tried to get trade unionists to boycott Marks and Spencer. Your company is growing by exploiting its workers.'

Simon quivered with anger, but I was enjoying myself. 'What's more, Margaret says it's firms like Marks and Spencer that give the Jews a bad name.' An uncomfortable few minutes of silence ensued while Simon digested this intelligence. Then he said: 'Have you any ideas to suggest? Can you do something about it?'

I was amazed and overwhelmed. A man of few words, Simon was inviting *me* to show how conditions of employment in his business could be improved! To be offered the possibility of plunging into work so worthwhile in an area that had for so long existed in my subconscious, seemed almost too ideal to be true. My thoughts raced. If I could be instrumental in transforming labour conditions in Marks and Spencer, with its army of employees, it could be a significant beginning for workers elsewhere in the country. I refused to allow my complete ignorance of industry to make me hesitate. Perhaps I would stumble and bumble, but if Simon trusted me for such a task, I had to take it on. I answered: 'Yes, I would like to.'

'Then go ahead.'

Margaret Bondfield, who was some twenty years my senior, had progressed from her draper's shop and eventually graduated to the post of Chief Woman Officer of her union. The 1931 election landslide, which had put a National Government into office and earned MacDonald the stigma of renegade, took her out of the Cabinet. I went to seek her advice about the assignment I had received from Simon Marks.

'Don't rush into it,' she warned. 'Take a good look at the stores first. And if you're wise you'll go across to Europe and investigate conditions there. You may pick up some ideas.'

This was excellent counsel, but first I had to settle my personal affairs. I was by no means destitute, but orderly housekeeping was so foreign to me that one day the gas was cut off in Hornton Street: I had omitted to pay the bill. Then, little by little, I disposed of my jewellery, which included the gems left by my mother. That was quite a relief, as I rarely wore jewellery.

The Blackamore Press, prestigious but financially a dead loss, of course had to go. But I didn't intend losing Mary Hanson; she was coming with me to Marks and Spencer. Ripley my butler went over to Elaine Blond, Simon's youngest sister, and she made him bailiff of her estate at East Grinstead. My personal maid Denise married the footman, solving that problem, while one of the chauffeurs entered Marks and Spencer as a waiter in the directors' dining-room. I sold Miriam Sacher a sapphire ring she had always admired and, being Miriam, she promptly lost it. Clive Garsia packed his bags as No 49 Hornton Street was taken by one of the Salmons of the Lyons catering company.

It was like general demobilization after a war. I moved into the upper part of a house of which the ground floor was let to my Aunt Tamara and her husband – named by Harold, ever unable to resist deriding what sounded exotic, as Auntie and Uncle Tomato.

I was an exotic spectacle of a kind myself as I began looking into Marks and Spencer stores. Armed with an authorization signed by the chairman I questioned sales-girls, interviewed managers, sniffed behind broom-cupboards. No-one gave me the impression that I was welcome. This preliminary work proceeded without my receiving a penny-piece in salary or expenses. The question of my being paid like any other employee had not even been discussed.

Frances Solomon's sister Amy Israel had married a German who owned the department store called Israel's in the centre of Berlin. So I betook myself there, staying with the family in the Tiergartenstrasse. Amy was a stalwart Briton. She had ensured that her sons had British nationality by coming to London for their birth, and now she would say of them, in the phrase once spoken with great pride, 'Made in England'.

The Israels were enlightened employers by the standards of the period, and Herr Israel impressed the importance of good management upon me. Through his introductions I was able to inspect other department stores as well as various clothing factories. But the Weimar republic presented a sorry picture, with many more unemployed even than in Britain.

Amy and her husband were active in a renowned Jewish charity organization, the *Hilfsverein*. They took me to a ball at the Kaiserhof Hotel, Berlin's most elegant, where funds were being raised for the poor and homeless. It was December 1932. We left about midnight, along with hundreds of other Jewish guests. As we boarded the Israels' car I glimpsed a short figure in brown uniform emerging from another entrance of the Kaiserhof, his arm raised in the Nazi salute.

Hitler and his Brownshirts had been in the same hotel, planning to make Germany *judenrein* while the *Juden* danced.

8 A Working Life

Religion, I believe, is a subject best left to the experts. I find it difficult to be absolute in my thoughts about the existence of God, and so have endeavoured to take life largely as it came. But if I think of God in relation to the three Benenson sisters it is as the Great Inspirer.

Fira and I, who once despaired of persuading our sister Manya to face up to the fact that she was the daughter of a multi-millionaire and should find ways of getting through money as effectively as ourselves, were now the poor relations. Let me hasten to add that I am speaking relatively. Fira had to sacrifice her loss-making couture house of Verben as I gave up the Blackamore Press, and seek out gainful employment. She entered Bonwit Teller of New York to design clothes at the top end of the fashion business while I enrolled in Marks and Spencer which, in the harsh realities of the early thirties, languished at the bottom. The company used plain paper bags to wrap its customers' purchases, for they were embarrassed to carry its name through the streets.

That the austere Manya had little use for money availed her nothing. She had married into riches, even by the standards of the latter-day dynasties of the Nile. When she insisted upon establishing her home in London her devoted husband began transferring ample supplies of the Harari fortune from Cairo, though he continued working at the great irrigation projects in Upper Egypt that were to earn him a certain international renown. Ralph had won a boxing Blue at Cambridge and took life in his easy stride. He donated his priceless collection of Islamic art to the Cairo Museum and began another collection, this time of the drawings of Aubrey Beardsley, then much neglected. Religion comes into the picture only because Ralph remained staunch in Judaism and its responsibilities. But while he attended synagogue Manya was taking instruction in Farm Street from the Jesuit Father Martin D'Arcy: his church was the

154

Mecca, if I may be pardoned the expression, of those Catholic aspirants who tended to regard Mayfair as their private village. Manya embraced the faith in 1932, stoutly averring that her conversion was of the spirit, not the body, and that she was still as much a Jewess as either of her sisters.

We already had a Catholic in the family. Fira, for whom the election of Franklin D. Roosevelt to the White House proved that God still guided the destinies of the New World, married Count Janusz Ilinsky, one of her Poles. Thus she realized yet another of her American dreams by achieving a title. While in her strictly professional incarnation she remained Fira Benenson, a despot with a mouthful of pins, scourge of her rivals Mainbocher and Valentina, she greeted the world outside her atelier as the Countess Ilinska, holding court, as it were, among her residual antiques in a spacious ground-floor apartment on East 57th Street. Bonwit paid her ten thousand dollars a year, a handsome salary for those days. She earned every penny.

Perennially attired in black, never without a cigarette, she adored her count with the same single-mindedness with which she pursued her career. Janusz was a cavalryman formerly attached to the Polish Embassy in Washington – not much of a qualification for a New York livelihood. Of course, before 1932 Fira could easily have kept him, but now he too had to work. A job was organized for Janusz through the good offices of Robert Dowling, Jnr, once an employee of our father's and now building a property empire of his own upon the ruins of the Wall Street Crash. Father had acquired the Benenson Building from Robert Dowling, Snr, and engaged his ambitious son as its manager. Junior was therefore able to return the favour and nominated Janusz vice-president of his latest acquisition, the Carlisle Hotel.

Fira proclaimed her continued affiliation to the Jewish fold. Thus, with my own liaison with Alexander Kerensky, a son of the Russian Orthodox Church, all three Benenson women now stood, as regards their ancestral heritage, half in and half out. We puzzled our friends by our complicated characters and conflicting loyalties, and inevitably were described, on both sides of the Atlantic, as the Sisters Karamazov. It was, I think, Louis Fischer, author of several books on Russian history and mores, who baptized me.

Ralph's cousin Georges Cattaui led Manya on her path to Rome, and not his Dominican relative Jean de Menasce (Father

Pierre), who was her first and probably most enduring love. Georges was now an acclaimed French poet and already engaged on his noted series of Proustian studies – his dedication to the gentle genius being superseded in later years only by his friendship with the warrior genius Charles de Gaulle, about whom he also wrote extensively. I have rarely encountered so hybrid a spirit as Georges: Jewish born, fervent Catholic, he was immersed in the Islamic as well as the Gallic civilization; he could also, with equal facility, address his analytical mind to the intricacies of modern English poetry and the wonders of architecture. Perhaps this *mélange* accounted for his lonely, somewhat tortured soul. Georges also ranked high at the royal court in Cairo, and in his capacity of cultural emissary-at-large for Egypt would one day be attached to its London embassy, creating an atmosphere there to make it a favoured haunt of the cosmopolitan intelligentsia.

Georges' interest in architecture, and his friendship with Manya, fructified unexpectedly in her discovery in Paris of Berthold Lubetkin. She found this young architect of the revolutionary avant-garde living with his Russian princess, Pasha, in the direst poverty. Manya invited them to London, setting Lubetkin to work designing a house for her in Hampstead. She gave Lubetkin a roof in her temporary home while I took in his companion. Fortunately for me, Pasha could use a typewriter.

The house Lubetkin conceived for Manya, based on a dramatic plan he had made while a student in Moscow, was never built, although the drawings are to be found in the architectural text-books. My involvement with Pasha proved more immediately productive. I had sketched out a memorandum for Simon Marks on what I judged to be wrong with his retailing empire, and kept Pasha up through an entire night to type it. I made so many alterations as she worked that it became presentable only after about the sixth draft.

This memorandum did not rank high as literature and I suppose most of it would today sound commonplace. But so would the writings of Lord Shaftesbury as he campaigned in the last century for a Factory Act. My investigation of conditions in the stores of Marks and Spencer brought me into a world not only of exploitation, but of apathy, condescension and fear. Its gloom dismayed me. I walked the High Streets of towns without number to scan the people entering shops large and small, and found the situation similar in other chains, such as Woolworth's and the Co-Op. The sight greeting my eyes was of a human mass miserably dressed, dull of expression, cheeks sunken by hunger. It was a period when a job of the most humble kind was regarded as a privilege, and it could be withdrawn on the least pretext. Those depending on the retail trades for their wages stood, because they were for the most part female and unskilled, on the lowest rung of the working ladder. After delivering my memorandum to the commissionaire at the proud new headquarters of Marks and Spencer at 82 Baker Street I waited at home in trepidation lest Simon Marks consider I had committed to paper a manifesto of revolution. Indeed it was. Fortunately, Simon was a man of compassionate understanding and truly exceptional vision. Three days later he endorsed every word. Provided I never troubled him personally I was welcomed as a member of his staff.

It was really happening to me, a purpose in life! I was to be allowed to function without striving to fill long, empty days. Goodbye, youth clubs (and night clubs)! Farewell, charity committees! Adieu, the ever-accommodating Flora! And thank you, destiny, for taking away my limitless bank account. Friends were amazed. What was she doing with herself, enlisting as a glorified draper's assistant?

Another week passed while I made the acquaintance of people in the various departments of the company and hesitantly enquired whether I could be found a desk somewhere. I was then handed a sealed envelope. It contained five pounds, and deserved a poem: the first money I had ever received through my own endeavours.

From the weeks I had spent visiting the stores I had learnt that any trader in Britain could, at that time, hold his staff behind their counters until late at night and provide no facilities for them to take rest during a break. He could tie them to premises without heat in winter or fresh air during the summer, and accept no obligations whatever for the most elementary requirements of hygiene. Legislation? The Shops Act stated that one lavatory must be provided for every twenty workers. Other rules existed, but were treated as the vapourings of amateurs and flagrantly disregarded.

Girls of eighteen earned a minimum of seventeen shillings a week, less if they were younger. How do you manage? I asked them. Often they remained dumb. This fat woman with the heavy accent could have been sent by the 'high-ups' to spy on them. Coaxing with a cigarette could sometimes elicit a reply, occasionally the blushing admission: 'If we can't last the week out we help ourselves from the till, or pinch a pair of stockings.'

The trade unions had been involved for decades with labour in the retail and catering industries, the biggest source of employment for women, but what had they achieved? I posed this question to my many friends in the unions. They did not seem to comprehend its point. Hadn't they agitated to reduce working hours, and to raise wages? Were they at fault if women regarded unions as organizations created by men for men? Life's realities forced girls to accept whatever jobs they could find, in the hope of ultimate rescue, like Janet Gaynor in the movies, by marriage. I was sternly reminded that this was a free country, that those dissatisfied with their work could leave – though if they did they would not receive unemployment benefit, and for each vacancy created a dozen jobless people waited in a queue to fill it.

These arguments concealed a failure on the part of the trade unions to realize that wages and working hours, vitally important as they were, should not be the sole criteria for judging employment. The unions had secured great advances in Britain before most other European countries in abolishing the horrors of the nineteenth century, but were now falling behind. The victims of their own history, they regarded the worker–employer relationship as a continuing war which more or less accepted, pending the inauguration of the socialist paradise, that the working class should fight on the economic level alone. Surely, they maintained, it was the task of the government to guard over standards of health! As for the *atmosphere* of the work-place, they had no thoughts on the subject at all.

My memorandum stressed a factor hitherto overlooked: human dignity. Marks and Spencer, not to mention their competitors, were providing work for women and girls under conditions that made it impossible for them to face the public as the female sex desired to be observed – presentable in appearance, relaxed in manner, worthy of respect. I found girls heaving bulky packages while in an advanced state of pregnancy, but they were compelled to continue working because pregnancy was not classified as an illness and did not qualify for sick-pay under the health insurance schemes. If they were unmarried they had an added reason for keeping on the job: the stigma of immorality to compound with the spectre of poverty.

Throughout Britain the branches of Marks and Spencer and

similar chain-stores were ruled unchallenged by men who were themselves overworked and poorly paid. A look from them could instil fear into the hearts of their subservient staffs. These managers of course had no training in management skills and their single compensation for their own lowly state among the musty merchandise was the consciousness of being the dominant sex. They trembled for their positions not if one of their employees injured herself falling off a lop-sided step-ladder, but if the week's takings showed a downward graph. What girl with a personal problem would go to such a superior for help? Why should a female drudge be presumed to have problems anyway?

I felt confident I could handle any question relating to staff welfare, and make the subject an approved management activity, if only I could suppress my natural impetuosity and proceed with tact. My aim was to avoid clashes with male executives (there weren't any others) by recognizing the sanctity of their territorial rights. I was not going to be labelled 'that interfering foreign busybody'.

Orderly office procedure proved a mystery, a Frankenstein monster refusing to be tamed, and after a few weeks I sat helplessly on the floor of my office surrounded by papers. A young woman came in and said: 'My name is Mrs Thomas and I am to be your secretary.' I leapt from the floor in relief. 'In that case, Mrs Thomas,' I told her, 'you can begin at once by filing all this stuff.' At first few in Baker Street deigned to grant me recognition, I was intruding into an organism arranged with all the masculine exclusiveness of a Pall Mall club. But it was obvious I had the exalted ear of the chairman and the club adjusted to the unfamiliar situation accordingly.

This didn't apply to Harry Sacher. He was 'family', being married to Simon's sister Miriam. Harry Sacher had joined the Board on leaving Palestine in 1931. The problem was, how to occupy him? He was a lawyer, a scholar, a writer; what he wasn't was a businessman. So Simon put any unspecified job that was judged as of no great importance his way. Naturally, one of Harry's responsibilities was oversight of the newly established Welfare Department, and this to him meant its budget. He demanded that I put my requests to him in writing. He had a red-ink and a black-ink pen. For 'No' he scribbled his replies in red. They were usually red.

Early in my career Harry exclaimed: 'If this firm comes to ruin it'll be your fault, Flora!' He took a negative view of almost every proposition requiring money that I put to him. Once this made me so angry I burst into Simon's office and loudly complained. 'Just carry on as you wish, girlie,' was all he would say, 'only please don't bother me.' So in the end I got what I wanted. Another problem related to the attitude of Becky Sieff, the eldest Marks sister and wife of the vice-chairman. She felt I was the wrong person for the job, asserting that she could do it better – and that was probably the truth. Simon would not dream of it. All his sisters had to seek fulfilment outside the family business, their daughters too. Some years later I placed one of the girls in a store as a welfare officer. The experiment was short-lived. Simon exploded when the news reached him.

Despite my ignorance of the commercial world, planning came easily to me because I concentrated on the elements which struck me as necessary for personal satisfaction in employment. For people spending virtually the entire day at their work, thinking about it while they travelled to and from the place, talking with their friends – two-thirds of one's life perhaps – respect and appreciation due to them as individuals must rank high. I compiled a list: bright, pleasant surroundings; the elimination as far as possible of fatigue; adequate arrangements for the maintenance of personal hygiene; a healthy, enticing diet at a minimal price; a person of responsibility to whom one could express private anxieties; a sense of pride in the significance of one's work. I had other ideas too, but Marks and Spencer were still emerging from the psychology of the counter-hand in the penny bazaar, so I knew I must bide my time.

My little department of five began with the introduction of subsidized staff canteens in every store (amazingly, such a thing was virtually non-existent in Britain, which went to work with a sandwich wrapped in newspaper). For this we engaged experienced cooks and kitchen-staff and had space cleared for the installation of proper equipment, tables and chairs. Emphasis was placed on the importance of colour, and comfort, and civilized washing facilities. We fanned out across the country to persuade each store manager to appoint a member of his team as welfare officer. Some of them stared blankly into space, wondering what the world was coming to, with this pampering of inferiors. Often they would nominate their least valued employee for the job. I didn't care, they could be trained. I knew that one day specialists would be appointed for such posts, full time.

160

The older stores were open to all weathers, for instead of doors they had shutters clamped down only at night. Instructions for warming or ventilating the premises as necessary evoked a conspiratorial chorus of objections from store-managers. You would think we were demanding the impossible, a change in the English climate. Nevertheless, by the end of that year a girl could have a substantial hot meal for sixpence – discreetly waived if she couldn't afford it – and tea in a cup with a saucer and a biscuit for a penny. Her lunch-hour could be passed in an easy chair in a pleasant rest-room, with a magazine. It doesn't sound particularly revolutionary today, but these innovations were condemned as offending a hallowed doctrine for the stacking of every available square inch of space high with merchandise.

Marks and Spencer divided the realm for administrative purposes into thirteen divisions. Staff supervisors were allocated to each of them, based at head office. Mary Hanson became one of these, while another was Sophie Podolsky, a warm-hearted girl who had worked in Germany as a receptionist in a 'people's advice bureau' for birth-control, and that gave me an idea for the future. I needed a title for myself, so that my letters should carry some weight and at least be honoured with an answer. I chose Staff Superintendent. When an advertisement was placed in the classified columns for an additional secretary to our department the doorman warned me the following day not to venture into the hall; it was being stormed by applicants.

One of my initial steps had been to form a Welfare Committee at Head Office, of which I appointed myself chairman. Members included an auditor, a member of the personnel department and a representative of the staff. To this committee hardship experienced by male as well as female employees was referred. An early decision related to creating a sense of security within the company: no employee with a minimum of five years' service could be given notice of dismissal without reference first to the Welfare Committee. Thus at a stroke we abolished the divine right of the master to fire his worker at whim. We then introduced gratuities for every girl leaving to be married or retiring after ten years' continuous employment. The committee gave personal loans and took over any human problem that could not be handled at store level. Our Welfare Committee came together every week, never missing a meeting even during the war. Like the famous Windmill Theatre, 'we never closed'.

My staff and I thought of ourselves as a little resistance movement, ever scheming against heartless company bureaucracy. We made a somewhat strange spectacle to trespassers from other departments – 'that noisy crowd upstairs, always laughing or crying'. We ourselves were available for consultation by anyone anywhere who had a grievance.

Recalling my association with the Butler Street Club, I enquired specifically about the arrangements girls made for their annual holidays, and of course discovered they invariably spent their time off at home. They hardly travelled away from their native towns. And so Dymchurch came once again in my field of vision. I knew all the right local people and sent Mary Hanson to organize holidays under canvas there, at a nominal charge. This proved so popular, particularly with the youngsters, we soon had Marks and Spencer camps at sea-side resorts across the country.

What of the staff who had never visited London? A swapping system was inaugurated in their private homes, so that in the summer, when stores on the coast were especially busy, the Londoners could be temporarily attached to them, for a change of atmosphere. We reversed the process in winter, to coincide with the seasonal London trade. Friendships were born, sometimes romance and marriage. The news spread that in joining Marks and Spencer you became part of an extended family. Mitsubishi and Spencer? But pre-war Britain hadn't the faintest idea how commercial activity was organized in Japan or, indeed, if it was organized at all!

Simon Marks enquired whether the staff ever expressed gratitude for all that was being done for them. He put this to me after I had attached doctors, dentists and chiropodists to every store, virtually a national health service in miniature for our employees, now approaching twenty thousand. 'Why should they be grateful?' I retorted. 'They're better, more efficient employees than before, and their loyalty is enhanced. They make the stores look inviting, they understand the importance of receiving their customers courteously. You rarely have to sack anyone, which means fewer staff changes, with all the expense that involves. And incidentally they create sales goodwill for millions of Marks and Spencer jumpers. You're getting the benefit too.'

Company results proved it, for Marks and Spencer leapt ahead of its rivals. During the middle thirties a vast building programme was under way, to display the merchandise on the

162

style of great department stores like Selfridge's and Harrod's, at that time only patronized by the well-to-do. Each new branch was allocated spacious personnel amenity areas with skilled welfare officers, now described as staff manageresses. We made arrangements with hospitals to admit members of the company at very short notice free of charge – it cost Marks and Spencer a mere two shillings a head. Few people outside the London School of Economics knew of the existence of a gentleman called Sir William Beveridge, but many were becoming aware of our medical service, which now included dental and optical treatment as well as special grants in sickness and a rest in a convalescent home. Simon Marks and his family endowed a benevolent fund that gave retirement benefits to employees not covered by the company's pension scheme.

In the course of my efforts to change the status of working women I was myself being turned into a different person. The reason could not be ascribed to Marks and Spencer alone. Adolf Hitler, and the birth of Fascist movements right across the European spectrum, shattered many of my illusions concerning the stability and superiority of Western democratic regimes. If an anti-Semitic tyranny could become acceptable in a country so respected for its civilization and creative genius as Germany, were the Jews safe anywhere? To my consternation, Hitlerism aroused little protest except on the Left, or so it seemed. In 1933 *The Times* published a series of extracts from the Nazi leader's *Mein Kampf*. I experienced a surge of disgust, and yet found this sentiment was not being shared by some of my closest friends. Germany's propaganda machine went into high gear among prominent Britons: Ethel Snowden, for one. Even she, my friend, came back from the Nuremberg Rally with nothing but praise for the discipline of the Hitler Youth, the shining faces of the boys and girls, the patriotic spirit of the New Order, the determination to eradicate every trace of the Weimar shame. Of the doctrine of Aryan racial supremacy she had not a word.

I asked her: 'How could you raise your arm in the Nazi salute?' She replied: 'I admire what Hitler is doing.' I would not see Ethel Snowden after that. Another friend, Sir Thomas Moore, a comrade of Harold's army days in Ireland and Serbia, later a Scottish Unionist MP, dilated on his generous reception by the Nazi leaders. He had had a most enjoyable time in Germany, he said. Tom Moore had been at my wedding. The protection of animals from human cruelty was his all-consuming passion. Well, I now threw him out of my house.

With my visits to Paris growing less frequent, Alexander Kerensky came more often to stay with me in London. I drank thirstily from the fount of his affections but was no longer so readily available to minister to his slightest want. Holidays at Annecy, where he reverted to the country pursuits of his youth, fishing and boating, invigorated us both and reminded me that a woman approaching forty could, with the man she loved at her side, retain her curiosity, her desires, her bloom. Still, Kerensky sensed that he was losing a part of me, and offered marriage. I could not do it. I wished to keep him always as he was at Annecy, the great-hearted man-god. I feared the tedium of the politician passé. Furthermore, I found his sustained vendetta against Moscow unattractive in a period when Russia alone evidenced determination to resist Hitler.

In his turn Kerensky railed against my preoccupation with the Jewish fate in Germany, and my belief that Hitler's imitators elsewhere, not the least of them Oswald Mosley in England, were endangering the future of Europe. Once, in a fit of pique, I accused Kerensky of anti-Semitism. It was a foolish charge against such a man, but he took it seriously.

'Me? The defender of Mendel Beilis in Russia! The leader who gave the Jews liberation from Tsarism!'

'In that case,' I replied, 'you must suffer for your people, and I shall suffer for mine.'

On the principle that the enemy of one's enemy is one's friend, I now see this exchange as the moment when Kerensky and I began drifting apart. Stalin, because he confronted Hitler, was to me a hopeful symbol, even though I was remote from Communism. But in Kerensky's calculations the other dictator, crusading against Communism, could be the agent of Stalin's downfall and the true liberation of Russia. It was an awesome choice to have to make, but in the thirties we were forced to one side or the other, avoiding the blurred areas in between where the philosophies of the two despots intermingled, and where many a lost soul became entrapped.

I had a muddle-headed friend, Dulcie Sassoon, precisely in such a position. She was a Franklin, married to Siegfried Sassoon's cousin, and though she declared her abhorrence of Hitler, she took it into her consciousness to admire his English replica, the lapsed Socialist Mosley. Visiting her in the country one day I came upon a man I had last seen when, as an eleven-year-old, he lunched with his parents at my house in Jerusalem. It was Kim Philby, still with traces of that childhood stammer. I reminded him of our earlier meeting but those days were now lost to his memory. He introduced me to his Jewish wife, the Viennese Litzi Friedmann, and I gave them my address (I was living in Addison Road). Gradually, a friendship developed.

It caused me no disquiet when my housekeeper, Bella Meyer, a refugee from the Continent, informed me that she had known Litzi's family in Vienna, and that Kim's wife had been a Communist. Only years later, after Kim's defection to Russia, did I learn with everyone else that he had a cover job with a pro-Nazi organization, the Anglo-German Fellowship. The Kim Philby I now got to know was not a talkative man; he had a gentle charm, never drinking to excess at my house, and mingled easily with my other friends. I had not discarded the habit, carried over from my Hornton Street days, of keeping open house. Office colleagues jostled with Labour politicians like John Strachey and Stafford and Isobel Cripps, and of course a liberal sprinkling of my Zionist contacts. I was using any opportunity to preach the justice of the Jewish cause in Palestine. This never worked with Philby. He evinced not the slightest interest in the Palestine conflict. Neither did Guy Burgess, who occasionally arrived with Kim. My recollection of the latter is borne out by what others have written of him: he was a grubby, uncouth specimen but a fascinating conversationalist.

Once the infamous Nuremberg Laws were introduced in Germany, classifying Jews (and half-Jews) as a breed something less than human, the trickle of refugees into Britain became a steady stream. Problems of their rehabilitation and resettlement brought an anguished Wyndham Deedes hastening from Bethnal Green. He was deeply affected by the tragedy and felt a Christian responsibility to help the persecuted. Together with Norman Bentwich and Chaim Weizmann, Deedes started up the machinery for the rescue of 'non-Aryans', and their employment in England and elsewhere. We all joined in, and the British people I feel deserve greater credit than they have received for the help they accorded. The work did not proceed so very smoothly, and loud complaints could be heard about refugees taking jobs away from the unemployed, in the professions as well as the ordinary labour force. Wyndham, with his influence in church and government circles, was able to do much in smoothing ruffled English feathers. Weizmann of course stressed the role of Palestine as the principal haven. Simon Marks, together with Herbert Samuel, led the international campaign to raise funds, while I knew I had Simon's blessing in bringing refugees into the Marks and Spencer organization.

From a stencilled magazine, written in German, I picked up useful ideas about the training of staff for the distributive trades. It was produced in Amsterdam by a refugee, Elsa Hertzberg, who had been employed in Cologne by the great department store of Tietz, now of course 'Aryanized'. I invited Miss Hertzberg to London. Her English was limited, but I placed her on my staff and thus she was able to bring over her elderly parents. She organized a brief training course in Leeds while we watched how the German speaker handled her class. She proved an important acquisition. At first the girls rebelled against their somewhat authoritarian instructor, who used her arms and legs to fill the gaps in her vocabulary. No English term even existed in those days for the now commonplace 'visual aids'. The girls were won over, and Miss Hertzberg led them through what was tantamount to a commercial education. We arranged to take the girls away from the stores periodically for a productive respite at Head Office, and had them escorted round the factories of our suppliers and shown how each article they sold had a little history of its own, starting with the raw material. A Training Department was born.

Naturally, we encountered opposition. 'How ridiculous!' one of the directors scoffed. 'If our goods won't sell themselves, training won't do it.' It was just one more hurdle to be overcome. Another, incredible though it now sounds, was to teach the sales staff to use make-up. Some thought lipstick not quite 'respectable', that it belonged to people of an alien kind, women who spoke in foreign accents perhaps and originated in societies which, unlike virtuous Britain, flaunted their sex.

So, having dressed the sales staff in becoming uniforms, with their feet sensibly shod while standing at the counters, and brought the stock-room personnel out of their dust-choked corners into the light of day – this by the establishment of gardens on flat roofs in case the sun decided to shine – we were now schooling those with the required aptitudes for promotion to more responsible tasks. Reproductions from the great masters were acquired to break the monotony both of the walls and the daily routine. An annual exhibition of the creative activities of the staff soon became feasible too, and in the process the divide between male and female narrowed: a job at Marks and Spencer could be a career, even for women. As a minimum wage, however, they still took home a princely seventeen shillings.

I was at my desk during Ascot Week when Simon Marks and his brother-in-law Israel Sieff popped their heads into my office on their way to the races, grey toppers held in an act of staged deference. Outside working hours they were my friends, here in Baker Street they were chairman and vice-chairman, and I made a point of respecting their status. But this was a moment too good to miss.

'It's going to be your lucky day,' I sang out. 'Let's celebrate by raising the minimum wage to a pound a week. It'll make it lucky for everybody.' They exchanged a momentary consultative glance. Their binoculars hung heavily on their shoulders, their women were waiting below, and they were itching to get away. They couldn't refuse me, and a pound it was. The difference of three shillings could buy the Sunday joint for a family, though many families in Britain had long foregone the luxury. I made a mental note that at the very next meeting of our Welfare Committee we would institute a ruling that henceforth employees would receive an increase every birthday.

While I was enjoying my little triumphs, humanity at large was making its great blunders: disintegration of the League of Nations, a war in Abyssinia, a war in Spain, a Japanese invasion of China. Britain turned her back to the storm, taking shelter in her ancient and apparently impermeable institutions. I had been warned by the headmaster while my son was at Summer Fields that Peter revealed 'revolutionary tendencies'. (In fact, he had complained about the food!) Dr Williams once stressed to me, in reply to my query as to the careers his pupils usually entered, that his educational objective was to turn out 'gentlemen'. Peter was now at Eton, a King's Scholar, and this I gathered marked an Etonian throughout his life, for the thing to be there was an Oppidan. King's Scholars paid no fees and everyone knew it. Even Eton had its class distinction.

What had been described as revolutionary tendencies in the self-satisfied cocoon of the prep school was in fact Peter's awakening social conscience. This I encouraged. His Classics master's report for 1937, which has miraculously survived among long-forgotten papers, is revealing for its insight into the man-to-be: 'He has, I should say, a first-rate general intelligence and should make an excellent historian. And I look forward to reading some day his first book. It will be very interesting and most vividly written. But I'm afraid that the scholarly and learned will greet it with many disappointing shakes of the head!'

Peter was nearly sixteen. Together with class-mates he organized Etonian support for the Spanish Relief Committee, which gave succour to children on the side loyal to the government who were bereaved in the Civil War. The effort was applauded by the headmaster, Dr C. A. Elliott, and a substantial amount was contributed. Subsequently they decided on a like project for refugees from Germany, though this time they were more ambitious. They would sponsor the education of two boys in Britain. Dr Elliott thought this too a splendid idea.

Refugee children could come to England only if 'guaranteed', that is, would not constitute a public charge. So they went about collecting the necessary funds, making a point of approaching each other's parents, not their own. Peter took care of some of the top Jewish prospects, among them my good friend Lionel Cohen (later a Lord of Appeal) who had two sons at Eton. Lionel contacted me to voice his displeasure. 'I'm not keen on what your son is doing,' he complained. 'We ought not to be so conspicuous at Eton, people will not approve of such direct association with Jews.' And yet the gentile parents thought it a marvellous scheme.

When they had raised sufficient funds to guarantee their first refugee Peter approached his headmaster with the proposal, so natural to the organizers of the effort, that the boy come to Eton. The Head was taken aback. 'Surely you're not serious!' he exclaimed. 'We support the oppressed of many races, Chinese, Hottentots, without discrimination. We can't bring them all to Eton.' The two arrived in London, one of them temporarily living with us before training as an engineer. The other had a different ambition. He became a chef.

Lionel Cohen's reaction reminded me of Weizmann's flagellating description of such gentry: 'They belong to the Order of Trembling Israelites.' However, Lionel redeemed himself late in life, after Israel's independence in 1948. He embraced the cause of Zionism and, like other Jews of similar background, it was with the uncontrolled zeal of the late convert.

My generation cannot think of the Spanish Civil War divorced from a flood of connecting recollections of a Britain sliding into an abyss along a path made of its own bungled intentions. When Victor Gollancz and John Strachey inaugurated the Left Book Club over a drink at the Café Royal I naturally signed up as a founder-member, affecting to belong to an intelligentsia that patronized rather than identified with the Left in politics. We were pacifist, yet at the same time demanded that Hitler be stopped, if necessary with a show of force. We worried ourselves into a tizzy about Mosley's sympathizers on the right wing of the Conservative Party, yet neglected to strengthen Labour except through a campaign of what we fondly believed was 'enlightenment' – those tomes in limp orange bindings. The Left Book Club won sixty thousand earnest subscribers; it exerted so little influence that when Ribbentrop arrived in London as Hitler's ambassador he was lionized in the upper reaches of society. Churchill, demanding re-armament, was among Britain's least popular politicians. Hyde Park oratory was just that – talk: a demonstration against injustice could bring thousands into the park, but at the first gentle hint of rain they would crowd into Lyons Corner House and drink tea to the music of a gypsy orchestra.

Kim Philby came to see me before leaving for Spain in 1937. I attached no significance to the news that he was to report the war from the Franco side. I remember the day well. I think he wanted to tell me more. 'I'm doing important work for peace,' he said. 'You should be doing it too, Flora.'

'I have my own cause,' I observed. 'Who's going to help the persecuted Jews, if not their own people?'

Developments in staff welfare and training at Marks and Spencer began to attract notice in the Press. I came upon various trade union officials at conferences devoted to industrial welfare who believed the treatment accorded our employees was disguising some ulterior motive. Did our workers have the right to strike? Would management allow them to be organized? The unions were welcome to hold meetings in our canteens and explain their objectives. A few of the girls joined, but in the main the unions registered little progress at Marks and Spencer. Indeed, some of their officials confessed that we were making their job much harder – if our example were copied by the retail trades in general they would have no members at all! Years later one union organizer ruefully informed the Board of his difficulties in making a dent in our company, and he passed a letter

169

over, signed by myself. It related to a cheque enclosed with good wishes on the occasion of the marriage of one of our girls. 'My wife,' he said.

Simon Marks had evolved from being an enterprising businessman pure and simple into a national leader imbued with a determination to raise general standards in Britain. In Israel Sieff he had a partner thoroughly schooled in economics and sociology. Israel's views on the future development of industry were formulated in a non-political study group of which he was the head, Political and Economic Planning (PEP). This body produced analyses of the steel industry, cotton, coal-mining and other staple activities which, if taken to heart at the time, might have spared Britain so steep a decline.

Between them the brothers-in-law demonstrated how any article, be it a garment or an umbrella, could be sold for little more if its quality was good rather than poor; the labour involved in manufacturing and selling it would be the same. Though it owned no factories the company tested everything it stocked in its own laboratories. I endeavoured to match this standard in my own field. I had my concept of the fulfilled woman – it was far from any obsession with sex equality but fell simply into the category of human satisfaction. Thus a policy was inaugurated in 1937 of a fortnight's Continental holiday for those with a minimum of ten years' service, at the nominal charge of three pounds. A holiday abroad was of course still reckoned a prerogative of the rich. We took groups to Dieppe for a few days, followed by a longer stay in Paris. Marks and Spencer employees were not to be confused with the scorned 'shop-girls' of tradition.

One day I was summoned to the chairman's sanctum and sensed trouble, for I was warned he was in a wrath. I was barely inside the door when he shouted: 'I hear you are introducing birth-control instructions to the staff!'

He was bound to find out sooner than later. I had contacted Marie Stopes – her name alone was then enough to evoke a prurient titter – at her clinic off the Tottenham Court Road. (She received me, I recall, reclining on a chaise longue in a burgundy silk dress and a magnificent flowered hat.) Now I had to explain it to this pillar of the bourgeoisie.

'Have you any idea how many of our girls become pregnant? They can't afford to give up working, so they keep it a secret till the last moment.'

170

'Is that my concern? Their husbands should look after them.'

'And if there isn't a husband? Single girls like that usually get thrown out of their homes.'

'You will be selling French letters over the counter next.'

'It may come to that too,' I replied. Simon burst into laughter. Another battle was won. His anger was never sustained. On another occasion, when he learnt that I had recruited two welfare officers at three pounds ten shillings a week, he reproved me with a reminder of his salaries' rule: only in exceptional circumstances could an employee commence above three pounds. 'I know,' I answered, 'but these women are highly qualified. They have university degrees.'

'Oh!' he grumbled. 'That means they ought to earn more than me. I haven't a degree.'

I adored the man, despite his peculiarities. His fetching humility was always in evidence. Commercial success had brought him out of his middle-class residence in suburban Cricklewood to a grand mansion, Cleave Lodge, in Hyde Park Gate. He remained the same Simon Marks, ever ready to share praise the company earned with others, yet accepting criticism for its failings as a personal dereliction.

One learnt to adjust to his phobias. He could not bear to be alone in his office, and always walked the corridors in Baker Street with a retinue of assistants. He once asked me particularly not to wear pearls; since a childhood accident, when he had witnessed a friend struggle with a boot button up his nostrils, he had a horror of anything of similar shape. When abroad he ate nothing but eggs and fruit, in the conviction that foreign food was not hygienically prepared and would poison him. With all this his domestic life was the most harmonious of all his family, his only source of grief being the failure of his son and heir to follow his footsteps into the business. Today a somewhat unconventional peer of the realm, Michael Marks has told me that if ever he were to write his memoirs he would adapt the title from the celebrated Paul Muni film and call it 'I am a Fugitive from a Chain Store'.

My attitude to male colleagues involved me in a careful science of relationships. Marks and Spencer sell very largely to the women's market, but as yet no woman has been elected to the Board. Not once did I raise the question of my own salary, which seemed immutable at five pounds a week. When I was asked to organize a luncheon-club for executives, which achieved the

171

comforts of a well-appointed West End restaurant, I was neither offered, nor did I request, membership.

It was an article of faith with me not to be concerned in the possible dismissal of a male employee. Dismissal, I told myself, was a greater disaster for a man than a woman, and should not be aggravated by destruction of the masculine ego. My most immediate superior, Joe Berger the Company Secretary, understood my objectives and invariably supported me. He was a pacifist in every fibre, and extremely left-wing. To my regret, on the outbreak of war he left Marks and Spencer for America, his divorced wife marrying the journalist MP Tom Driberg. That gave rise to a notorious aphorism, ascribed to Churchill: Buggers can't be choosers.

Another colleague with whom I was on terms of close friendship, Neil Furse, an accountant, approached me with the request that I find a position in my department for his cousin Aileen. Though not short of money, and highly intelligent, she was subject to depressions. Her doctors thought she should have a job. Aileen was appointed to our Marble Arch store as a staff manageress, and I undertook to keep an eye on her well-being.

Aileen Furse soon established herself as one of my principal assistants, all of whom dropped in at my home for the occasional drink. She was there one day when Kim Philby arrived, now separated but not divorced from his Litzi. Kim plonked himself in an easy chair and began talking about Spain. He found an avid listener in Aileen, and the two left together. The next I knew they were sharing a flat.

Kim appeared to me to be concentrating on making a reputation for himself in journalism. Aileen belonged to the class, now out of fashion, called 'county'. She was typically English, slim and attractive, fiercely patriotic, but awkward in her gestures and unsure of herself in company. I was pleased for her. As they left a party in my home – this must have been some time in 1938, just before Munich – Kim took me to one side, looking morose. 'I want to tell you,' he said, 'I'm in great danger.' It dawned on me then that he was still associated with the Communist Party, the cause he had espoused at Cambridge. The statement was extraordinary, perhaps, but the intimation of his affiliation provoked no suspicion. What was dangerous in Britain about being a Communist? In some circles of the intelligentsia it was the done thing.

Between Hitler's incorporation of Austria in his 'Greater Germany' and the return of Neville Chamberlain from Munich with his ridiculous piece of paper fluttering in the wind, my years of work at Marks and Spencer achieved the cachet of official approval, as it were, in the construction of specially designed staff rooms at the new Pantheon store, the company's largest, in Oxford Street. On the site had once stood a 'Palace of Pleasure', meeting the crude requirements for relaxation of Londoners before the French Revolution. Then it became a combined market-place and fair-ground, and lastly a morass of parked cars, stables, street vendors, all standing in a litter of rotting fruit. Now Simon's goal of an establishment to make shopping for the working classes an enjoyable excursion, and my own ambitions for the staff, came together, and I was gratified to read in the trade magazines as much about the second feature as the first. We had three hundred employees at the Pantheon. Oxford Street had previously been famous for a few great stores only, patronized by a West End clientele. Our arrival brought an invasion by the masses, to give this thoroughfare a standard unknown elsewhere in the United Kingdom.

Where Oxford Street faded eastward into a drab redoubt bordering on Holborn and the City, a giant bee-hive hummed with a very different business. Bloomsbury House, converted from a sprawling hotel, had become the centre to which refugees from Hitler, clad in long black raincoats and clutching Continental-style briefcases, repaired to receive a weekly subsistence; perhaps also to learn about possible employment and the likelihood of visas to distant parts. They also needed hints on the British way of life: how, for example, the British kept warm when the coals you placed in those open fireplaces would not respond to a lighted match (the refugees had mostly inhabited centrally-heated blocks of flats but we had yet to catch up with such luxuries). Thousands upon thousands, forlorn as they displayed their diplomas in engineering, in music, in law, dreaming of the *gemütlich* coffee-houses back home, they wrestled with our peculiarities, beginning with the English tongue. These were the lucky ones. Within a year or so millions would be left to die in Europe. One perplexed soul who turned up at Bloomsbury House in search of help was the nineteen-year-old George Weidenfeld. Over in Germany Lola Hahn, daughter of the banker Max Warburg, now my dear friend, and Wilfrid Israel, my late husband's cousin, stayed with some others almost to the end to ensure the safe departure of unaccompanied children.

Peter refused to abide the playing fields of Eton a moment longer than absolutely necessary and went to work at Bloomsbury House alongside Norman Bentwich and Wyndham Deedes. Britain offered sanctuary to ten thousand children under the age of sixteen. Peter's task was to find homes for as many as possible overseas, so as to keep the British quota up to strength. We thought we did all we could, but none of us did enough. Palestine was a thorn in Britain's flesh. Chaim Weizmann, now returned as leader of the Zionists, pleaded for the entry of as many as possible into the homeland, though with the oncoming shadows of war the Chamberlain Government feared repercussions in the Arab world and kept the flow down to a minimum.

Amidst the depressing events of that period my relations with Kerensky took a decidedly cooler turn. With no other man could I attain a similar degree of intimacy. He was growing more handsome with age, he might have been a Shakespearean actor with those features chiselled from generations close to the climatic extremes of Russia's heartland. Clive Garsia, ever hopeful, now lost patience with me as he perceived how my devotion to Kerensky, despite our many differences, would not be replaced.

In November 1938 a Polish-Jewish youth, a refugee in Paris, penetrated the German Embassy in that city, pointed a gun at a junior official and shot him dead. The assassination of this Vom Rath provoked a pogrom in Germany and Austria, with destruction of synagogues, shops and private homes. The noise of splintering glass gave the moment its name – *Kristallnacht*. Thirty thousand Jews were deported to concentration camps, thirty-six were killed. This was the regime with which the British Government hoped to live in enduring peace. Kerensky was with me as the news was reported in London. He observed my anguish but seemed strangely unmoved.

'Such happenings are occurring all the time to the Russian people,' he said. 'They don't find their way into the newspapers.'

I could not contain myself. A bitter, wounding quarrel ensued. He was stung by my summing-up: 'If war breaks out in Europe it won't be caused by Russia, but by Germany.' Kerensky left my house in anger. So this was, I thought, the end. Weeks later he returned, apparently mollified. But he brought an ultimatum. Though of the Russian Orthodox faith, he could arrange a dispensation for divorce. We either marry, or we separate for ever. He could see my answer in my expression.

I heard from Kerensky intermittently after this. He sent Vladimir Nabokov to me, asking my help to obtain an academic post in Britain for the writer. Nabokov, son of one of Kerensky's liberal supporters in the old Provisional Government, was struggling for a livelihood in Berlin, producing works in Russian under the pseudonym Sirin. But there was no place for a Russian émigré writer in Hitler's Germany. Chaim Weizmann's niece Eva Lutyens – she was married to the son of the architect, and once confessed to me that her greatest shame was to be born a Jewess – had been quite close to him in Russia and told me of his qualities. I used what influence I had to secure a post for Nabokov at Oxford. I failed, and he moved on to New York. (Nabokov, an exceedingly handsome young man, had obviously captured Eva Lutyens' heart at one time, but when we both met him again years later, at George Weidenfeld's party to launch his novel *Lolita*, the plump and successful novelist decided not to recognize us.)

Garsia could not take the place he hoped for in my life. With Kerensky gone I did not feel starved of affection; I was able to relegate sex to a minor role. Clive remained one of my cavaliers unconsummated and uncomplicated by passion. Another was the psychiatrist Eric Strauss, celebrated for having introduced treatment by shock therapy in Britain. Long associated in medicine with Russell Brain, his lectures at Bart's Hospital challenged the accepted Freudian wisdom of the day and enjoyed a tremendous vogue.

Eric Strauss provided the intellectual stimulation my years with Kerensky had lacked. I followed his guidance in dealing with welfare cases at Marks and Spencer though, like so many psychiatrists, he was something of an emotional mess himself. Jewish by birth, he too had converted to Catholicism, I believe at Oxford, and yet he suspected anti-Semitism for the strangest reasons. Eric composed music for the piano and had ideas relating to the nervous disorders of his favourite saints. Some of the oddest specimens of the aristocracy consulted him at his Wimpole Street practice, perhaps because he was such a delightful raconteur. Both smoking heavily, we would pass long hours through the night together, as he unveiled the mysteries of the human mind. Eric confessed his physiological shortcomings to me, as regards women, so I accepted an unspoken admission of his homosexuality. Whenever we travelled his first requirement was to find a church for his Sunday Mass.

It was now March 1939, and the curtain rang down on the life of Grigori Benenson. Impatient to the end, his face puckered like a map of the world he once bestrode, and still rearing against the infirmity of old age, father died in a London nursing home. When Manhattan collapsed about him he returned to Europe and, yes, made money again, lost it, made some more, and departed this world owing not a penny. Even by his standards he left a tidy sum: you could buy a fine mansion for a tenth of the amount. The *Financial Times* that gave him his daily ration of Stock Exchange intelligence cost twopence, and anyone with an urge to own a mink coat (I already had one) could get it full-length for a hundred guineas.

Father's money was in the form of scraps, or rather scrips, of paper and Lena Goldfields promissory certificates (more valuable as collector's items than currency), bequeathed many times over. It would take years of tedium and a cataract of buff-coloured envelopes, during the war and later, to comprehend the lawyers' letters and untangle the estate before a final disposal could be achieved. Ancient trusts were invoked, history stalked. I do not recommend the experience.

His natural force all but spent, father made a last request for immortality: he wished his grandson to retain the family name. Peter tagged Benenson on to Solomon and took himself double-barrelled to Balliol, then into the army, and finally to the secret intelligence unit Ultra at Bletchley Park. He married at the age of twenty, whereupon, merciful to his progeny, he pruned the awkward growth. The world would know him as Peter Benenson.

The summer moved forward as a season of oppressive sunshine for those like Clive Garsia, Eric Strauss and myself, at the threshold of middle age, waiting for the war that we prayed must not come. That other World War, still so fresh in our memories, so pointless, mocked our thoughts as we proceeded mechanically with our affairs. Could a providential intervention save the younger generation from another sacrifice? Two years earlier German dive-bombers had swooped upon Guernica. Must they now descend upon London?

Late in August I travelled with Hadassah Samuel, my adventure-loving friend from Jerusalem, to the Haute Savoie for a brief holiday. We stopped over in Paris and wandered through the Tuileries, basking in its customary touristic calm, the languages of the world murmuring in the background, a babble of friendliness. Then on to a little place close to Annecy. As I ate the famous peaches of the region thoughts of Kerensky tugged at me. How we used to enjoy them in times past, during those carefree holidays of my joyous womanhood!

Seated at the lake-side with Hadassah I searched out the latest crisis news in the Continental edition of the *New York Herald-Tribune*. And there, briefly, was the announcement I never dreamed I would ever see: the marriage of Alexander Kerensky to an Australian divorcee. I cannot pretend it didn't sadden me.

Hadassah and I motored on to a depressed Zionist Congress in Geneva. Weizmann made his familiar speech, of Britain's goodness and her perfidy, her help and hindrance of the National Home, his faith that, in the end, the Arabs would sit down and negotiate with the Jews. David Ben-Gurion, his head between his hands, listened despondently. They all looked tired.

Hitler's pact with Stalin extinguished every last spark of interest at that Congress. Delegates wished only to hurry back to their homes and families. Chaim movingly embraced his colleagues on the platform in a last farewell and, with Vera and Blanche ('Baffy') Dugdale – she the niece of Lord Balfour and Chaim's political confidante, perhaps his closest – drove towards the French frontier. I could not prevent the silly, wicked thought entering my head of gossip so often exchanged with Vera Weizmann, as to whether that remarkable assortment of auburn curls on Baffy's head was really her hair, or a wig. Then we left too. Many of the Congress delegates were never to be heard of again.

A much-changed Paris now: streets empty, hotels full, taxis straining under tourists' luggage. Hamburg 1914? It could easily have been. I was nineteen then. What had my generation learnt in twenty-five years? Squeezing the remaining dregs of influence out of my old contacts at the Meurice, I was conceded a room in the hotel for Hadassah and myself. Tomorrow it would be September. The Germans proclaimed Danzig for the Reich and a pall of black-out hung over the rue de Rivoli. The next day we joined the endless convoy of snailing motor-cars for Calais and at last, thankfully, we reached England.

On Sunday, 3 September, Britain was at war. Hadassah's

father-in-law, now Viscount Samuel and a Liberal leader in the House of Lords, was due to speak that morning so we decided to witness history in the making. We left Addison Road by taxi and at Hyde Park Corner the sirens wailed. We drew to a halt outside St George's Hospital, the taxi-driver declaring, 'This is as far as I go.' We darted into the hospital shelter to await the crunch of bombs. Nurses hastened to and fro filling hot-water bottles and preparing beds for the wounded. Who will ever forget that first false alarm!

We decided to skip the House of Lords and made our way to the Dorchester Hotel. The Weizmanns had given up their Kensington home and were now in residence in Suite 210, where Chaim conducted himself almost as a Prime Minister-in-Exile. Vera coolly dispensed drinks to an unceasing stream of secretaries, advisers and tanned visitors from Jerusalem who comprised her husband's unofficial Cabinet. Vera's well-tailored mind adjusted perfectly to the role of grand lady even, I think, while she slept.

The bustle was comparable to the waiting-room of a busy railway station. Chaim and others talked of the war in terms of grand strategy – keeping the sea-lanes open, defence of the Nile, the attitude of Mussolini. Two figures sat silent by a window, holding tin helmets and what seemed to me like Kodaks in square leather cases on their laps. They were Baffy Dugdale and her husband Edgar. It took some time before it dawned on me that here at the ready they had their gas masks.

9 The Lady of the Ladle

Wars induce all kinds of obsessions in otherwise normal people. Mine was with the nation's stomach. Britain, traditionally so static, was now a society of changed occupations, separated families and clashing civilizations – townspeople confronting city-folk for the first time in their lives. We were enjoined in radio talks to dig for victory, cut out waste and ask ourselves whether that journey was really necessary. At Marks and Spencer departments were dispersed as the men began disappearing. Hardly anyone was getting killed, so it all proved rather exciting. Musically, we hung out the washing on the Siegfried Line, though we wondered how long the country's honeymoon with itself was going to last. My thoughts worked overtime and kept returning to the subject of food.

My job at Marks and Spencer took me along many different avenues, but I was mostly associated in the public mind with staff canteens. My department installed them, provisioned them, supervised them. One of the weapons of war, surely, was a good hot midday meal. Then why did one have to work at Marks and Spencer to qualify for it? Didn't the entire home front deserve one? It could be provided cheaply, I knew the economics. On the outbreak of war Simon Marks, at a meeting reviewing emergency arrangements, turned to me with just one instruction: 'You carry on as you think fit, Flora, only don't leave us. Do whatever you want.'

It was the most formal authorization I received from anyone, and I decided this gave me *carte blanche* to try an experiment: a communal restaurant. Now, don't greet this statement with a yawn. Restaurants existed, and so did communities; but put the two together in those days and you were introducing a practice so alien to the mentality of the British people it could be likened to replacing the brick walls of the Albert Hall with glass and turning the place into a nudist colony. This was Britain in 1939, during the 'phony' war, and for the masses eating one's food

179

was strictly a private affair. Soldiers took their meals together, out of necessity, paupers and tramps too, behind grim portals known only to the destitute. For the rest of us, civilization was deemed to have advanced too far. No-one seemed to recognize that this country was an island, under siege. Rationing had not yet seriously begun but, we were informed, when fully instituted it would ensure adequate supplies and fair shares for all. When I read this in the newspaper I hummed a ditty brought home by my son from Eton: *And the band played believe it if you like!*

I spied a disused community centre with an archaic Aga cooker in Dalgarno Gardens, near the gas works in the shabby section of the so-called Royal Borough of Kensington. It was ideal for the purpose and my Welfare Department descended upon it in a body. We scrounged crockery from the Marks and Spencer stock-rooms and had leaflets printed which my staff and I personally distributed in the neighbourhood. Aileen Furse, who now had a Philby child and changed her name by deed poll accordingly, was particularly enthusiastic. Kitchen expertise, and this never failed to raise a laugh, was provided by our two specialists, Miss Cater and Miss Duck. I had willing helpers from outside too, among them Maidie Weizmann, married to the Weizmanns' elder son.

'Have a hot lunch at your communal restaurant', the leaflet read. 'Two courses, eightpence. Tea, one penny.' As with 'The Drop of Milk' of my Jerusalem life, people passed furtively by, curious but suspicious. Gradually they filtered in, and the enterprise actually became profitable. Soon we were placing restaurants at various locations in London and other towns, practically commandeering church halls and other empty premises and borrowing Marks and Spencer personnel to set up each little establishment until the locals could be persuaded to run it.

We thus engrossed ourselves while Western Europe came under Nazi control, and the nation at home felt the chill sensation of being abandoned to an isolated fate. One of the first bombs to fall on London crashed into Dalgarno Gardens. Luckily, our restaurant was empty at the time, but our precious Aga cooker succumbed. Walking over the site the next morning I observed the aftermath with a sick feeling: men and women gazing in stupor at their destroyed homes, gas mains blown, charred timbers still sending up trails of smoke, a silent queue at

180

a stand-pipe waiting to fill kettles and saucepans. And rescue teams burrowing through the rubble to bring out the living, whether this be a human or a mewing cat. Nightfall again, and a glow hung over the sky to proclaim the message that London was burning. We now knew we were truly at war.

My personal war was with town clerks, borough councils, the Whitehall bureaucracy. Perhaps we were all in a state of shock, all except the professionals dishing out the propaganda of heroics. The East End caught the brunt of the attack, and I hurried down to Spitalfields, an area I knew well from my girls' club days. Soldiers were clearing paths through the devastation to keep the traffic moving, street-wardens rotated around each other in search of something they could usefully do. A scheme for civilian protection lay somewhere in orderly office files, and early in the war many thousands of Londoners had been evacuated to safer areas, along with the capital's schoolchildren. During the lull before the storm a great proportion had drifted back, plans had gone rusty, precautions lackadaisical, and the entire metropolis caught unawares.

Beneath the girders of a huge covered area, part of Spitalfields wholesale fruit market, citizens took possession of the warehouse and huddled together for warmth and solace. Others clamoured for information from any official-looking person they could find as to where they might obtain food, or an aspirin. Across the road, in the crypt of a church, people were camped around, and even inside, the ancient tombs, as though the division between life and death had disappeared. The scene could have been stolen from Dante's *Inferno*. Everything a person needed for his day – a change of clothing, a hot beverage, a sense of order, had been blown sky high, along with the friendly neighbourhood grocery store.

In the horror of it I found myself talking to three of the most remarkable men it has ever been my good fortune to encounter. One of them, Ritchie Calder, was ostensibly reporting the scene for the *Daily Herald* but he had shed his journalistic detachment to become a partisan. He angrily proposed organizing a march on Whitehall. He was putting this to Father John Groser, a local priest who took his ministry into havoc's maw, recognizing that here was a time when a lavatory was more important than an altar. And between them the impelling figure of Mickey Davis, four feet high. His home was not destroyed, for indeed he never owned one. 'Mickey the Midget' as the East End knew him lived

181

as a Spitalfields stray, but in this crisis he was the commander, self-appointed. Joining these three I thought to myself, goodness, another committee!

Tea was being handed out to rescue teams, demolition workers and others with white initials stamped on their black tin helmets; for the masses, nothing. Ritchie Calder went off to telephone a report to his paper. No doubt it would be heavily subbed, to show how bravely London was 'taking it'. What about food for the people? I asked. Mickey thought this would need an age to organize. A siren wailed. 'It's the banshees,' croaked an old Irish lady pushing a pram filled with bedding.

Next morning, instead of going to Baker Street, I made my way to the Ministry of Food in Page Street. I had not before penetrated any of those bastions of government but entered unchallenged, determined to speak with – anyone! Sidling past a commissionaire I pushed open a door and into a roomful of clattering typewriters. I was confronted by a tall figure who described himself as the Public Relations Officer and enquired after my business. (He was, in fact, Howard Marshall the broadcaster, later a BBC war correspondent. Marshall was Britain's leading exponent in the art of trout- and salmon-fishing. Why the Ministry required a specialist in such luxury foods when its concerns rarely extended beyond miserable creations like powdered egg and spam, I never knew.)

'You've got to get something going for the homeless down the East End,' I warned him, 'or they'll rush this place and tear it to bits.' What Marshall thought of the sudden appearance of this apparition with her peculiar way of speaking English I cannot surmise. Even my attire must have given him cause for wonderment. My generous frame was covered in a camel-hair coat into which my mink was sewn for a lining. But just then an air-raid alarm sounded, and we hustled with everyone else to the basement shelter.

'That's Lord Woolton, the Minister,' Marshall said, indicating a grey-haired man in a corner. 'Why don't you tackle him?'

I did. Woolton was not unfamiliar with persistent females of my kind, for he had been in business with Rex Cohen of Lewis's, the Liverpool department store. He heard me out until the 'all clear!' and invited me upstairs to his office. Summoning his personal assistant John Maud, later Lord Redcliffe-Maud, he boomed an instruction: 'This lady is Mrs Solomon. Find out what she needs, and make sure she gets it.'

Maud made notes. I wanted everything necessary to equip emergency field kitchens. Once again my Welfare Department, with Simon Marks's approval, took the lead. Volunteers were enrolled and we installed canteens in the largest shelters. Steaming plates of rich stew could be had for the price of the proverbial packet of Woodbines. The East End first, and then wherever we heard of a need.

The Spitalfields shelter developed a life of its own. It was my favourite, I was practically a member. We tried to smarten the place up, got some entertainment going, even a library. For weeks on end it became home for many of the three thousand people sleeping there; many of those without a place of work to go to hung around during the daylight hours too, for the bombers' menacing throb could be heard at any time. Each day was different, but twilight brought its own routine: men and women, or children, marking out a patch of ground with a blanket to secure their family space. Petty criminals loitered among the law-abiding citizenry, but if fights broke out Mickey and his band of deputies, armed with megaphones, could generally make peace, in the forthright language of the East End. More serious incidents brought the police. After a while tiered bunks were introduced, but until then the least forgivable offence was to step upon someone else's blanket.

We improvised a medical service. The doctor I knew best lived in Suite 210 of the Dorchester Hotel, Park Lane. Vera Weizmann hadn't practised since her Manchester days over twenty years earlier, but together with others she now formed a roster for the sick-bay organized by the Red Cross. Before long they had delivered a baby, whom we privately baptized Shelterina. Nothing would induce me, not even the hollering of the wardens, to wear my tin helmet. It swung from my hand by the strap, like a glove. A lump of shrapnel once struck it with a nasty clink. I would have sustained an injury had that helmet been on my head.

Scotland Yard loaned me Inspector Caine. I first made his acquaintance during the 'Fifth Column' scare after the fall of France in June 1940, when a branch of Intelligence took over the top floor of Marks and Spencer's headquarters at Baker Street. Anyone of German or Austrian origin was suspect. My department had a secretary with such a past and Arthur Caine wanted an eye kept on her. Ironically, Kim Philby worked upstairs for a time but who dreamed that the really dangerous traitors could be upper-class Englishmen vintaged from William the Conqueror?

Each evening as the sirens heralded a visit from the Luftwaffe the inspector picked me up in his police-car and we raced through the traffic lights towards another scene of destruction, death, and the occasional hysterical woman tearful over her lost budgerigar. Within the hour we would be dishing out our soups and sandwiches from our mobile canteens.

I don't suppose I shall ever forget that dawn with London shaking the dust from another sleepless night, people moving dazed among the ruins in search of some possessions as if to re-assure themselves of their lost identity, and I stood with my girls ready with our containers of soup. A man looked up and ever so casually observed: 'There she is, the lady of the ladle.' Ritchie put it in an article (and later in his book *Carry on London*). The name stuck.

Ritchie Calder, Arthur Caine, Mickey the Midget, John Groser, we forged a bond never to be severed. Come the day-time and we would often repair to my new flat off Curzon Street for a drink, and perhaps a sleep – my home in Addison Road had itself caught a fire-bomb so I had to salvage what I could and find another billet. London had settled into its eerie routine by November 1940, when suddenly I received a phone call from Zina Jackson (she was one of the graduates whose salaries had evoked protest from Simon Marks), speaking from Leamington, in the Midlands. 'Coventry is destroyed,' Zina reported. 'The entire town centre has gone, the cathedral, our store. There's no bread and no water. I've brought all our people here to Leamington.' I drove up at once.

Coventry's was, outside London, the worst air-raid of the blitz. I found a dead city. We set up a mobile canteen – the only other one to be seen belonged to the Women's Voluntary Service (WVS) – while Marks and Spencer sent up van-loads of merchandise. It was government policy to keep shops open, for nothing raised morale more than a show of normality. Head Office personnel looked round the town and discovered a garage, large, cold and disused. The ordeal of Coventry began on a Thursday night, and endured for twelve hours. By Friday the place was in the icy grip of shock and fear. On the Saturday, to the amazement of the City Fathers, our store was operating from that garage. It filled up with shoppers, Coventry's survivors. We were the first business to return. Raids were then directed upon Southampton, and Plymouth. A dozen Marks and Spencer branches in provincial towns went up in smoke within a matter of weeks, with others extensively damaged. Wherever our girls were left without a store they were put to work in a communal restaurant.

I was now a regular visitor to the Ministry of Food. Lord Woolton grew a little tired of my mink-lined coat, and my restaurants. He passed me over to his assistant Jock Menzies, in charge of community feeding for the entire population – he sent me letters from all over the country that always began 'Dear Mata Hari'. A few doors beyond Menzies' office along the corridor Barbara Castle, as yet bearing her maiden name of Barbara Betts, sat among other civil servants in a state of perpetual exasperation. In 1944 she asked: 'Can't you rescue me from this mad-house? I'd love to work at Marks and Spencer.' By this time I knew her well enough to understand she was a political animal, through and through. 'You won't be happy with us,' I replied. Barbara was already a borough councillor, endowed with good looks as well as brains, and a certainty for eminence in the Labour Party. She ended the war with a job on the *Daily Mirror*.

Woolton was himself no mean politician of course, and he summoned me to his private sanctum. 'I have a message for you, Lady of the Ladle,' he announced. 'It's from the Prime Minister. Why do you describe your feeding centres as communal restaurants? Are you a Communist? Mr Churchill wants them to be called "British Restaurants".' That was all right with me, but I too had a complaint.

'While the working classes have to make do with their weekly ounces of meat, and fortnightly egg, and a measly ration of butter, those with money enough can gorge themselves sick on the un-rationed luxuries in hotels and restaurants. That's not fair!' He saw my point. I recommended that catering establishments be ordered to place a maximum price on their meals, feeding their clientele accordingly. No-one would go hungry on, say a five-shilling menu. Woolton implemented the idea, and the system remained, like the British Restaurants, throughout the war, and in fact for a few sorry years afterwards.

I had the idea also of canning our famous stew as a 'blitz broth'. The recipe, based on beetroot, carrots, potatoes and soya beans, bore a faint resemblance to Russian *borscht*. I sent the first six tins to Woolton. It was Christmas-time, and he presumed

185

they were intended as a personal gift. No, they were for his approval as an emergency ration. Well, he liked the stuff – so did I. Before the end of the war his ministry produced hundreds of thousands of cans and secreted them in remote food camps. How many were used never came to be revealed. Perhaps they are still awaiting excavation by some future archaeologist digging in the Pennines, or the Scottish moors, or under Mount Snowdon!

Repeated attack from the skies could not bring Britain to submission, but it infected the national character with a kind of sullen lassitude. A dispirited Philby had assured me, on the fall of France the year before, that the intervention of Russia alone could save us from inevitable collapse. Russia? The ally of Hitler who had grabbed half of Poland and swallowed the Baltic countries? People like me hated everything associated with Communism. 'Yes,' Kim insisted. 'Only with Russia's help can we defeat the Fascists.' In June 1941 Hitler moved against Moscow, Churchill made his great speech and Stalin was now good old Uncle Joe: whisper a word against him and you incurred distrust.

I was on a train going north and fell into conversation with a humbly dressed old lady entranced by the idea of meeting a Russian in person. As she left the train at her station she begged me to take her week's sweet coupons. 'Please, I so much want you to have them, you're such a wonderful people. And your Red Army is so brave.'

Willy-nilly, my Marks and Spencer Welfare Department was swept into the general affairs of Britain at war, in contrast to other departments condemned to conduct business as usual. They resented our being in the thick of things. Apart from the chairman himself and Teddy Sieff, Israel's younger brother, I don't recall any executive of Marks and Spencer taking an interest in what we were doing. This was understandable. The young and healthy went off to fight, leaving these others to hold the boring commercial fort. I did receive a somewhat left-handed compliment on a questionnaire we left around at the British Restaurants for patrons' suggestions. Asked what arrangements the person made for midday meals prior to the opening of the restaurant, a male clerk aged forty-eight wrote: 'Sandwiches, or in cafés run by foreigners and Jews, and we can do without both of them.' That one I retained for posterity. I enrolled Hannah Marks, Simon's daughter, at one of the cash-desks, for the restaurants were none of *his* business. She lived on an allowance not far below my own in an earlier incarnation, I suppose, pound-notes melting around her like snow in the tropics. My, what a head for figures that girl revealed, just like her father! She never closed the till until the last penny was accounted for, though it could mean remaining behind alone for hours at her post.

Inevitably, the big battalions were on the prowl. On the establishment of the earliest British Restaurants I was invited by Lady Reading, head of the WVS, to join forces with her people. She asked me over to their headquarters, solemnly presented me with a badge and offered their uniform. I wasn't having a uniform, and I refused to shelter under her benign umbrella. I admired Stella Reading for her qualities as a fantastic organizer. If only Britain appointed women generals she would have run the whole war and, I've no doubt, shortened it by a year or two. Nevertheless I preferred my freedom, for I could barge in anywhere while I had the Marks and Spencer name behind me, taking over premises without authorization, heaving reluctant officials into action.

Naturally Stella was displeased. And my reputation spread as an awkward customer throwing her considerable weight around (nothing I tried, nor the meagre ration allowance of the government, could slim me down). This didn't terrify one of her deputies, Barbara Wallace, in the least. She asked Lionel Cohen to arrange a meeting. I turned up at the Ritz and there was Barbie, as she was called, looking absolutely stunning in that drab green WVS uniform. She said, as though propitiating one of the gods: 'My brother Robert is married to a Jewess, a relative of your Dr Weizmann.' Now I knew she was a Lutyens. We pledged to keep in touch, and I won a friend who was to enrich my later years and teach me the true meaning of courage.

Barbie was fated to a life of tragedy, but she had the English-woman's heart of oak. With her three sisters and brother she had been raised practically motherless after Lady Emily Lutyens fell headlong into the arms of Annie Besant and the Theosophists to become besotted with the boy prophet Krishnamurti, supposedly the personalization of all the deities past and future. In the process of following that beautiful, solemn youth across the world, Emily had no time for husband, home or family. Edwin Landseer Lutyens, the eminent architect, placed an H in front of his initials, turning E.L.L. into HELL. Barbie's husband, Capt.

Euan Wallace, one of Chamberlain's faithfuls in his 'appease-ment' government, died early in the war and Barbie gave her mansion near Petworth to the authorities for a maternity home for evacuees. When the bombing intensified she offered me one of several cottages on the estate as a bolt-hole. I had neither desire nor need for a bolt-hole; I lived in a fairly new block boasting that rare luxury, an underground shelter.

I took the cottage just the same, furnishing it as a weekend tuckaway for Marks and Spencer staff so that they might have an occasional respite from the blitz. Adjacent to it another cottage was occupied by Pamela Churchill. She lived there with her baby Winston, having already left Randolph – she was still black and blue from the brief experience of being his wife. Barbie worried about red-haired Pamela, so much was evident. The girl needed to do some work to stabilize her, she was opting for a career of reckless bohemianism, but was far too young for such a life. She could be a gracious, witty hostess, and it didn't surprise me at all when, as Mrs Averell Harriman, she was anointed queen of the American Democratic Party. In the meantime here she was, bruised all over, and little Winston Churchill crawling under the kitchen table.

With Barbie Wallace as my scout, an unending trail of volun-teers came to me for a job in the British Restaurants. To many it was just a game: Anne O'Neill, still married to her Irish peer but later to be widowed and become Lady Rothermere, and after that Mrs Ian Fleming; Dodo Hankey, sister-in-law of the Cabinet Secretary; and Freda Casa Maury, better known as Mrs Dudley Ward, who was for many years, until replaced by Mrs Simpson, the constant companion of the Prince of Wales. All the purple-named rushed to help, some of them doubtless because the restaurants were classed as national service and spared them conscription into a dirtier job. Freda Casa Maury got her own back on me – she roped me into her Feathers Club, founded in the thirties by the Prince of Wales, for working-class youth.

My war seemed to be speeding by. I had little time to be defeatist, or to listen to those eternal bomb stories, or even to attend my sister-in-law Vera Benenson's concerts at the Wig-more Hall – she alternated with Myra Hess and Harriet Cohen to give recitals against the tumult of the blitz, and the pilot-less 'doodlebugs', and the volleys of rockets that were Goering's last fling over London. (In 1983, at the age of ninety-five, Vera Benenson was still entrancing audiences at the Wigmore Hall.)

But the struggle was exacting its uneven toll. Barbie had three sons of her own and two step-sons. Three of them were killed in the battle, another died soon after demobilization. Sadly, she even survived her youngest, Billy Wallace, Princess Margaret's one-time escort. We wept together.

To all my world I was a food person, a kitchen organizer and, incidentally, a person privileged with an ample supply of petrol coupons for her motor-car. So I also became a taxi-driver of sorts, and among my passengers during London's ordeal Chaim and Vera Weizmann registered as a priority. They could take occasional refuge at the country home in Bosham, near Chichester, of their friend Sigmund Gestetner, whose father had built a great business with his invention of the duplicator process. Chaim both served and fought Britain. He was the Ministry of Supply's honorary consultant on chemical matters, a position of great responsibility, but he also chastized Britain for keeping Jews out of Palestine and obstructing the raising of a Jewish Army as a formal ally under its own flag. In this second endeavour he pressed for the appointment as commander of Orde Wingate, the soldier venerated by the Jews for his passionate devotion to the Zionist cause and his bravery in leading an Anglo-Jewish force during the Arab rebellion before the war.

To conquer Palestine for the Jews was Wingate's dearest wish, but such enthusiasm rendered him *persona non grata* at the War Office. In the calculations of the Army Council he could just as readily command a Jewish force against the British. This devout Scottish Christian, who studied Hebrew, was into the bargain somewhat unbalanced; he had attempted suicide while stamping his feet in Cairo after his successful campaign against the Italians in Abyssinia. No matter how hard Weizmann laboured on his behalf, no-one would dream of letting him back into Palestine.

I was deputed to take the Weizmanns, with Maidie (an ex-daughter-in-law now, marriage to Benjamin Weizmann having proved an impossible state) to join Orde Wingate for a weekend at Gestetner's, whose own wife and children were evacuated to Australia. Sigmund Gestetner proved the most considerate of hosts, with a lively sense of fun, and his house fronted the loveliest coastline: this meant Bosham was richly supplied with excellent fish, while poor London only offered fish queues. Further, he had spare accommodation in the form of a large adjacent house named Four Winds; I made a mental reservation to acquire it as a holiday-home for Marks and Spencer employees.

The evening of our arrival saw a fine catch of gleaming plaice. 'If only I had a dressing to go with it,' the cook said, 'this would be a banquet. I can produce a couple of eggs and some lemon juice, but we're out of cooking oil.' Vera challenged me. 'You feed the masses, Flora. You've invented a blitz broth. Why not mayonnaise?'

Vera's hearing was bad – that's why she never learnt Hebrew and only went to see foreign films, with sub-titles. She couldn't have heard my reply properly when I spotted a bottle of medicinal paraffin and wondered aloud whether this could substitute for the oil. She merely said 'Yes', absently, as deafish people do, with a mechanical nod of her head.

They smacked their lips at the tasty dressing I produced for our feast. However, that night we all met frequently in the corridor, in a fish-queue of sorts. How was I to know that liquid paraffin was a prescribed laxative? 'Flora's mayonnaise' was never to be forgotten.

Shortly afterwards Chaim and Vera left for America, but while waiting at Bristol for a plane to Lisbon, the way VIPs were generally routed in those days, word reached us in London that their younger son Michael, an RAF pilot, had not returned from an operational mission over the Bay of Biscay. Simon Marks broke the news to them, by telephone from Baker Street. They returned to London, in the hope of Michael's rescue, or to learn perhaps of his safe arrival in a prison-camp. It was not to be. I knew the boy from his birth, and that famous occasion in 1916, recounted earlier, of his circumcision. It was subsequently established that he might have been found, but the planes out searching for him were ordered back to go after the battle-cruisers *Scharnhorst* and *Gneisenau*, then preying upon the shipping in the Atlantic. Both parents aged visibly under their ordeal.

Resuming the journey, Weizmann pressed his cause for a Jewish Army in the more favourable climate of the United States. It was after Pearl Harbour and America, yesterday a benevolent neutral, became transfigured into the senior ally. Chaim extolled the virtues of Wingate to all and sundry, making particular impact on General Marshall. This had some effect, though not in the way Chaim intended. Orde was summoned to join the ship taking Churchill to the Quebec Conference as a member of the

Prime Minister's staff. Caught completely by surprise, he had no time to get his luggage together, for the vessel was on the point of sailing. A tailor on board fitted him out with a change of clothing.

Orde eventually received a command. It was as far away from Palestine as the War Office could catapult him, to lead the Chindits in Burma. He died there, following a plane-crash, in the jungle. One of my armchairs was henceforth regularly occupied by Gladwyn Jebb, of the Foreign Office, hoping, as he day-dreamed of being appointed Ambassador to France, for a glimpse of Orde's wife Lorna. She rented an upstairs flat, and Gladwyn Jebb was one of the countless men captivated by her beauty.

A bereavement more deeply personal to me was the loss, in 1943, of Harold's cousin the gentle Wilfrid Israel, of the Berlin department-store family but 'Made in England'. He visited me prior to a trip abroad on a mission of Jewish rescue. His plane was shot down over Europe (a fellow-passenger was the actor Leslie Howard).

One never knew what work people did; one never asked. My sister Manya was recruited into the Political Intelligence Department at the Foreign Office, no doubt because she was that rare jewel in London, impeccably bilingual in English and Russian. She and her chief, Marjorie Villiers, had two things in common: the Catholic Church and a passion for animals. On such foundations fruitful partnerships can be built, and theirs was the Harvill Press, established in 1947. Ralph Harari also joined his wife's department. Ralph had been economic adviser to Wavell while the General commanded the Middle East Forces, returning to England on the latter's 'banishment' by Churchill to India.

The Harari son and heir, fourteen-year-old Michael, attended Ampleforth College, the Catholic school near York. One day, on my way back from a trip to the Midlands, I heard on the radio-set in my car of an explosion in an express train travelling north, in which boys from Ampleforth sustained serious casualties. It was the end of the Easter holidays so I knew Michael was on that train. I turned my car round and after an interminable journey reached Grantham station, where the train was halted. Manya had already arrived. Six boys lay dead on stretchers in the waiting-room, among them two sons of the Belgian Prime Minister-in-Exile, M. Pierlot. Seven others, including Michael, were terribly burnt. Packed in the room parents swayed and prayed, with Ampleforth school-masters, all of them priests, administering last rites. Lourdes, I felt, must be something like this. I stared at poor Michael, mutilated and bandaged, and remembered the face of his grandfather.

An inquest revealed a story of the boys larking with matches while lighting cigarettes, setting their compartment on fire (the compartment was locked, the railway witness said, to prevent passengers moving from third-class to first-class carriages). Michael was commended for pushing his school-mates through the window to safety, thereby incurring injury to his hands as well as his head. Five years later, his face restored after a series of graftings by Sir Archie McIndoe, brilliant plastic surgeon of the RAF 'Guinea Pigs', Michael received the Belt of Honour at a passing-out parade of Tank Corps cadets. Thankfully, the war was then over.

Pamela Digby, to give her original name, for I never think of her as Pamela Churchill, or Pamela Hayward, or Pamela Harriman, has herself spoken of the impact upon London of the American invasion following Pearl Harbor. Indeed, England as a whole suffered from culture-shock. Our new allies blew a fresh wind through our tired society with their easy manners and that youthful earnestness touched through with naiveté. They couldn't understand our rules, we were outraged by theirs. The great ballroom at Grosvenor House was transformed into a huge cafeteria where mountains of unconsumed food went daily into the slop bins, ironic comment on those Ministry of Food notices in the Press to the British housewife on how to spread a potato round an entire family. Americans were not strangers to me, my sister Fira was one herself and I had a constant overflow from her New York connections. The activity generated by the Americans took some time before it had any actual impact upon the war, but from the very beginning it created a vast new industry on the home front – looking after them, keeping them amused, all under the slogan of hospitality.

Here in London sat the Drexel Biddles, amidst a display of wealth that was the talk of this war-scarred, undernourished city. From their suite at the Ritz Tony Biddle held a position of sorts as US Ambassador to the various governments-in-exile from Central and Eastern Europe. His main task was to stop them quarrelling among themselves over ancient rivalries which history had ostensibly settled in the Thirty Years War. His chief preoccupation was to squeeze in a daily game of tennis, in which he excelled. His wife Margaret, daughter of the copper magnate Schultze, wore a Red Cross uniform designed by Molyneux.

Margaret Biddle had taken charge of the American nurses' home in Mayfair. When she asked around for a person to set up its restaurant her spies directed her to the Lady of the Ladle. Margaret's office in Charles Street was adorned with two Coramandel screens and other Orientalia that betokened a long heritage of piracy. Her qualities of administration impressed me, though not half as much as I was impressed by the nurses – very superior they were, with top-grade diplomas, and all uppishly parading their military grades. Margaret had comestibles on order of a standard to feed the gods, and I found her a Cypriot cook equal to the challenge. After the war he was too good to lose: needless to say, I brought him and his wife over to Marks and Spencer, for the directors' dining-room.

Sir Harry Brittain, founder of the Pilgrims, progenitor of the Anglo-American 'special relationship', and Sir Edward Grigg of the War Office – my 'White Knights', I called them – asked me to organize a club for American officers. I looked warily at them. I already served on a Ministry of Supply committee dealing with hostels for factory girls, and an Appeals Tribunal for those seeking exemption from national service. But I could think of only one question: 'Who's going to pay for it?'

'Don't you worry about that,' they replied. 'Brendan Bracken fathered the idea, and he's got the money from the banks. We can use Westminster School, in Dean's Yard – the boys are evacuated.' So I agreed, provided Barbie Wallace came in with me. She needed no second bidding, and enlisted Pamela who, having produced the mandatory Churchill grandson, was now underemployed. The three of us had lunch on it, total cost fifteen shillings, constituted ourselves the committee, and the Churchill Club for American Officers was born. It was fitted out with all the amenities we considered attended the American way of life, though I've no doubt many a lieutenant from some Dakotan hick-town could, with an effort, have adjusted to quarters slightly less luxurious.

We furnished the Churchill Club with fine antiques, all provided free, and pictures loaned from West End art dealers. Catering? Women clamoured to work there just to take home the left-overs to their hungry families. My Russian soul dwelt on food for the spirit, and we arranged lectures and musical soirées.

The first to come and lecture, sent by the American Embassy, turned out to be Herbert Agar, the Pulitzer Prize winner who had just written *A Time for Greatness*. At the end of the war Barbie and he were married.

And if the reader is wondering about me I shall have to speak of George Backer, the man described by Theodore White in *The Making of the President 1960* as 'one of the finest minds of the Democratic Party'. Anglophile almost to a fault, George wrote plays with Robert Sherwood and S. N. Behrman and did his bit for victory in London together with William Paley, Chief of CBS, in the Office of War Information. George schemed up ideas for psychological warfare in collaboration with Ritchie Calder, Richard Crossman and John Strachey. I would often place the whisky bottle in front of the four of them in my flat and then leave the room.

George Backer, being so close to Averell Harriman – in fact he was to champion the Governor without avail in a celebrated 'Stop Kennedy' campaign for the Democratic nomination – confessed his greatest ambition to me – to become an ambassador. He certainly had the brains, and the means, and the connections, but apparently these were not qualifications enough; George lacked the single-mindedness. He was handsome, and though something of a snob, in the American, intellectual sense, I might have been persuaded to marry him. All New York knew of his memorable ten years as Dorothy Schiff's husband. Together they founded the *New York Post*, though she kept it in her name. When she took up with Tom Thackeray, another journalist, out went George Backer, both as editor and spouse.

He hung around my flat without actually asking me to be his wife – he was waiting for *me* to propose. Soon after the war he told me of a girl he'd met, widow of a flyer. Should he marry her? 'George, you have my blessing,' I said. Certainly, I could have had him at that moment, but he sounded so feckless. I have never regretted it. More preferable to me was the relationship I formed with Albert C. Barnes, the self-made millionaire who invented the formula for the antiseptic Argyrol and converted his fortune into a great museum of art in Merion, Pennsylvania. Our friendship began well before the war.

Albert Barnes must be classed among the world's originals. He worked his way through medical school by playing basketball and then practised in a hospital for the insane; that, he said, equipped him for life. At his chemical works his employees had to stop whatever they were doing for two hours every day to study his favourite philosophers, and when he opened his renowned museum in Philadelphia, containing no less than two hundred Renoirs and countless other Impressionists, he allowed hardly anyone in. Should a visitor ring for admission his servants were instructed to call out, 'The house has an infectious disease!' Well, he couldn't take the pictures with him, so Pennsylvania got them in the end. Albert created the Barnes Foundation and engaged Bertrand Russell to lecture after Russell was barred from City College of New York as an immoral influence. The story goes that the sage had to fight for the paltry eight thousand dollars a year Albert granted him. Ours could be called an *amitié amoureuse*, I suppose, brought to a sudden halt with Albert's death in a motor-car crash.

All kinds of characters seemed to find an excuse for sleeping at my flat with its convenient air-raid shelter. Among my self-invited lodgers Frank Pakenham, later Lord Longford, deserves the accolade for staying the longest. He occupied my spare room for months, sharing my fond belief that the flat was safe – in fact, being over the entrance arch, it was the reverse of secure – while he worked for William Beveridge on the latter's social security plan. Frank would go to his family in the country for weekends. He found in me an object of absorbing interest and plied me with questions about my background, but, strangely, he never once referred to those times at our later meetings. He was a little like Clive Garsia in some respects. Clive, an old soldier, offered to help out on the roof during my turn of duty at fire-watching, which no-one was supposed to avoid. Clive brought a deck-chair up only as far as the top-floor corridor and slept through the night every time, awakening by coincidence on the break-fast-call.

Frank Pakenham's post in the social services gave him some responsibility for the hostels to which women called up for work in the armaments' factories were accommodated. Lord Beaverbrook put me on the appropriate committee so it was in this area that Frank and I became colleagues. My visits to the hostels, and the factories, could be a disheartening experience. Some girls thrive in strange environments, while others will feel uprooted and insecure. This can cause depression, with nervous indigestion, a fear of the factory floor and a tendency towards absenteeism. In those days it was difficult to explain to the men in authority that women were not weaker than the other sex, their emotions were differently distributed.

It was therefore arranged for Marks and Spencer girls to be called up together. They could then travel as a group to their new accommodation in a distant town, and be accompanied until properly settled in by one of our trained welfare workers. We were thus able to maintain contact with them as a body, send them news of old colleagues and organize hospitality by Marks and Spencer staff in their new environment. Where applicable, the scheme was adopted by other large companies. We would go up to greet them and show they were not forgotten by the old firm, at the same time looking over their factories and the facilities provided in them. One of my suggestions, adopted by the Ministry of Supply, was to paint those grim machines in bright colours, even giving them names, as was done with war-planes.

Filling shells with explosives, a most unpleasant task, was mostly women's work. The ingredients contained sulphur, which tinged skin and hair a peculiar yellow, evoking the First World War description of 'canary girls'. I told my committee about this but my report was shrugged off, in the hope that somehow the problem would solve itself. I was stubborn, and skin creams were distributed for the girls' use, together with scarves to wear as turbans. Details such as this involved me in the most ridiculous battles of will.

The reactions of working people under war-time stress, bombing, rationing and so forth, particularly interested the American social anthropologist Margaret Mead. Already somewhat over-conscious of her reputation, she had come to Britain to give some lectures, at the same time studying the 'natives' roughly as she had scrutinized the tribes of New Guinea. I was deputed to take her to a mining area, and chose Newcastle. Margaret Mead had a friend and admirer in one of my colleagues, Marie ('Mitzi') Jahoda, an Austrian refugee with experience of similar work in the United States. The three of us travelled north together.

Barbie Wallace's sister Ursula had married Lord Ridley and lived in Northumberland, not far from Newcastle. She tended towards melancholia, not surprisingly for a daughter of Emily Lutyens. I agreed to call on her. Ursula had established a children's hospital at her house, and Barbie wished me to see the work. It was based on a principle then considered an innovation, that infants in hospital benefited if their mothers remained with them.

We three from London, accompanied by an official of the National Union of Mineworkers, visited several mining villages, interviewed the men at the pithead and had tea with their wives in those grim ranks of back-to-back cottages. Come the weekend, Margaret and Mitzi rested up while Lord Ridley collected me to stay at his home for a couple of nights. Ursula laid on a marvellous lunch, with grapes and peaches from their hot-houses. My mind pictured another kind of lunch: cold sandwiches eaten by the miners from a tin box, and a bath after work in the kitchen – we had noted it all, with anything escaping our attention filled in by the man from the Miners' Union.

Ridley politely enquired about my business so far north of Baker Street. I described what we had seen, and the disgrace of it. Well, that started something. Did I not realize those cottages belonged to him, asked Ridley, and that those miners were his employees? The Ridleys had lived in Northumberland for centuries, he was chairman of practically everything in these parts, and what had all this to do with three ignorant women, one an American, one an Austrian, and one a Russian?

They gave me a room at the end of a rambling passage. That evening I changed and, absolutely miserable, came down for dinner. A strange atmosphere permeated the great house. I was due to remain until the Monday morning, when Ridley was to take me back to Newcastle. It would be interminable, so I telephoned Mitzi and got her to ring me back on some pretext of being required urgently in Newcastle. Early on Sunday morning I crept out like a mouse, without saying goodbye to anyone and leaving a note of apology behind, along with half my possessions. A flash of my petrol coupons and I was able to hire a taxi all the way back. I never saw that children's hospital. Shortly afterwards Ursula died suddenly – another tragedy for Barbie.

In the meantime, the British had cause to raise a cheer as the Germans fell back at El Alamein and became a trapped force in Stalingrad. Not the beginning of the end, Churchill said, but the end of the beginning. I now waited with bated breath as the armies of Uncle Joe gnawed their way through my childhood turf in the deliverance of Russia: across the Don Valley to Rostov and Kharkov, round the Sea of Azov and down to the Crimea. I could sense the lash of the winds sweeping across the frozen wastes between colliding multitudes of men, and the thaw that held up the Soviet advance across the Dnieper. I trembled as Leningrad was at last relieved, and when Kiev, then Minsk and Pinsk, were recovered in the inexorable progress of the Red Army. It was a trembling of pride, as though this was my personal vindication, repayment to Britain for accepting such a woman, with all the peculiarities of her Russian personality, as one of its own. I did not as yet know enough, though suspected much, of the other side of the epic then unfolding – how all Europe was made into a cemetery, and especially so for my own folk, the Jewish people.

My duty, I thought, pointed me towards those politically-minded friends who remained unconvinced that the Jews were entitled to a homeland of their own, doubting still that we were the stuff of which nations are made. Many would listen courteously, in the English way, conceding the argument outwardly while secretly nurturing an opposite belief. I recall particularly John Ward, of Anthony Eden's staff and after the war Ambassador to Italy. He came back from a conference in Moscow in 1944 with a case of caviare and – another luxury – a dozen lemons. We had a banquet, and I was sure I had made a Zionist out of him. Suddenly one night he telephoned. 'Flora,' he said, 'before you read it in tomorrow's papers I want you to know that Lord Moyne, our Minister-Resident in Cairo, has been assassinated. By your Zionists.'

My Zionists! Jewish murderers were mine; Jews doing their normal duty on every war front, or contributing their expertise while hidden away as boffins, were not mine, just British, or American, or Russian. The balance must ever be weighted against us.

Of course it was a shocking crime, and a Jewish tragedy. Winston Churchill turned cold towards Zionism, Moyne being his close friend. Chaim Weizmann once told me, 'If I am ever assassinated it will not be by an Arab, but a Jew.' He had his Jewish Army in the end, dwarf-sized, as a Brigade Group, a gesture thrown at him just in time for the concluding battle of the war.

How typical, that in fighting this war in the defence of freedom, the British people had learnt to live without it, almost contentedly! We cared hardly at all that there had been no General Election for ten years. More civilians died than soldiers, as many problems were created as were solved. Alongside my block of flats Shepherd Market straggled like a bazaar. It was

198

noted less for its fruit and vegetables than for the ladies offering their delights to the passing fancier. The Union Jack now fluttered proudly from their unwashed windows, sanctioned no doubt by the smartly dressed gentlemen who controlled their trade.

Cries of 'good old Winnie' filled the air. With the rest of Britain I venerated Churchill; though I wonder, in retrospect, if the flags hanging out from the windows of the prostitutes reinforced my conviction to go into the polling-booth and cast my vote not for *Geroi nashevo Vremeni*, the Hero of our Time, but for the politician described as the Invisible Man, the Socialist Clement Attlee.

10 My 'Brave New World'

As the ragwort and thistle thrust and twisted through the crumbled limestone of our cavernous bomb-sites, the men returned from the war – among them a Marks and Spencer generation for whom a cliché was waiting, the Young Turks.

Simon Marks gained recognition for his multifarious good works on the home front and was rewarded with a knighthood, later a peerage. He had run the company virtually alone, with Teddy Sieff, Israel's younger brother, at his right hand. Israel himself spent the major part of the war seeking markets for British exports in America. I was awarded the MBE for my contribution – Kim Philby's OBE appeared in the same list – and must admit to a measure of surprise and pride to find myself singled out for a picture on the front page of the *News Chronicle*, with the anticipation of my first peep into the recesses of Buckingham Palace. I never got there, however. The Court was in mourning at the time, for some obscure royal apparently, and my medal arrived in the post along with a crop of advertising mail and an invitation to subscribe to an organization concerned with the welfare of camels aging in some remote corner of Arabia Deserta.

(When, many years later, the Beatles were similarly honoured, some recipients of the MBE returned their decorations in resentment against association with pop musicians, no matter how celebrated. Personally, I was delighted; after all, I had received mine for feeding the masses, so why shouldn't they be recognized for entertaining the masses?)

In 1946, on returning from a visit to Palestine, I discovered how the MBE could function as a protection against the clumsy rudeness of petty officials. Palestine was in turmoil at the time, and I reached London the day following the bomb outrage upon British headquarters at the King David Hotel in Jerusalem. There had been a large number of deaths, and the airport was alive with CID men on the look-out for terrorists.

200

'What have you been doing in Palestine?' a customs officer queried.

'I've been on holiday there.'

'On holiday! To a country in a state of armed revolt? Where exactly did you spend this holiday?'

I had as a matter of fact been with the Weizmanns at Rehovot, but I was not going to submit any further to this public catechism. Drawing myself up to my full importance I asked the customs officer: 'Are you a Member of the British Empire?'

'Why do you ask?' he stammered, surprised.

'Because I am a Member of the *Order* of the British Empire. And if you've any further questions please call on me at my home, and I shall be glad to answer them.' That was the end of it. Since then I have placed my decoration where it might have impact, on my passport.

Marcus Sieff, son of Israel and Becky, returned from army service intent upon taking war-weary Marks and Spencer in hand. His was a distinguished record, front-line service alternating with staff work, so in surveying the situation within the family firm, he led with his strong chin. Marcus described himself to me as 'ruthless, ambitious and energetic', but I also found him compassionate. Hannah Marks' husband Alec Lerner, whose romance with the chairman's daughter was born of his war-time enjoyment, as a Canadian medical officer, of her parents' hospitality at their country home in Sunningdale, now emerged as Simon's blue-eyed boy: a surrogate for the son who avoided Baker Street like the plague. Michael Sacher, as Harry Sacher's son, ranked perceptibly lower in the hierarchy. A veteran of Eighth Army battles, he was younger in years and of gentler disposition than his cousin Marcus. His considerable talent for administration took him to the heart of problems associated with development of the business in the post-war world.

The family tradition of charitable works, including support for the arts, and for working in the Jewish cause (now revealed as poignantly necessary in the loss of a third of the people in the European holocaust), was faithfully maintained in this new generation. Not altogether unreasonably, some people mistook the great commercial house – 'Simon Marks and the Forty Sieffs' Dick Crossman dubbed it – for a branch of the Zionist Organization.

I do not propose dwelling on the catastrophe that overtook the

Jews during the war except to admit to a feeling of revulsion towards the Germans which required years before it could be exorcised. Frank Pakenham, minister in the Attlee Government responsible for Occupied Germany, invited me to go and help 're-educate' German women out of their Nazi past. I would be most suitable for the task, Pakenham said, because of my war-time experience. I greeted the suggestion in disbelief.

'You seem to have forgotten I am a Jewess.'

'That's precisely why I want you to do the job,' Frank replied. 'Look at Victor Gollancz. His campaign on behalf of the hungry Germans is a great act of reconciliation.'

I wasn't ready for reconciliation. Victor was in any case dispensing the conqueror's charity, a noble gesture of course and in keeping with that aspect of his character that concentrated on love. (Other aspects, such as his peculiar blend of Judeo-Christianity, had more to do with his conceit.) But it was too soon for me to look upon any German in middle life, male or female, except as an agent of the Nazi extermination process. The wound was still open.

The new mandarins of Marks and Spencer, anticipating their future control of the company and full of ideas imported from service life, shared few of the memories of my battle for a Welfare Department and knew little of its war-time activities. They regarded me as a sort of aging aunt and, like aunts everywhere, to be treated with respect, humoured perhaps, but not to be taken too seriously. My ideas of human relations in industry, a subject to which I was now ideologically committed, found no echo in their brief experience. It would come, eventually, and Marks and Spencer would be offered as an object-lesson for Britain as a whole. For the moment, however, my department appeared in their eyes an indulgence the company could ill afford in a period of economic crisis, acute shortage of manufacturing materials, and the emergence of threatening competition in the new names above High Street department stores. Simon Marks still ruled the roost – 'when I leave this place they will have to carry me out feet first,' he averred – and he remained my anchor.

The myriad little changes in British society brought about by the world cataclysm, when taken together, did not add up to one decent Balkan-size revolution. Clement Attlee, in the process of dismantling the Empire and nationalizing basic industries, left the nation largely as it was. Work was still compartmentalized, privilege still reigned, the classes settled back into their rigorous strata. I saw it all on the building sites where blitzed Marks and Spencer branches were being reconstructed. They were a microcosm of the country at large.

Permits to obtain bricks and mortar involved in every instance a clutch of forms that would lie in office trays at the Board of Trade inert as a Crusader's tomb. Architects controlled their designs remote from the scene, rarely risking a visit to the actual site for fear of soiling their boots. Workmen squelched through the mud, performing their tasks with as much concern for what it was all about as the ancient Israelites must have felt in erecting the Pyramids. We had our mandatory strike. I tried to keep a close eye on everything to do with staff quarters, which I was going to ensure were of the highest standard – wash-rooms particularly. In one town the electricians gave trouble, and I went to investigate.

'We are wiring up these fancy facilities for your people,' they told me, downing tools, 'yet we have to work in absolute squalor – no place to eat, nowhere to take a break. If we need to relieve ourselves we have to do so here on the spot, like cattle in a field.' I was horrified. I got the backing of Simon to warn our building contractors to install adequate facilities for their employees or they would lose the business. This worked. Going around with the architects also proved an education. I had stipulated lavatory-seats to be horse-shoe in shape; a trivial thing you may think, but I was mindful of the demands of hygiene. An architect protested: 'You're spending enormous sums, many thousands, on your buildings, yet you want to economize on a minute quantity of wood, or plastic, for the lavatories.' He simply did not get the point.

The Young Turks began cutting expenditure with an attack upon 'Four Winds', our holiday home at Bosham, shutting it down as an expensive luxury. Nevertheless I pushed through a most controversial innovation – so far, that is, as the directors were concerned: a staff hairdressing service in all newly built stores. This involved me in protracted conflict, with a plenteous flow of red ink. Patiently I needed to explain to men whose own wives – and I knew most of them – spent small fortunes on cosmetics and beauty 'aids', how important proper hair-styling was to a woman's morale. True, the practice is now disparaged, especially among the young, but a session at the hairdresser's was then a luxury most women used to dream of; it demanded as much care and thought as the purchase of a new hat. Arrangements were made for the coiffure to be performed in the lunchhour, with a meal served on a tray. 'No time is being lost,' I assured my superiors.

Our first hairdressing salon was installed at Plymouth, where the store re-opened to a fanfare from the local dignitaries headed by the mayor and his lady. For this civic occasion the entire Marks and Spencer Board of Directors descended upon the city. I shall ever be grateful to that mayoress; in a little speech to welcome the magnificent emporium now opening its doors she said: 'What I appreciate most of all is the staff hairdressing service. Such a marvellous idea!' This resulted in handshakes all round, the mayoress's own bouquet for me, with employees under the drier photographed for the staff magazine.

Once won over, Marcus Sieff proved, to his credit, as aware of the human aspect of staff management as I was myself. He preached on the subject at conferences throughout the world, and later, following his father in the House of Lords, warned of the entrenched deficiencies in British labour relations.

Eleanor Roosevelt placed Marks and Spencer on her itinerary during a tour of Europe. Impressed by our welfare facilities, she invited me to America to compare notes with department stores over there. I was shepherded round Bloomingdale's, Lord and Taylor, Orbach's, Macy's, then at their commercial zenith. Though they had much to teach Britain in merchandising, they had little for Marks and Spencer on conditions of employment. We were streets ahead.

I don't suppose anything occurring in Britain in those early post-war years so completely epitomized this nation's noblest intentions and cheated hopes as the creation of bright new towns to banish the shame of slum-life and Victorian survivalism from the landscape. They would nurture healthy communities in the country air. They would give scope to adventurous ideas in city-planning and the dispersal of industries. That phrase 'improving the quality of life' was creeping into the language and seemed tailor-made for a concept to liberate rolling acres for neighbourhood use. Of the architects equal to the challenge, one particularly seemed to fit the bill: Berthold Lubetkin, erstwhile protégé of that unassuming woman passionate in such causes, my sister Manya. He was then at his peak, a practical visionary who could inculcate social commitment into building design.

204

The first name in new towns at that time belonged to Monica Felton, with whom I formed a friendship before the war. She had a close relationship with the Minister of Town and Country Planning, Lewis Silkin. He appointed Monica to direct various new town schemes, and it seemed to satisfy every ideal when she made Lubetkin architect-in-charge of Peterlee in the Durham coalfields. But then the sparks began to fly. For Lubetkin, affiliated to every progressive cause though he might be, turned the people associated with him into victims of his tyranny and moods.

Visiting Monica Felton at Peterlee I was treated to a long account of her woes, how the man's outrageous requirements for the implementation of his architectural philosophy exasperated the officials in London, placed her in the cross-fire and reduced progress to a limp. Lubetkin could not abide interrogation by committees, he was secretive and, not to put too fine a point on it, said Monica, he was unreliable. I had the feeling they deserved each other.

Peterlee was eventually completed, no thanks to Lubetkin. Contemptuous of the bureaucrats he resigned from the project, gave up architecture, rejected his old friends, and engaged in farming. Three decades later he returned from oblivion, accepting, in a grand gesture of reconciliation, the Royal Gold Medal for Architecture. Monica Felton herself never made a secret of her Communist proclivities.

Our friendship came to an abrupt halt in 1951. Though she loved the power which responsibility for Peterlee and other new towns gave her, Monica suddenly disappeared from the scene, only to turn up in North Korea at the height of the war against America's puppet in the South. From there she travelled to Moscow and broadcast a furious anti-Western tirade. She angered me by exploiting her official position to procure a visa for North Korea, following this with an attack upon her own country. I shunned her when she returned to London with her Stalin Peace Prize. In the end she settled in Madras, marrying an Indian.

New towns were scattered all over Britain, but not for a long time would families, even the poorly-housed, sample the life they offered. Dramatic though they appeared to the visitor, they took on a forbidding, drear aspect to their residents. Their bare avenues and artificial lakes could have been created for ghosts. The planners had failed to foresee how the television era would glue families to their armchairs, and put cinemas and pubs out of business.

I knew a little about the strains in the new towns through Dame Caroline Haslett, who had partial responsibility for the development of Crawley in Sussex. My colleague on the Council of the Industrial Welfare Society, Caroline fully shared my sentiments on the subject of labour relations. She does not figure prominently in the usual accounts of the feminist movement because she never contemplated throwing herself under a race-horse or chaining herself to anybody's railings, yet she struck a hundred blows for the rights of women. As a girl Caroline obtained work as a secretary in a boiler-making company and this encouraged her to train privately as an engineer. In the process she learnt how certain industries took it as axiomatic that women were somehow the wrong shape and had the wrong mentality for creative employment.

The lessons of the war notwithstanding, women were once again engaged in smoothing paths to enable men to do the significant thinking, as though important work was theirs by God's law. Caroline dramatized this injustice by claiming a role for women in such male preserves as the electrical and engineering fields, and business management. Her book *Problems Have No Sex* analysed the vicious circle condemning women to eternal inferiority long before Simone de Beauvoir and the 'Women's Lib' movement reduced the subject to parody.

In 1947 Caroline Haslett and I travelled together to a conference in Stockholm arranged by the International Labour Organization, she representing the Women's Electrical Association, I as head of Personnel and Staff Management at Marks and Spencer. We were a large delegation of business executives and trade unionists – the usual flock of investigators who spent a little time touring factories and schools so as to justify an abundance of relaxation and sight-seeing. Our group was in the charge of a polished young man of tireless energy and with a slight Viennese accent, who was described as our public relations officer. Caroline knew him well, referring to him as a *Wunderkind*.

'Who is this *Wunderkind*?' I asked her.

'George Weidenfeld,' she said. 'He was at the BBC during the war, involved with broadcasting to Occupied Europe.'

He co-ordinated, animated and inspired our entire programme. I met his parents in London, his mother intelligent and worldly, his father, once a banker, now a classics tutor. Solemnly, the latter notified me that his son George was a genius.

Ambitious, certainly. Young Mr Weidenfeld possessed the foreigner's quality of viewing the British and their society with an eye unjaded by familiarity with the scene, and he fathered new ideas sublimely unaware of the traditional British resistance to innovation. His BBC record, and his talent for friendship in circles of influence, brought him close to Gerald Barry, Dick Crossman and Kingsley Martin in the Press, Harold Wilson as an up-and-coming Labour politician, and Randolph Churchill, *enfant terrible* of the Tory establishment – not a bad score for one who arrived in London in 1938 penniless and barely able to utter a word in recognizable English. George Weidenfeld started a large-format news-magazine in hard covers titled *Contact*. Where he obtained the paper to print it in those frustrating times of rationing remains a mystery.

After a couple of issues the project collapsed, and I brought George to Marks and Spencer and introduced him to Teddy Sieff, whose daughter Jane he subsequently married. Together with Marcus Sieff George worked out a programme of children's classics, for sale at the apparently impossible price of five shillings. He was thus launched on a career in publishing that became the envy of the trade. It wasn't all smooth going, of course, and I sometimes found him sick with worry; but his determination never wavered. He had, in his youth, been associated with the Zionist movement, and I encouraged George to revive his interest in it.

Immediately following the searing war in which the newly-born nation of Israel repelled an onslaught of five Arab armies, not to mention the guerrillas operating within its territory, I landed at a small military airport near Haifa, in the company of Simon and Miriam Marks. While being confronted by a passport official, I caught sight of the Israeli flag and burst into tears.

The passport official said: 'There's no need to cry, you are safe now.' I was weeping with joy at the fulfilment of the dream I had nurtured for thirty years, but he thought they were the tears of a bewildered survivor of the concentration camps finding peace at last.

Out of nowhere Marcus Sieff appeared. He was one of many Jewish volunteers who had rushed to Israel's aid in her hour of danger and was at this time adapting his experience as a British

Army colonel to the needs of Ben-Gurion, war leader and Prime Minister, in the procurement of supplies for the Israeli forces. We were on our way to Rehovot and the presidential residence where Chaim Weizmann, now Head of State, and his wife Vera awaited us. Built as a private home by the celebrated architect Eric Mendelsohn, this lovely pale-stoned building was located on the science campus established by Weizmann with Marks, Sieff and Sacher endowments.

As we drove through road-blocks along the coast towards Tel Aviv, through ancient Ramleh, captured that July, and into Rehovot village, the talk came round to the depth of Weizmann's chagrin and his disappointment in the new Israel. This was born of Chaim's realization that his office of President was purely honorific, while David Ben-Gurion as Prime Minister filled every corner of the stage. So embittered was the older man that he seriously contemplated resignation.

Weizmann contended that the gulf between himself and Ben-Gurion was so wide he was not even granted the courtesy of being shown Cabinet papers; he was only scantily informed of the government's decisions in this crucial period when nation-building was starting from scratch. I listened as a neutral to this sorry account. I greatly admired Ben-Gurion and saw that he had a case in this tough climate when the existence of the new state hovered in the balance – no Arab power was prepared to make peace – and there was too much to do too quickly for strict adherence to the constitutional niceties. Then I thought of George Weidenfeld.

Why shouldn't he come out as a personal aide to Weizmann, acting as liaison between the President and the government? Simon Marks endorsed the idea, we tested it out with Chaim, and then with Moshe Sharett, who as Foreign Minister was on excellent terms with his President. The plan was accepted. George agreed, and remained for a year. I met him frequently during a further visit I paid to Israel. In his new role, which he liked to describe as Chef de Cabinet, George displayed a taste for the diplomatic scene. He escorted a trail of ambassadors along the pock-marked road – a narrow coil of asphalt over rough country, really – from Tel Aviv to Rehovot where they presented their letters of credence. A chore he performed with rather less dedication was to read to the almost sightless President. It included reading *Trial and Error*, Weizmann's memoirs that had been re-drafted and burnished by many hands. One day George fell asleep over the book, incurring a thorough dressing-down from Vera.

George returned to England in 1950 to direct all his attention to his publishing company, in which Nigel Nicolson, son of Harold, put some family money. Their first significant title, on the coal industry, was written by the then unknown Harold Wilson. Soon George was performing usefully behind the scenes for this politician, who dropped into the leadership of the Labour Party by stepping into the shoes of two dead men – Aneurin Bevan and Hugh Gaitskell.

Generous to a fault to his friends, Wilson lavished honours on his publisher: a knighthood, then a peerage. I told George, on his elevation to the Upper Chamber, that I preferred his persona as a commoner. His position in public life had no need of such a crutch as a lordship, and it was signally unfortunate for the new Lord Weidenfeld to appear among a crop of Wilsonian favourites which evoked newspaper comments varying from the ironic to the condemnatory.

Wilson's celebrated dictum, 'a week is a long time in politics', received a certain piquancy when George, having briefly made his mark as a Labour peer, defected to the newly-begotten Social Democratic Party. However, the change was more appropriate to his baroque personality, what with his undisguised enjoyment of life's pleasures and a marriage (his third) consecrated in the American Embassy, courtesy of David Bruce. He has frequently stated that he owes all his success to me, as the fairy godmother who touched him with her wand back in 1947. I am still exceedingly fond of George – but I accept no responsibility for his conversion to the epicurean centre in British politics.

My activities in the Industrial Welfare Society introduced me to another young man of high promise, Peter Parker. Observing his stewardship of the Duke of Edinburgh's 1954 Study Conference on Human Problems in Industry, I assumed my talent-spotting role for Marks and Spencer and invited him to join us. He thought about it, was interviewed, but declined a post at Baker Street – this to my regret, if only for the reason that he might have adopted our standards of cleanliness for the trains when he later became chairman of the British Rail Board!

As I recall the period immediately after the war my thoughts centre on Aileen Furse, or Philby as she now preferred to describe herself. She had long ceased to be an employee of Marks and Spencer and was producing babies with an almost monotonous regularity; the tally was three in 1946, progress being duly reported to her delighted old colleagues. We seemed to be ever on our way to Carlyle Square bearing gifts. Kim, a happy and devoted father, was making a successful career in the Foreign Office and Aileen seemed stable and content.

More than anything she wished to be properly married. It need not now be long delayed. Litzi Friedmann, partner in Philby's first uneasy exercise in matrimony, had lived the war out in London with another man. In 1945 he took a post in East Berlin and before joining him there she and Kim were divorced. So it was at last possible to do the right thing by Aileen. Would I, Kim asked me, be a witness? Aileen was pregnant again, he was due for a posting to Turkey, and Chelsea Register Office stood just around the corner from their house. It was a very private affair, and appeared to be a happy ending. I was of course entirely ignorant that Kim's Foreign Office job was a cover for his membership of the Secret Intelligence Service. His buddy Guy Burgess was also in the Foreign Office at the time, though he did not put in an appearance at the marriage. As his second witness Kim enlisted his close friend the art-dealer Tomas Harris. Communism in Philby's case seemed to belong to the misty, juvenile past. ✓

Subsequent episodes in the Philby story are now common knowledge, from studies written by authors who evidently took in large quantities of each other's washing. The uproar resulting from the escape to Russia of Burgess and Maclean in May 1951 brought Philby's career as a senior Foreign Office man to a dramatic close, and although I saw little of him and Aileen subsequently, I knew of his difficulties in re-establishing himself in journalism. A helpful eye was kept on Aileen by Stuart Lisbona, of the Marks and Spencer Pensions Department. A godfather to one of her children, he visited their home, now outside London, to find Aileen depressed, and a marriage gone rickety.

Of the icy relationship between the British and American intelligence services resulting from the defection of the two officials, with suspicion focused also on Philby, the general public was sublimely unaware. Pressure to 'explain all' regarding the missing diplomats, as stories of their decadent life-style emerged, grew irresistibly, and a White Paper in 1955 failed to assuage concern, for it was so obviously white-wash. Marcus Lipton, in the shelter of the House of Commons, named the

'Third Man' involved as Philby: Kim was in the news again, via the headlines in the evening papers.

Together with the friends we had in common, I took the view that this was a witch-hunt McCarthy style, engineered by a publicity-hungry MP. Justice appeared to be done when Lipton, challenged by Philby to repeat his allegations outside the House, made a complete retraction. I was satisfied, though a little surprised, when Philby was engaged by the *Observer* and *Economist* in 1956 as their correspondent in the Middle East. Poor Aileen, abandoned by her husband, was found dead in the house at Crowborough which she maintained in the hope of a reconciliation with her errant Kim, while I endeavoured to strike him from my memory. This, however, was not to be.

But first I must return to the atmosphere of the new State of Israel. All the apparatus of nationhood was being superimposed high-speed upon a scene of blinding confusion. Ships berthed, aeroplanes landed, bringing thousands of immigrants daily. No homes as yet existed for these newcomers, their reception being in the hands of flurried officials who despaired of making any semblance of order out of the chaos.

I received a call from Golda Meir asking my help with the problems caused by the influx of newcomers. In the first year of independence the population had doubled. The immigrants mostly arrived without possessions, resources were strained, experienced social workers thin on the ground. Golda was then Minister of Labour, and the immigrants were her prime concern. I crossed the Mediterranean by ship, bringing my own little Ford. Private cars barely existed in Israel, and people stood for hours in the fierce sunlight awaiting the heavily overcrowded buses. In Haifa I was directed to Sha'ar Aliya, a sprawling encampment where miserable groups of people complained in a babel of tongues at being stuck away in crude hutments and old British Army tents. Inadequate medical supplies, short-tempered officials, ill-equipped kitchens, all combined to make a mockery of the Promised Land.

After finding myself a room in a small Haifa hotel I travelled down to Tel Aviv, then the administrative capital, to talk to Golda Meir. How she coped I do not to this day know. Her office was under siege. Call her Minister of Labour if you like, but this was Israel, with Jewish authority a novelty. Golda was being harangued in all the languages she knew, or didn't know.

'You may requisition anything you need,' she told me in that broad American accent, 'so as to prepare the fit people for work. I want to settle them in different parts of the country, but they all insist upon giving me in person their reasons for living in the large towns.' Then a brief hug. 'And thank you for coming.'

At Haifa I observed how, in the end, and amid much argument, things had a way of getting done. Food was distributed, doctors moved deftly among the sick, documents were completed, cashiers issued money. The camp had no ambulance and my car was constantly on the road fully loaded. Once I left my tent, which made do as an office, to find I was covered in lice. The rains came that winter to turn the immigrant camp into a quagmire. And every so often *Hatikvah*, the Israeli anthem, rang out in a lusty prayer of hope.

Thanks to the idealism of the younger generation of Israelis, no one doubted all would come right. I was taken by Teddy Kollek, not as yet the international celebrity he would become for his role as Mayor of Jerusalem in winning the confidence of both Arabs and Jews, to the *kibbutz* of which he and his wife Tamar were among the founders. Ein Gev stood on the shore of Lake Tiberias hard by the Syrian frontier. Its inhabitants lived by fishing, and we went out in the dawn to join the young people at work. A sunrise in Galilee viewed from the lake is an experience never to be forgotten. To have witnessed it together with these young pioneers compelled re-enaction of the story of Jesus bidding his disciples to put away their nets, so that they might be 'fishers of men'.

Golda Meir went abroad that year raising funds to meet the nation's bills, so I took my problems to Ben-Gurion direct. No Prime Minister could have been beset by greater difficulties, but he always found time to see me. I needed his help specifically when I arranged for shipments of medicines from England. Penicillin, for example, was in woefully short supply. But the consignments remained locked in a shed because I couldn't produce the right piece of paper to satisfy the customs officials for their clearance. A word from Ben-Gurion was of course enough.

Paula, the wife the Prime Minister had married while a young man in America, struck me as a uniquely original person, much less predictable than the husband over whom she stood guard to ensure that he ate and slept. Coming from Minsk, Paula saw herself as superior in some respects to David, whom she would describe with an affectation of scorn as a mere 'Galician'. Endless stories were recounted of her oddities, and her failure to live up to her elevated role, whereas Vera Weizmann lacked none of the graces. One characteristic the two women shared in common: they expected presents from all their guests. Visitors came from far and wide to claim audience, on the flimsiest pretext, so they might return home with the proud report of a conversation with the wife of the Prime Minister or President (usually both).

In 1953 David Ben-Gurion decided he had had enough as defender, builder and leader of the nation, for a while anyway. He and Paula retired to a *kibbutz* of young people in the Negev. I was invited down in the company of the writer Leon Uris, already renowned for his novel *Exodus*, and a photographer who with Uris was producing a guide-book of the Holy Land. We were joined by an American businessman and his wife. The occasion coincided with the Passover *Seder*, and after the communal meal we escorted Paula alone back to her little dwelling. Then the inevitable question: 'What have you brought me?'

We delivered our gifts, the businessman's wrapped to make a bulky parcel. Paula opened it with great anticipation. It contained dozens of brassieres, for it transpired that this American manufactured them. Paula, oblivious of being in a crowd, took a brassiere, stripped to the waist and tried it on for size. Suddenly, perceiving the comedy, she emitted a gale of laughter in which we all joined.

Ill-mannered Paula Ben-Gurion may have been, but her perceptions were accurate. At their official residence in Jerusalem she could often be seen gossiping with the guards at the gate. She sent one of them shopping for her, saying, 'I'll hold your rifle.' A Prime Minister could walk down a crowded street in those days without thought of possible assassination, and Israel, once all those newcomers were absorbed into her society, had a cosiness unmatched by any nation. Unhappily, a new chapter opened with her venture into *Realpolitik*, alongside Britain and France, in the Suez War of 1956.

Back in London I found myself engaged in a little war of my own at that time. Marks and Spencer had reached a peak in its reputation, and my Welfare and Training Department was enjoying a smooth passage, culminating in our affiliation to a group medical scheme, one of the nation's earliest. We also had a medical officer of our own, of course, under the jurisdiction of my department. That however was until the arrival of Dr Oldershaw. She, one might say, 'knew not Josephine', and refused to acknowledge that she came within my aegis. Perhaps I was foolish, but I deeply resented being up-staged by an outsider, even a qualified doctor, who insisted upon studious detachment from my department.

The company was then introducing its 'Good Housekeeping' policy, which Marcus Sieff espoused with great determination. It began with a blitz on paper-work, and was so successful as to be emulated, with considerable saving of public money, by the government (Derek Rayner, now Lord Rayner and Chief Executive Officer of Marks and Spencer, being seconded to direct the operation). I was among those accused of using too much paper – it was nonsense, I hardly wrote anything down. An instruction then reached me to share my responsibilities with Dr Oldershaw. Everything to do with health would be hers, while I would remain as chairman of the Welfare Committee established before the war. I protested, threatening resignation, but Simon Marks assured me all would work out to my satisfaction. One or two of the younger directors chose this moment to let me know that many of the benefits originating with the Welfare Committee were absurd, and not justifiable in the trading conditions then prevailing. They made this allegation without proper investigation of actual costings, but purely as a pronouncement from above.

Dr Oldershaw, a former Home Office doctor in an institution for delinquent girls, was my antithesis, and very well organized. She came to work early, I invariably arrived late. I had little sense of order, liked to dress for comfort not style and was informal with subordinates. She was regimental and immaculately turned out, never a hair out of place. The next I knew, during my absence for a couple of days, she had moved into my office.

I received an ultimatum: 'Share responsibility, or leave!' Silently, I cleared my desk of the accretions of twenty-four years. Sophie Podolsky and my loyal personal assistant Violet Moore helped to stuff it all in the boot of my car. There was mention of a handsome 'golden handshake', perhaps a year's salary. That certainly was an original way of formulating a dismissal and, to add to the injustice, my handshake, when it ultimately materialized, proved to be of a much baser metal, nickel perhaps. It was the moment when the Suez War broke out, so I decided to go over and make myself useful in Israel. Too late – that war lasted barely a week. I felt caged like a lion.

In the midst of this depressing episode Eric Strauss, my

214

dearest friend, fell ill. Lung cancer was diagnosed. He took the terrible blow bravely – rather better than I, in fact, for Eric had brightened my life for years. Another of his friends offered him use of his house in Barbados for a holiday. Eric would go only if I accompanied him. Well, what was there now to detain me in England? This could be our last excursion together.

My abrupt separation from Marks and Spencer had its special irony. Throughout my career I had preached the importance of consultation between management and staff in industry. Even the humblest employee was entitled to such a courtesy, and my company was a model in this regard. Yet I was removed by a humiliating *fait accompli*. I would not sanction such treatment to a school-girl working at the counter for pocket-money during the Saturday rush! I knew right was on my side when dozens of telegrams and bouquets of flowers awaited me at the airport, from colleagues at Head Office, branches throughout the country, and including individual messages of appreciation sent by people I hardly knew. The stewardess was convinced I was a film-star, or some other celebrity, travelling incognito!

Incidentally, disquieting characteristics soon developed in Dr Oldershaw, who had completely taken over my reins. She ceased to be the ultra-efficient staff doctor and began to lose interest even in her personal appearance. She then suffered a breakdown and entered a mental hospital where, before very long, she died.

The Barbados house, called 'Glitter Bay', was fully staffed, not excluding a traditionally attired black butler. Eric was still quite strong (he died five years later) and I could see he drew consolation and calm from his Catholic faith, regularly attending service. But that calmness turned him inward, and I was required to take long walks alone while he retired to his room to work on his chosen subject, a psychiatric study of St Paul – a task he was not destined to complete.

At the United Nations in New York a fierce debate was in progress to compel Israel to withdraw from the Sinai, which she had conquered in a swift campaign. Golda Meir, as Foreign Minister, led the Israeli delegation. Eric had little interest in such matters, but I was intensely concerned at the outcome and missed the company of my Jewish friends.

During a walk one morning I was bitten by some insect on my leg, producing a swelling that refused to go down. A local doctor treated it, but to no avail. Eric seemed much too preoccupied to be concerned, and in any case disclaimed knowledge of this branch of medicine. Not so the butler. 'Not uncommon in these parts,' he informed me. 'Probably from a tarantula spider.' By now the leg was ballooning and my panic mounted.

'You can cure it in no time,' promised the butler, producing two bottles of rum. One bottle I was to drink, the other to be used for bathing the wound. In my agony I was ready to try even this idiotic cure. It was the reverse of successful, and my leg expanded to a frightening size. This was stupid, so I decided to fly at once to Fira in New York and consult a specialist, leaving Eric in Barbados. I touched down in New York in a blizzard, feeling generally debilitated and thoroughly miserable – one leg minus its stocking and shoe.

I cannot say what helped my recovery most: proper medical attention, or New York's excitement over the Suez controversy – at the UN Israel ranged herself beside Britain and France, America beside Russia. In any event I recovered, and sat in the UN gallery to hear Golda Meir make that eloquent statement of Israel's unconditional withdrawal from the Sinai, following the assurance of a UN international force to end the Egyptian blockade against Israel. The arrangement held for a decade when, sure enough, Nasser expelled the UN force, reinstated the blockade and thus provoked the Six Day War of 1967.

She was still the unspoilt, very feminine Golda I had always known, though now a star of the television channels and the Boadicea of America's Jews. (It was only later, years later in fact, when she was called out of retirement to be the compromise Prime Minister of her country, that she developed those traits of blinkered certainty, unforgiving to anyone who crossed her, and hard as a stone towards the Arabs. But I rarely saw Golda in that latter period, deliberately distancing myself from the sycophantic circle by which she was surrounded. I preferred the old Golda, happily baking cakes for her Sabbath family reunions.)

And Fira. Sometimes, after she swept her guests out of her salon, we would talk a sisterly version of politics. Having lived through the Russian revolution she had groomed herself to be completely anti-Soviet, suspecting Reds everywhere. Hers was not a totally insignificant voice, for she moved among leading politicians – one of whom, Senator Fulbright, was particularly close. Fira had been awarded the ultimate establishment accolade with a ten-page profile in *Fortune* magazine. She could dispense favours: Larry Spivack, who conducted a highly regarded television forum, would consult her for possible candidates to appear on his 'Meet the Press' programme. She had taken Kerensky under her wing too, as much for my sake as for his, I imagine. His later years were spent mainly in America, reliving ancient history, collecting professorships, and writing the books for which Fira acted as his unpaid literary agent.

Highball in hand, bracelets dangling from her wrist, she was the Countess Ilinska and I her wild sister from the backwoods. If she had solid Episcopalians to supper, that was it – no Jews invited. If she marked out the day for Polish Catholics her Manhattan apartment rang with the conversation of nineteenth-century Cracow. In London she could not remain happily with me for more than a few days at a stretch, so much did my friends and my dislocated ways bother her.

An odd situation arose shortly after my return from New York. Vera Weizmann was staying with me on one of her periodic visits to London. Simon Marks and Israel Sieff were at all times at the beck and call of the woman still regarded as Israel's First Lady. They were her oldest friends, and naturally we passed long hours together mulling over the past in my flat. But not a word was exchanged about that unhappy affair at Marks and Spencer. Vera had no interest in cooking, though she enjoyed preparing tea for the four of us, and while she was thus engaged in the kitchen one afternoon Simon said: 'Look, Flora, this must stop. We need you back with us. I'm appointing you our consultant, as of now.' I concurred, and that was how my personal Suez crisis ended, with a strategic retreat through *force majeure*.

With Fira the complete American, and me an unclassifiable *mélange*, Manya, third of the Sisters Karamazov, placed herself in a world uniquely of her own creation. I find it quite in keeping with her individuality that Manya, the Catholic among us, should be the only one to return to Russia, to peer through the windows of our old home on the Moika, and to board a little branch-line train to Redkino, putting out her easel and making a picture of the crumbling mansion, scene of our happiest childhood life.

Totally without artifice, taking people only at their best, Manya was the intrepid wanderer into the unknown, as when she arrived with just a haversack at a *kibbutz* in Palestine and, not knowing a single person there, requested permission to stay and work in the orchards. Go where she might in the world, she

217

accosted strangers, discovered their innermost secrets, took over their problems, gave them money, made them her friends. Her first journey to Russia, in the harsh climate of the cold war, must have horrified Fira, with whom I once left a Washington party at Senator Taft's in a car driven by arch-Commie-hunter Joseph McCarthy.

Manya's publishing house the Harvill Press claimed many a *succès d'estime* by the early fifties but was exhausting the generosity of her husband Ralph Harari. Furthermore, it irked him, a straightforward Jew, that his money went into so many works by Catholic theologians, some of whom spent long hours with his chain-smoking wife in their Westminster home. Manya's conversion he accepted; fuelling the forces of Catholic propaganda he did not consider part of the bargain. He decided in 1954 that he had paid out enough. If Manya wished to continue publishing then she must find another patron. Harvill's future looked bleak.

Fortunately, Manya's partner Marjorie Villiers (their combined surnames formed their publishing imprint) won the interest of William Collins, who took Harvill under his company wing. This was the moment when Harvill began showing a profit, for it coincided with the inauguration of the Kruschev era in Russia and the beginning of what we all hoped was a general thaw in East-West relations. Manya travelled to Russia with Billy Collins to establish contacts with the government publishing house for a beneficial exchange of titles. Not too much official business was transacted, I gather, but in the process the Harvill–Collins imprint developed a field hitherto barely touched, perhaps untouchable – the translation of the finest contemporary Russian writing.

It was at Manya's that I encountered Ilya Ehrenburg, whose novel *The Thaw* she published as the first profitable Harvill title. Ehrenburg's stay in London was a landmark both literary and political, an augury that at last the ice-cap upon Russian society was truly melting (unhappily, a false token). We left together, and I felt he must be so busy I should spare him a hunt for a taxi and take him to his next appointment in my car. But the destination Ehrenburg requested was Cruft's, the dog show. Seeing the surprised look on my face he explained: 'Two-legged creatures don't interest me half as much as four-legged ones.' Now I understood how Manya won his book for Harvill.

Her instinct for significant fiction was almost uncanny,

perhaps because she never looked at her books in commercial terms. When whispers crossed the Channel that Feltrinelli, the inventive Italian publisher, had the manuscript of Boris Pasternak's *Doctor Zhivago*, Manya beat all the competition and plunged into a translation. She did this in collaboration with Max Hayward, then the leading Russian scholar in the English language. Hayward was not, however, a man to be trusted alone with a manuscript. His weakness for whisky compelled one to stand guard over him lest the pages drowned in the liquid chaos that was his habitat, whether at Harvard or Oxford. Manya, Marjorie, Hayward and Leo Labetz (the scholar who discovered *One Day in the Life of Ivan Denisovitch* and got Max to translate it almost at gunpoint) operated as a team of all the talents. Through them the British public was introduced to a range of outstanding authors – Andrei Amalrik, Andrei Sinyavsky, Evgenia Ginsburg, Mikhail Bulgakov – whose works could not see daylight in Moscow. Harvill failed to win Solzhenitsyn's *Ivan Denisovitch* but was handsomely recompensed with British rights to his *First Circle*, the masterpiece that led him, after Pasternak, to the Nobel Prize (renounced of course by the latter through governmental pressure).

Harvill rescued from oblivion works less epoch-making politically but which became equally memorable. The oft-rejected manuscript of a poorly written story reached Harvill in 1959 and both Marjorie and Manya knew they had to publish it. It was the biography of a lioness!

Joy Adamson's *Born Free* appeared in 1960 to become one of the publishing sensations of the decade. Elsa the lioness lived in distant Kenya, though her existence pervaded the atmosphere of Manya's house in Catherine Place as if she were some important relative expected on a visit complete with luggage, smelling salts and gifts at any moment. Once I arrived there to be enjoined by the butler (yes, they kept one) to be absolutely quiet, everyone was upset. Elsa had died; it could have been a family bereavement.

My consultancy at Marks and Spencer was proceeding in particular harmony with Teddy Sieff, who assumed the chairmanship after the two inseparable brothers-in-law passed on. The kindest, most considerate of men, Teddy also revealed great reserves of courage. In 1973 an assailant (suspected to be Carlos, the international terrorist engaged on missions of murder on behalf of the Arabs) penetrated the bedroom of his home and shot him in the head. Teddy's resourceful wife Lois, through prompt action and devoted care, probably saved his life. He miraculously recovered, returning not only to the company but to the Jewish service which had marked him out for assassination in the first place.

Following Teddy's retirement from Marks and Spencer his nephew Marcus, now Lord Sieff of Brimpton, assumed command of the patrimony, which takes over two billion pounds a year across its counters. To my great satisfaction Marcus promoted the basic principles laid down as early as 1933. His developing appreciation of good labour relations, with their impact upon the economy of the country, enabled him the more fully to appreciate my initial achievements in that field. I must resist the strong temptation to make of this book a Marks and Spencer advertising campaign; much is being written to mark this year of 1984 as the company's centenary. But now that I myself have reached a certain venerable age, how can I conclude reference to its working conditions without speaking of its concern for its pensioners, of whom I am probably the oldest? We continue to be regarded as family, not less than when we were active members of the staff. We are never over-looked – should they not hear from us they will make contact. They say this is the Japanese way; if so, the more British industry emulates the Japanese the better.

11 Retrospective

The aircraft, a Boeing 707 called Whisky Echo, lifted purposeful-
ly off the runway with a full complement of passengers: first stop
Zurich, then on to the Middle East, Australia, New Zealand. It
was April 1968, and I was seated tourist class at the rear beside a
friend who had changed his flight so that we might travel
together. The plane rose towards the sky, sounded the usual
bumps as it gathered height, lurched and banked and then
performed a wide curve to offer a glimpse of the slanting
landscape. Now we were fully airborne, suspended between
heaven and earth, an isolated little community of 126 souls
encased in metal; barely a minute out of Heathrow, piped music
still filling the cabin, seat belts fastened. Absently, I stared at one
of the portside engines and noticed it was spurting smoke and
flames.

Almost immediately, black fumes penetrated to the interior
and we had difficulty in finding breath. White-faced but calm,
the crew moved swiftly through the plane informing us we were
returning to London. We must place our heads on our knees. All
was silence, except for the murmurings of those at prayer, my
companion, a Quaker, among them.

Flames began licking round the fuselage, the crippled engine
hurtled to earth, and soon intermittent explosions rocked the
plane. But the crew were superb, and kept panic at bay while the
pilot, Captain Charles Taylor, steered the burning hulk to a
crash-landing on a little-used runway at Heathrow. In a matter
of seconds the escape chutes were operating and we were made
into an orderly file to be pushed to safety. I was the last person to
leave the plane alive, for soon after I reached the ground it gave
out a deafening bang to become, tragically, a funeral pyre for five
people, one of them a stewardess, trapped within the molten
carcass.

In the airport lounge I demanded brandy and a cigarette, then
a car to take me home. My Quaker friend accompanying me, I

arrived at my flat, switched on the television, and we watched ourselves dropping from the plane. He and I decided that our brush with death would be a bond keeping us together always, yet I have rarely seen him since that day.

As I pondered over the fates which decide who should die and who should live, I received a call from Barbie and Herbert Agar. They insisted on my flying off with them to Venice, where they were about to go on holiday. But, they said, I would be returning alone. It was an admirable procedure as defence against any fear of air travel that might otherwise have developed.

Such a fear was unlikely in my case, for death has no terror for me. I do however value life, and since that experience on Whisky Echo my conviction that we are on this planet for a purpose has been reinforced. It caused me to deliberate the ways of destiny: the eldest of the 'Sisters Karamazov', I have outlived the other two, and indeed most of my contemporaries. An obsession to live positively, born of my frustrated girlhood, has accompanied every turn in my fortunes; Whisky Echo only dramatized and justified this philosophy.

Earlier, as the word spread of my ceasing daily, formal employment at Marks and Spencer except as a consultant, I was besieged with invitations to put my experience to service elsewhere. This included, naturally enough, investigation of conditions in other major companies. I produced reports on two of the largest commercial houses in Britain and went to Malta for a similar task with a ship-repairing concern. As to the adoption of my recommendations, I was never informed. This neither surprised nor disappointed me. The job was worth doing for its own sake and granted me the only recompense I desired, personal satisfaction.

Paramount in any individual's nature is the ego; offend it and you inflict more hurt than physical pain. This is the element often lacking when the trade unions come into conflict with management, for each believes their differences must concern money, or hours of labour. But I have never yet encountered a person, even one doing the most insignificant and menial work, who doesn't achieve an infusion of new interest once that worker understands the part he occupies within the whole.

It is not that I am oblivious of the importance of money. Quite the reverse: by being born rich and then losing my wealth in maturity I can make a true assessment of its value. Life has taught me that this is limited. I was no happier with a bottomless bank account than I became when it evaporated and I depended upon my own efforts for a regular income. Disappointment awaits those who slave to work their way to riches, for they are unlikely to attain contentment. On the contrary, money is attended by its own complications and can lock you into relationships that are better discarded. This by no means signifies that poverty has its benefits; it can bring squalor, misery and its own brand of cynicism. But we each have problems that money, no matter how abundant, cannot solve and will frequently exacerbate.

The reader will have observed how this narrative mostly places my son Peter and his family where they would prefer to be, out of the picture. But I feel entitled to make an exception in the case of one aspect of Peter's character – the instinct since his youth to take up cudgels on behalf of the underdog. Though as mother and son we have frequently disagreed, a major achievement of his warrants inclusion if only as a reminder to myself that, had I done nothing but produce such a son, my existence would not have been in vain.

Disenchantment with the state of the post-war world had moved Peter to try to enter Parliament as a Socialist. On three occasions he was near the top of the poll but not successful. In 1956, following the notorious 'treason trials' in Hungary and South Africa, he had, largely out of his own pocket, founded the non-party organization of lawyers called Justice. Advocates of the rank of Gerald Gardiner, and Hartley Shawcross and others came on to the council, individual cases were defended at trials in distant realms, and appeals against wrongful decisions lodged in British courts. Through Justice, agitation began that brought to this country the institution of Ombudsman as a new kind of public official, a legal watchdog, in our national life.

On a grey November morning in 1960 Peter, then thirty-nine years of age, was crammed into the London Underground on his way to his law chambers when his eyes caught a brief item in his newspaper. It referred to the imprisonment for seven years of two young Portuguese for the crime of raising their glasses in a public restaurant and drinking a toast to liberty.

Peter felt a cold rage because a trial of sorts had already taken place, and an appeal, if any, dismissed. Nothing had been revealed until too late; sympathizers were impotent. Or were they? Supposing enough private individuals in other countries raised a clamour of protest, might not the authorities in

Portugal (it was the era of dictator Salazar) be moved to review the case? And similar cases elsewhere? Here was work in plenty for ordinary citizens, provided a framework to co-ordinate their efforts could be established. No great sums would be required – Justice conducted its affairs with a minute staff of two or three people – and it could become a *moral* watchdog.

Peter wrote an article which appeared simultaneously in the *Observer* and *Le Monde*. It was published on Trinity Sunday, 28 May 1961 – deliberately so, because its author wished this religious holiday to be invested also with a secular significance. My son had converted to Catholicism when he was thirty-seven, and believed that concern for the oppression of others pointed equally to the sin within oneself. In what proved an historic statement, the article told of the millions in prison for no reason except holding beliefs unacceptable to their governments. It made an appeal for amnesty on behalf of 'prisoners of conscience' within the meaning of the Universal Declaration of Human Rights. Its impact was explosive. Groups formed spontaneously in towns large and small throughout the world, with members simply writing letters – to governments, to ambassadors, to leaders of opinion, exploring any channel of communication to fasten on their plight. 'Prisoner of Conscience' became a rallying-cry; Amnesty International was born. Peter developed the theme further in his Penguin book *Persecution 1961*.

The organization's determination to detach itself from any ideology exerted particular appeal. Each group adopted three prisoners, one in the West, one in the East, and one in the Third World, no section working on behalf of a person imprisoned in its own country. Frequently, Amnesty would be attacked in the West as a front for Communism, in the East as a tool of imperialism, and in the Third World as an agent of colonialism. In fact it criticized no government, for it offered nothing by way of doctrine beyond that of human rights, and thus refused to condemn one regime by the standards of another. In this regard it compared with the International Red Cross, whose function is respected because it seeks not to remove the causes of war (the role of the United Nations) but to mitigate the suffering caused by war. Amnesty International was awarded the Nobel Peace Prize in 1977.

How many prisoners has Amnesty succeeded in liberating since its foundation? How many, though remaining behind bars, have had the worst horrors of their plight reduced?

Amnesty does not know. It does not proclaim its achievements, nor does it place offending regimes in the direct spotlight of international opprobrium. Or rather it did not, as a matter of policy, pursue such a course. Peter, once it was truly launched, left the organization to the professionals, not all of whom wished to keep it on strictly humanitarian rails. Previously, Amnesty limited its scope to the disinterested idealism of volunteers assembled in a living-room, but now its headquarters staff has expanded to some two hundred, with the consequential computerized accoutrements. Can it therefore retain that old philosophy of homespun effort, or will it turn into a political machine with a mission to change society, obsessed with its own grandeur and bidding for a voice among the organizational batteries in world affairs?

I am grateful to my son for not harbouring ambitions to be an empire builder. He has the consolation of his religion, and to him that is enough. I do not share his religious faith, but my satisfactions too have come in seeking to help people; and if this doesn't sound too priggish, it has brought its own reward.

One of the more distasteful episodes of my life resulted from my friendship with a man who indeed presumed to change society, to the degree of betraying his own country, and this will be my final word on the Kim Philby story. The despatches he sent from the Middle East to the *Observer* were causing me distress. To anyone with eyes to see they were permeated with an anti-Israel bias. They accepted the Soviet view of Middle East politics: 1960 was the year of the Eisenhower Doctrine, which placed Israel firmly in the Western camp. The thought occurred to me that Philby had, after all, remained a Communist, notwithstanding his ascent in the Foreign Service and his clearance by MI5 of possible complicity in the Burgess–Maclean scandal.

In 1962 I was again in Israel at the Weizmann Institute of Science in Rehovot, by this time a great research centre administered by my dear friend Meyer Weisgal, who had created the Institute on his chief's behalf. The gleaming campus, with its comfortable faculty club for guest accommodation, all set in exquisite gardens, owes everything to Meyer's devotion, while his wife Shirley must hold the world's record for the cups of tea and coffee she has dispensed in the course of their unending hospitality.

During that visit I encountered Victor (Lord) Rothschild. Distinguished scientist that he is, Victor has demonstrated his

225

admiration for the work of the Institute with generous benefactions, albeit declining Meyer Weisgal's invitation to assume its presidency. His war record, in which he was decorated for bravery, included service in Military Intelligence. He had been with Guy Burgess at Cambridge and also knew Philby well. According to Malcolm Muggeridge, Victor had shared some hilarious times with Philby in Paris following the liberation of France.

In my exasperation with the Philby articles I suddenly exclaimed to Victor, 'How is it the *Observer* uses a man like Kim? Don't they know he's a Communist? You must do something!' Victor appeared startled, replying: 'I will think about it.' On my return to London he telephoned, to seek my consent to a meeting at his flat with a security official. Being assured of absolute confidentiality, I agreed. In truth, I knew nothing of Philby's professional life and could only speak of hints he had dropped to me in the distant past. I recalled his invitation before the war that I join him in 'important work for peace' and the belief he expressed after the fall of France in 1940 that only with Russia's help could we defeat the Fascists; then his intimation of being in great danger.

The security man questioned me further. Did I suspect anyone else? I offered the name of Tomas Harris, the well-known art-dealer, who was then living in Spain. While I had no evidence, nor any knowledge of Harris's war-time involvement with Intelligence, those two were so close as to give me an intuitive feeling that Harris was more than just a friend. Apparently this was enough to complete Philby's dossier. The rest we know: Philby disappeared from the scene, turned up in Moscow, received citizenship, wrote a book, and entered the chronicles of treachery as the 'Third Man'.

Strangely, I had never been approached before this to reveal what I knew of Kim Philby; neither had those at Marks and Spencer who were acquainted with him through Aileen. I had not volunteered information as every public statement had pointed to his innocence. I was too remote from official circles to be aware of surviving suspicions. I was now also asked to meet a member of *Mossad*, the Israeli Secret Service, in the belief that I might have further information to divulge and would perhaps say more to an Israeli than to MI5. The two services, I was informed, operated in close harmony. Of course I knew no more, and deeply resented an implication questioning my first loyalty to Britain, but I agreed to the interview nevertheless. Somehow the fact that I had spoken leaked as an insignificant news item in an Israeli newspaper. The Third Man was hardly news any more, Fourth and Fifth Men having by this time emerged to reveal how clubmanship and the Old School Tie could protect their own.

The news item was picked up by the journalist Chapman Pincher, who made quite a meal of it in a book published in 1981. The British Press then took up the scent. Eighteen years had gone by, but reporters banged on my door, cheque-book hawks offered money for my story and I had no rest from the incessant ringing of my telephone. It was persecution, as anyone unfortunate enough to have been the victim of such an experience will recognize. Recalling his promise to stand by me, I appealed to Victor Rothschild – alas, to no avail. He did not come to my assistance then, and I haven't heard from him since. However, when Miriam Lane, Victor's sister and in her own right a brilliant entomologist, learnt of my ordeal she collected me at once, like the faithful friend she has always proved, and gave me sanctuary in her country home. To elude the hovering journalists I veiled myself like one of the Moslem women who inhabit this part of town, and so made good my escape. Only then was my peace restored.

About 'doing good', I must confess to failure in one particular field of activity, and it related to hospital work. Various regional health boards invited me to serve on hospital management committees. Endeavouring to direct my experience in that worthy direction I applied myself to the care of Mongol children and adolescents with severe psychological problems. My colleagues were the usual crop of 'quality' folk and though I do not disparage their contribution I found that for them being busy was a goal in itself. Fulfilling themselves in managing institutions for Mongoloids they might just as well have applied their attention to stray animals – their attitude to the unfortunates was as to their own domestic pets, whereas I could not sustain an interest indefinitely in an obviously hopeless task. The cases I encountered filled me with despair; they were heart-rending and martyrdom does not become me. I need to see the positive results of my efforts.

Thus I cherish friendship as the only gift we choose ourselves, more precious in fact than love, which must include an element of selfishness and unequal contributions by its partners. I have

227

always made a point of keeping my relationships in good repair, particularly with younger people; the older ones, forever discussing their ailments and their grandchildren, can become crashing bores. Not only is true friendship an armour against loneliness and self-pity, it helps to conserve a sense of proportion.

The female sex has shown a tendency to lose that sense of proportion in an absurd agitation for equality with man in every facet of life. How can this be desirable when men cannot be neutered to eliminate the ever-active masculine drive from their senses? Proponents of 'women's liberation' retreat from the consequences of absolute equality, for it would demand suffocation of their own emotional impulse. Of course women have rights that still remain to be won, and I have no doubt that ultimately we shall achieve them. But will they make us happier? I doubt it.

A male companion is more important to women than the reverse, though I long ago concluded that marriage imposes unfair, sometimes intolerable, obligations upon women. In widowhood men remained necessary to me but it caused me no regret that I never remarried. By all means have men around to unzip a dress, organize travel arrangements and to ensure that boring correspondence like the telephone account is not ignored – after all, a woman is usually available to men who affect a helplessness in their domestic chores. But marriage? I wonder whether the institution merited the reverence it formerly received. Today's formula of couples living together provisionally has much to commend it.

The male 'machismo', related to his sexual role and instinctive fear of impotence, should not be entirely disregarded by women, or glibly identified with oppression. One important advantage women have over men is their greater receptiveness to new ideas: being more practical they reveal greater adaptability. Further, their nature tells them that even minor changes in one's life-style can make for a more bearable existence.

Having been blessed with excellent health in a long life, I can accept the inevitable biological process. If my eyes have lost some of their keenness I feel it is merely as though I am looking through misted windows. My hearing is perfectly adequate for all I wish to hear and my mind retains its interest in whatever I judge of importance going on in the world. I can therefore be useful, helpful and independent today as in times past; and, recalling that Russian saying 'habit is heaven-sent as a substitute for happiness', I feel I have grounds for continuing to live.

Finally, I feel I must voice my gratitude to the country of my adoption. The British, it is frequently said, are an intolerant race, yet I have seen enough of this country and its people to know that being a foreigner is no obstacle to fulfilment here. My Russian accent has never proved a disadvantage. The British must surely rank as the most exasperating, illogical, hypocritical of peoples. But they have a generosity of mind too, and a humility, and a capacity for endurance which is necessary for true greatness.

I don't expect my English grandchildren to endorse this declaration of love of country. The young appear to be embarrassed by patriotism. But then, my grandchildren were born here while for me the odyssey from Baku has been a long, winding trail. Given the chance, and fortified against life's hazards by my personal trinity – Russian soul, Jewish heart, British passport – I would do it all again, the same way.

Index

235

225–26
Philby, Harry St. John, 110
Philby (*formerly* Friedmann), Litzi, 165, 172, 210
Picasso, Pablo, 106
Pierlot, Hubert, 191
Pincher, Chapman, 227
Pinsk, 16–17, 20, 25
Pobedonostev, Constantin, 17
Podolsky, Sophie, 161, 214
Polack, Joseph, 92
Political and Economic Planning (PEP), 170
Populaire, Le, 121
Potemkin, Battleship, 27
Potemkin, Grigori, 35
Potter, Beatrix, 117
Poulenc, Francis, 106
Pouterman, J. E., 140–41, 145
Primrose League, 139
Prince of Wales, 188
Proust, Marcel, 125, 147–48
Pushkin, Alexander, 29, 39; his *Queen of Spades*, 36, 141

Quebec Conference, 190

Rasputin, Grigori, 35, 49–50, 61, 82
Rath, Ernst vom, 174
Rayner (*later* Lord), Derek, 214
Rasvyet, 38
Read, Miss, (maid), 99, 104
Reading, Lady (Stella), 187
Red Cross, 68, 183, 224
Redkino, 39–41, 43, 56–57, 63, 217
Reitlinger, Gerald, and his *The Final Solution*, 55
Reitlinger, Henry, 55
Reitlinger, Nellie, 69, 73, 80
Renoir, Pierre-Auguste, 125
Ribbentrop, Joachim von, 169
Ridley, Lord, 196–97
Ridley (*formerly* Wallace), Lady (Ursula), 196–97
Rikarna, (governess), 34–35, 53, 61–62, 68–69, 75, 86, 91
Ripley, (butler), 144, 152
Romanov family, 32, 35, 38, 56, 141
Roosevelt, Eleanor, 204
Roosevelt, Franklin D., 155
Rothschild, Baron Edmond de, 82
Rothschild, Dorothy de (Dolly), 82

Rothschild, James de, 82
Rothschild, Lord (Victor), 225–27
Rothschilds (of Paris), 22
Rozovska, Zoya, 104–5; her fate, 106
Russell, Bertrand, 195
Russia, conditions there, 15–16, 21, 24–25, 37, 141; her Jews, 16–22 *passim*, 41–43, 50, 89, 164; pogroms, 26–27; war with Japan, 26, 43; Black Hundreds, 27, 41, 116; Duma, 37, 42–43, 51–52, 82; in W.W.I, 63, 77, 82; Russian emigrés in England, 79–80, 87, 93; Kerensky's Provisional Government, 82, 86, 88, 137, 146, 175; and Lenin, 88, 90–91, 115, 134; Lena Goldfields, 132, 138, 142; in W.W.II, 186, 197–98; Kruschev era, 218
Rutenberg, Peter, 110–14

St. Helena, 84
St. Petersburg (Petrograd, Leningrad), 15, 27, 29–51 *passim*, 57–58, 63, 67–69, 86, 121, 138; Bloody Sunday, 27, 111–12; Romanov tercentenary, 56; Benenson scandal, 61
Sacher, Harry, 78, 80, 149, 159
Sacher, Michael, 201
Sacher, Miriam, 78, 152, 159
Sachs, Maurice, 127
Salazar, Antonio, 224
Samuel, Beatrice, 72–73, 75, 99
Samuel, (3rd Viscount), David, 116
Samuel, (2nd Viscount), Edwin ('Nebi'), 73, 102, 104
Samuel, Hadassah, 102–3, 116, 176–77; her father, 102
Samuel, (1st Viscount), Herbert, 72, 79–80, 95–96, 178; as High Commissioner for Palestine, 98–100, 107, 109, 124; and refugees, 166
San Remo Conference, 96
Sandhurst, 86–87
Sarajevo, 63
Sarel, Rev., 128
Sassoon (*formerly* Franklin), Dulcie, 75, 164
Sassoon, Siegfried, 164

237

Savoir (Posnansky), Alfred, 125; his
   Bluebeard's Eighth Wife, 130
Scharnhorst, The, 190
Schiff, Dorothy, 194
Schiff, Sidney, *see* Hudson, Stephen
Schiff, Violet, 148
Schiller, Friedrich von, 32, 63
Schultze, Mr., 193
Scott, Robert F., 83
Secret Intelligence Service, 183, 210
Sert, José-Maria, 126–27, 131
Sert, Missia, 125–26, 131; her
   memoirs, 127
Sharett, Moshe, 208
Shawcross (*later* Lord), Hartley, 223
Sheglovitov, Ivan, 41
Shereef of Mecca, 111
Sherwood, Robert, 194
Shochat, Manya, 114
Shops Act, 157
Shopworkers Union, 151
Sieff (*later* Lord), Israel, 78, 167, 200,
   217; and PEP, 170
Sieff, J. Edward ('Teddy'), 186, 200,
   207, 219–20
Sieff, Jane, 207
Sieff, Lois, 220
Sieff (*later* Lord), Marcus, 201, 204,
   207–8, 214, 220
Sieff, Rebecca ('Becky'), 78–79, 160
Silkin, Lewis, 205
Simon, Oliver, 140
Simpson, Wallis, (Duchess of
   Windsor), 188
Singer Sewing Machine Company,
   56
Sinyavsky, Andrei, 219
Smellie, Mrs., 139, 142
Snowden, Ethel, 115–16, 120–22,
   139, 143, 147, 163
Snowden, Philip, 115, 120–22
Sokolow, Nahum, 41–42, 71, 77, 94
Solomon and Company, 84
Solomon, Arthur, 146
Solomon, Col. Harold, 83–84, 88, 90,
   92–96, 101–4, 106–8, 111–12,
   114, 116, 130, 132, 140, 144, 152;
   meets future wife, 81–82; army
   service, 86, 88, 163; marriage, 92;
   as Jerusalem official, 99–100, 110,
   140; riding accident, 117; as
   invalid, 118–20, 136, 138, 145–46;

seeks parliamentary seat, 139,
   141–43; death, 146–47
Solomon family, 84–87
Solomon, Flora (Feodosia, 'Fenya'),
   birth, 18, 21; childhood in Baku,
   21–25, 29, 31; schooling in
   Wiesbaden, 28–33, 38–39; in St.
   Petersburg, 33–39, 43–51, 56–58;
   first visit to London, 52–55; and
   father's injury, 58–61; in Jena,
   62–63; in Hamburg, W.W.I, 63–67;
   settles in London, 68–72; as VAD,
   73–76, 89; meets future husband,
   81–82; concern for family in
   Russia, 88–91; marriage, 92; in
   Jerusalem, 98–102, 107, 114;
   pregnancy, 101, 103–4; son's
   birth, 106; at Degania *kibbutz*, 116;
   an invalid husband, 117–20; and
   Philip Snowden, 120–21; in
   Geneva, 122; a Palestine visit,
   123–24; in Paris, 124–26; and
   Missia's memoirs, 127; and East
   End poor, 128–30; Kerensky
   liaison, 133–38, 146, 155, 164,
   174–75; electioneering, 139,
   142–43; as publisher, 140–41, 145;
   husband's death, 147–48; and
   Zionism, 96, 148, 198, 207; father's
   financial collapse, 149–50; and
   Marks and Spencer, 77–79,
   151–52, 154, 156–63, 166–67,
   169–73, 179, 196, 202–4, 213–15,
   217, 219, 222; Philby connection,
   110, 165, 169, 172, 183, 186,
   210–11, 225–27; and German
   refugees, 165–66; in W.W.II and
   London Blitz, 177–84 *passim*,
   190–98; communal restaurants,
   180; British Restaurants, 185–88; in
   Israel, 211–13; and a U.N. debate,
   216; aeroplane crash, 221–22
Solomon (*formerly* Adler), Frances,
   81, 84–86, 92, 147, 149
Solomon, Gladys, 81, 84, 92
Solomon, Henry, 81, 84–85, 92–93
Solomon, Peter, *see* Benenson, Peter
Solomon, Solomon J., 81
'Soph', (nurse), 147
Solzhenitsyn, Alexander, his *One
   Day in the Life of Ivan Denisovitch*
   and *First Circle*, 219

Soskice, David, 137
Spanier, Ginette, 120
Spanish Relief Committee, 168
Spivack, Larry, 216–17
Stalin, Josef, 164, 186; pact with Hitler, 177
Stopes, Marie, 170
Storrs, Ronald, 109, 116
Stow Hill, Lord, 137
Strachey, John, 165, 169, 194
Strauss, Eric, 175–76, 214–16
Strauss, Richard, 52
Stravinsky, Igor, 52, 104, 127; *Rite of Spring*, 105; *Pulcinella*, 106
Suez War, 213–14, 216
Summer Fields Preparatory School, 145, 147, 149, 167
Sviatopolk-Mirsky, Prince Dmitri, 140–41

Taft, Robert, 218
Tamara, (aunt), 152
Tatler, The, 69
Taylor, Capt. Charles, 221
Tchaikovsky, Peter Ilitch, 36
Tempest, Marie, 52
Thackeray, Tom, 194
Thomas, Mrs., 159
Times, The, 85, 88, 106, 163
Times Literary Supplement, 140
Tolstoy, Leo, 1, 42; his *War and Peace*, 32, 45; his *Anna Karenina*, 39
Tottenham, 143; its Conservative Party, 139, 142
Tottenham Weekly Herald, 142
Trades Union Congress (TUC), 121
Tree, Beerbohm, 55
Tree, Maud, 55
Tsarskoye Selo, 146
Turgenev, Ivan, 39
Tutankhamen, tomb of, 123–24

United Nations, 215–16
Uris, Leon, and his *Exodus*, 213
Ussishkin, Menahem, 114
USSR, *see* Russia

Valentina, (designer), 155
Vallotton, Félix, 137
Vevey, Jewish cemetery there, 147
Villiers, Marjorie, 191, 218–19
Vinaver, Max, 42

Volkonsky, Prince, 36–37
Voluntary Aid Detachment (VAD), 69, 73–74, 89

Waley, Arthur, 140
Walker, Mayor Jimmy, 126
Wall Street Crash, 148, 155
Wall Street Journal, 97
Wallace, Barbara, *see* Agar, Barbara
Wallace, Billy, 189
Wallace, Capt. Euan, 187–88
Warburg, Max, 65, 67, 173
Ward, John, 198
Wavell, Gen. Archibald, 191
Webb, Beatrice, 53
Weidenfeld (*later* Lord), George, 173, 175, 206–9; as aide to Weizmann, 208–9
Weisgal, Meyer, 225–26
Weisgal, Shirley, 225
Weizmann, Benjamin (Benjy), 77, 180, 189
Weizmann, Chaim, 20, 78, 82–83, 95–96, 98–100, 102, 108–9, 111, 114, 131, 148–49, 168, 175, 177, 187, 200; in W.W.I, 71, 76–77, 79–80, 87–88; Hebrew University inauguration, 123–24; and refugees, 165, 174; in W.W.II, 189; a Jewish army, 189–90, 198; loss of son, 190; as Head of State, 208; his *Trial and Error*, 208
Weizmann Institute of Science, 225–26
Weizmann, Maidie, 180, 189
Weizmann, Michael, 82; lost on RAF mission, 190
Weizmann, Vera, 20, 76–80, 82, 102, 148–49, 177–78, 208–9, 213, 217; in W.W.II, 183, 189; loss of son, 190
White, Theodore, his *The Making of the President 1960*, 194
Wilhelm, Kaiser, 28; his Kaiserin, 66
Wilkinson, Ellen, 127, 150
Williams, Dr. (of Summer Fields), 147, 167
Wills, Helen, 130
Wilson, Harold, 207–9
Wingate, Lorna, 191
Wingate, Orde, 189–91
Wissotsky family, 137

239